A-Z OF INDUSTRIAL MARINE FISHERIES IN ASIA

A-Z OF INDUSTRIAL MARINE FISHERIES IN ASIA

A.C. Long

CYBER TECH PUBLICATIONS
4264/3, Ansari Road, Daryaganj, New Delhi-110002 (India)
Ph.: 011-23244078, 011-43559448 Fax: 011-23280028
E-Mail: cyberpublicationsdelhi@yahoo.com
Website: www.cybertechpublications.com

A-Z OF INDUSTRIAL MARINE FISHERIES IN ASIA

A.C. Long

First Edition 2011

Published by :

G.S. Rawat for **Cyber Tech Publications**
4264/3, Ansari Road, Daryaganj, New Delhi-110002 (India)
Ph.: 011-23244078, 011-43559448 Fax: 011-23280028
E-Mail: cyberpublicationsdelhi@yahoo.com
Website: www.cybertechpublications.com

CONTENTS

Preface

Cage culture has become an increasingly important sector of this industry, and significant opportunities exist for continued expansion of cage culture in regions of China that have underutilized natural and man-made reservoirs, lakes, ponds and other catchments. Upon completion, the Three Gorges Reservoir in Sichuan Province will impound an estimated 67,000 hectares with a cage production potential of nearly 20 million kilograms.

In addition to freshwater cage culture, the LVHD system has also shown to be effective in both brackish- and saltwater environments. As the amount of marine fish caught from the wild either stabilizes or declines, increases in demand for marine species will be at least partly met though cage culture.

The ASA has now gathered more than ten years of experience with demonstrations and feeding trials in China, and based on these very successful experiences a new program was initiated in India and Southeast Asia in 2003, called the Soy-In-Aquaculture program. Working with local farmers, feed mills, and universities, the LVHD technologies developed in China are being introduced into these regions.

India and Southeast Asia have strong and growing aquaculture industries. The four target nations of the Soy-In-Aquaculture program - India, Indonesia, Vietnam, and the Philippines - all rank in the top ten of the aquaculture producing countries in the world with over 4.6 mmt of production annually. The American Soybean Association recognizes the region's growing aquaculture industry and the opportunities to aid farmers and feedmills with advanced technologies.

The Soy-In-Aquaculture program aims to realize similar outcomes as the LVHD program has demonstrated in China. The program focuses on the acceleration of the adoption of more profitable and environmentally sound technology and the associated growth of the aquafeed industry in Southeast Asia and India.

This manual has been prepared as a practical guide for aquaculture production, extension and associated industry personnel involved with the culture of fish in cages. It presents principles and technologies for production of fish in LVHD cages as a technically and economically viable alternative to other fish culture systems, particularly traditional cage systems that rely on high cage volume and low fish density. The manual emphasizes the four key elements of successful fish culture in today's market driven economy - quality stock, water, feed and management.

—Author

1

Introduction

This summary of the history of marine fisheries in Southeast Asia traces the development of fisheries in the region from basically subsistence activities in the nineteenth century to large-scale industrial fishing in the latter part of the twentieth and early twenty-first centuries and examines the impact that this development has had on fish stocks and fishing communities in the region. The work is based substantially on the comprehensive review by Butcher (2004) although other sources have also been used as appropriate. Units of measurement have, where possible, been standardized to metric units to facilitate comparisons with current and other data, although Butcher's (2004) units for weights and measures of measurement are already quoted in metric units except where other units are referred to in a statute, law or other legal instrument. However, there are instances, particularly for the measurement of vessel tonnage, where such standardization has not been possible and these instances are highlighted and discussed as they occur.

The geographical area covered by this history includes all of the countries of Southeast Asia, excluding China to the north and Australia to the south. The time period covered is approximately from the mid-nineteenth century to the present day (2005).

Although inland and estuarine fisheries are also important in Southeast Asia, the seas of the region have been particularly important and have long provided people with a variety of fish, shrimps, squids, whales, pearl oysters, sea cucumbers and a multitude of other animals that they have collected and captured for medicine, oil, jewellery and most importantly food.

Prior to the early 1900s, the population of the whole of Southeast Asia was about 40 million with the majority of that population living in villages. The countries of the area were not yet urbanized to any great extent and therefore fishing (both marine and inland) was directed mainly at the need to supply food for these village communities. There was some limited trade (often between coastal and inland villages) and simple preservation and processing methods such as salting, drying and the manufacture of fish sauce which were developed and used to facilitate this trade. The supply of fresh, preserved or processed fish for large centralized markets, either domestic or international, was largely unknown.

As a result of this subsistence fishing by coastal villages in the nineteenth century, the region's marine fish stocks were almost certainly lightly exploited and, although no detailed surveys were carried out until after 1945, several contemporary nineteenth century records comment on both the quality and the abundance of fish in many areas and on the simple fishing methods used in marine fisheries.

Restricted by the simple fishing gear and vessels, and with abundant coastal fish resources, most fishing was undertaken in near-shore waters. When the demand for fish and other marine animals rose or the supply fell (often as a result of natural causes, such as the monsoons), it was a relatively simple matter to expand operations into new coastal fishing grounds since there were very few barriers to such expansion.

As fishing moved away from a subsistence-level activity and became increasingly oriented towards supplying more remote markets in the late 1800s and early 1900s, a spectacular growth in catches occurred (Sugiyama *et al.*, 2004). This expanding demand for marine products was created above all else by urbanization and the growth in population but also by the development of transport and marketing systems and changes in the techniques in preserving fish, shrimps and other marine life that prompted people to produce for the market.

This expansion of marine production accelerated after the Second World War as fleets were mechanized and fishing activities expanded to new areas, particularly those areas offshore that had previously been unfished or, at least, only lightly exploited. The expansion of marine landings in Southeast Asia has been so spectacular that two nations in the region (Thailand and Indonesia) are now among the world's top 10 fish producing nations and marine fisheries production accounts for more than 1 percent of GDP in almost all countries of the region (Sugiyama *et al.*, 2004).

With this expansion in landings through the twentieth century came an expansion in the areas fished by national fishing fleets, a decline in the abundance of many fish stocks and, accordingly, an increase in interest at the regional, national and international level, in administering, controlling and regulating fishing activities in the region. States, and since the late 1940s, international organizations have all influenced the scale and location of fishing in the region and, until recently, fishing often took place beyond the reach and grasp of state powers.

The ability to expand landings by moving to new areas was curtailed in the latter part of the twentieth century not only by the lack of new fishing grounds to move to but also very much by this increasing interest of national Governments (and the legal obligations and powers conferred by the UN Convention on the Law of the Sea, UNCLOS) to control fishing activities, particularly fishing by other nations' fleets, within a nation's territorial waters. Such recent attempts at regulating fisheries have not been wholly successful since they are built on a long history of a lack of government intervention and control in the marine fisheries sector. However, as Butcher (2004) points out, the era of opening of new "frontiers of fisheries has ended. The challenge now is to exploit the seas in a sustainable manner that preserves the diversity of marine life while providing the people of the region with a source of food long into the future". In examining how the various sectors of marine fisheries in Southeast Asia have developed since the nineteenth century and how they have contributed to the overall rapid expansion of landings, the individual components that comprise the region's marine fisheries sector will be examined. These components include: (a) pearling; (b) trawling; (c) purse seining; (d) shrimp trawling; (e) tuna longlining, poling and purse seining; (f) driftnetting; (g) trolling; and (h) other industrial fishing operations, including failed types of industrial fishing. In addition, the current state of each of these sectors and the resources upon which they rely will be examined so that an assessment can be made for each sector of the likelihood of being able to move from an expansionist mode of fishing (where landings were increased by exploiting new areas) to one of sustainability, based on existing resources.

Pearling

In the nineteenth century, prior to the development of the cultured pearl industry in Japan, mother of pearl shells and pearls were some of the most valuable marine animal products of the time, and the demand for these products had been increasing rapidly in Europe and North America. In Southeast Asia, there was a thriving pearl shell and pearl industry in the early 1800s, based in the islands surrounding the Sulu and Celebes Seas which sold or bartered its products to China. So great was this trade that providing sufficient labour was a problem and therefore slave raiders were employed to capture slaves in the islands and coastal villages of the Malay Peninsula and bring them to Manila and Jolo. At the height of the trade in the 1830s, as many as 68 000 people were employed in diving for pearl shell in the area, more than the number of fishers in the whole of Java and Madura. About 730 tonnes of pearl shell was exported from Jolo each year. The pearl shell and pearls that were not exported directly to China (either by Chinese traders or by British East India Company vessels) were sent to the market at Makassar for sale.

The pearling areas around the Sulu and Celebes Seas, the majority of which is now encompassed within the Philippines, is still by far the major producer of pearl shell and pearls (as opposed to pearls from the pearl culture industry) in the region with pearl shell production in 2002 being about 25000 tonnes or over 99 percent of total production in the region (FAO, 2004). This production is, however, about the same level as the 1960s although landings have fluctuated considerably during that time.

The early, rapid development of the pearl shell and pearl industry in the eastern islands area (which almost exclusively used Japanese and Filipino divers) quickly resulted in the more easily accessible stocks coming under pressure and, as pearl stocks in shallower waters were intensively harvested, it became necessary to find ways to harvest in deeper waters to maintain and increase supplies. In 1839 Augustus Siebe developed diving gear which was eagerly adapted by companies with sufficient capital to purchase the necessary equipment. The addition of diving equipment not only enabled divers to reach greater depths (up to approximately 54 m) than had previously been possible with free-diving, but also to increase the proportion of the year in which it was possible to collect oysters from three to nine months. The development also enabled stocks in deeper waters to be exploited and, by the late 1800s, areas in the Aru Islands, the Mergui Archipelago and the Sulu Archipelago were being fished. Faced with the high costs of the pearling operations, pearlers generally adopted the strategy of extracting as much as possible as quickly as possible and then moving on to another oyster bed. This strategy was adopted in all three of the main pearling areas.

The first area where diving equipment resulted in an increase in yields was in the Mergui Archipelago where, according to an official report by Rudmose Brown and Simpson in 1907, there was "no systematic pearling in the archipelago before 1891 when the attention of the Government was drawn to these banks by a Queensland pearler [presumably from the Torres Straits]." To manage this fishery, the Government of Burma immediately introduced a "block system" whereby the government auctioned the rights to collect pearl oysters in five "blocks" covering the richest pearling grounds. As a result of this system the mentality was adopted that it was imperative to extract as much pearl shell as possible during the year as the same company would not necessarily secure the same block the following year. Official figures indicate that yields rose dramatically from 26 tonnes in 1891/92 to 340 tonnes in 1894/95, leading to the emergence of Mergui as a boomtown. By 1900/01 the yield had fallen to 66 tonnes, and the government abolished the block system and replaced it by a system under which pearlers bought a licence for each pump they used. There was apparently no limit on the number of licences used.

During this period the accepted view was that there was little danger of overexploitation of the Mergui pearl beds as the beds were continually restocked by the offspring produced by oysters in deeper waters beyond the reach of the divers. It was argued that there was a "natural balance" between the number of divers and the quantity of shell available for, as yields fell, divers would leave and the stocks would recover. As a result it was concluded there was no need for any sort of regulation of the Mergui pearl fishery.

Pearling also expanded into the Aru Islands where Australian pearlers, using Japanese and Filipino divers, adopted diving gear in the 1870s. The richest grounds were those along the eastern side of the Islands which, after a few failed attempts at development, were developed by the Australian pearlers from Torres Strait in 1905, under a three-year concession granted by the Netherlands Indies Government. These grounds had hardly been touched by divers and, initially, catches were about twice what they were in the Torres Straits. In addition, the operations were significantly more profitable because licence costs, labour and the cost of living were cheaper than in the Torres Straits fishery. This Aru Island fishery quickly expanded and by 1906 there were

150 vessels working in the area, operating as a fleet with multiple diving vessels supplying a schooner which acted as a "floating station" where sorting, cleaning and packing was undertaken. In 1906, indigenous divers in the area (who, under the terms of the concession, had exclusive access to pearl shell in waters less than 5 fathoms) supplied only 13 percent of the total 950 tonnes that were taken in the area. The company operating the fleet was the world's largest producer of pearl shell and, in the same year, supplied 37 percent of mother-of-pearl shell imported into London.

However, within a few years, yields began to decline as the three year concession provided no long-term incentives for preservation of the stock and contemporary anecdotal evidence appears to indicate a reduction in catch rates per vessel of about 50 percent between 1905 and 1908. Although the concession was actually renewed several times, the company operating the fleet had withdrawn most or all of its vessels by 1916. However, this withdrawal did not end pearling activities in the Islands with the indigenous, shallow water fishery continuing and a few diving vessels operating well into the 1930s. These activities continue today from smaller, motorized vessels.

In the Sulu Archipelago, the introduction of diving technology came later and in a milder form than in other areas and, in 1914, there were 73 pearling vessels operating there, 40 of which were owned by a Japanese company and the rest by individuals of various ethnicities. Only two of the Japanese vessels had motor-driven pumps for diving. By 1930, there were only 24 vessels operating, five of which were equipped with engines and moto-driven air pumps. The Sulu Archipelago area appears to have exported about 300 tonnes of pearl shell in 1914 and, throughout its development, was distinguished by a greater reliance on indigenous fishers operating in shallow water for most of its production. Yields do not appear to have declined as precipitously as other areas where mechanized diving operations were more important, and Butcher (2004) suggests that this may have been a result of the more extensive nature of the pearl beds and the apparently less intense exploitation.

The introduction of mechanical diving technology in the late nineteenth century therefore led to a boom-and-bust development of the pearl shell beds of the region with pearl beds being sequentially depleted. Throughout this period of development, however, it is interesting to note that little concern was expressed for the long-term sustainability of the stocks since it was commonly believed that depleted adult stocks would be quickly replenished from untouched "deeper water" stocks. The decline in abundance of pearl shell helped drive an increasing demand for trochus shell and other gastropods as a substitute for pearl shell which was used in the manufacture of buttons. But, after the Second World War, it was the development of cheap plastic substitutes for button manufacture that resulted in the decline of the industry although it continues today as a small, artisanal fishery in the Philippines.

TRAWLING

Mechanized trawling requires a vessel that is powerful enough to tow a large net through the water at a reasonable speed (typically 2-4 knots) and therefore the development of trawling did not generally take place until after the development of steam-powered vessels in the latter part of the nineteenth century, although a limited amount of beam trawling using sail-powered vessels was undertaken, including that by Japanese fishers in Manila Bay. It was at this time that the "first industrialization" of fisheries began in the British Isles. At first, steam-powered vessels were used to tow fishing boats out to fishing grounds and take catches to markets, but later the power of steam engines was harnessed to drive fishing boats and haul in nets. The most important fishing gear at this time was the trawl net, which fishers employed to capture the abundant demersal populations of the English channel and then of the North Sea. As the fishery expanded the beam trawl, which is kept open by a beam at the entrance to the net, was quickly replaced by the otter trawl, which is kept open by the flow of water over the otter boards (or "doors") on the tow lines as the boat pulls the net through the water. In the late 1800s British trawlers moved further and further into the North Sea to maintain their catches, but fishing companies made great profits, as the income from the sale of fish to the rapidly growing market far outweighed the cost of sailing to more distant fishing grounds.

The profitability of steam trawlers and their ability to land large amounts of food to feed the growing urban populations of Europe planted the idea in the minds of a few entrepreneurs and officials that trawling might prove just as successful in the Southeast Asian waters. The first person to consider the possibility of capturing demersal fish in Southeast Asian waters by means of a trawler was apparently a

Captain Eddie, the captain of a steamship. During discussions with British officials in 1894 Captain Eddie proposed that he be granted a monopoly on trawling in the waters around Penang and off the coasts of Perak and Selangor for two to four years and that he would pay the government a certain sum for the privilege. Eddie had experimented with a trawl net and had apparently had very good results, but he dumped his catch before returning to port and said he would not reveal where he had fished or what he had caught or order a steam trawler from England until the Government agreed to his request. The areas for which he had requested to be granted a monopoly had great potential for trawl fishing, but because they had so little information to go on and they were in any case reluctant to grant a monopoly, officials refused Eddie's request and no one took up his idea of trawling in this area for many years.

The design of trawl nets in Southeast Asia may have some precedence in the fixed nets, known as *payang,* that were used off the coasts of Java and Madura and the Malay Peninsula in the nineteenth century to catch small and medium-sized pelagic fish. These nets were similar in design to a trawl net, with wings and a "cod end" and the upper part of the net supported by floats and the lower edge secured with weights. Similarly, fishers in the Philippines used a pair-trawl type net design, locally known as *sapyaw,* to also catch pelagic species. These nets, however, were not towed nets but fixed or lift nets. Therefore, perhaps their greatest importance in the development of trawling that was to come in the future was to provide the net making skills and familiar net patterns for manufacturing towed trawl nets.

The first attempt in the region at surveying demersal fish stocks and testing demersal trawling as a method of capture was made in 1907 when the Netherlands Indies Government refitted a steam barge, the *Gier,* to undertake surveys in the Java Sea and nearby areas using a small otter trawl. The trials that were undertaken were hampered by operational difficulties such as the net often becoming stuck in the soft mud and large cup sponges clogging the net. Despite these difficulties, some areas with good potential were identified by the end of the trials in 1911 and the conclusions of the survey were generally optimistic. In the report to the Government, which recommended a more commercially-orientated survey, it was emphasized that the *Gier* was not designed as a trawler since it used a small net and the vessel concentrated on surveying a number of areas rather than concentrating on the areas that were found to have high fish abundance. Despite these recommendations, no follow-up surveys were undertaken and, in fact, the Government actually reduced its commitment to fisheries surveys and research.

Other similar trawl surveys were being undertaken at about the same time, including the *Golden Crown,* which surveyed the Arakan coast of Burma in 1908-09 and later, under new ownership, surveyed the waters off the Straits Settlements, the *Albatross,* a steam beam trawler belonging to the U.S. Bureau of Fisheries, which surveyed demersal resources in the Philippines in 1907-08 and the steam trawler *Tongkol,* which surveyed possible trawling grounds in the Straits of Malacca and the South China Sea in 1926-27. None of these surveys proved encouraging enough for further surveys or commercialization to be undertaken although, interestingly, all suggested that the use of otter trawls and other "modern" fishing methods operated from small motor trawlers in inshore areas and landing on a daily basis may have some potential rather than the larger, European-type trawlers in offshore areas. This recommendation had a cultural and commercial focus as well as being a response to the abundance of fish found. Local markets preferred their fish fresh rather than frozen and prices in local markets were not high, which made it difficult to operate large trawlers profitably.

As noted earlier, Japanese fishers had been operating beam trawls from sail-powered vessels in Manila Bay since about 1900 and, in the late 1920s, this fishery began to expand as the fishing companies operating there introduced diesel-powered vessels. By the early 1930s, virtually all of the beam trawlers had diesel engines and the trawlers had extended their operations well beyond Manila Bay. This expansion of activities prompted one of the first suggestions that trawling was adversely affecting other fisheries when Filipino fishers in San Miguel Bay complained to the President of the Philippines that the Japanese trawlers were reducing fish stocks, a claim that was supported by subsequent research.

However, trawling activities in San Miguel Bay continued and, by 1980, 89 trawlers of various sizes were operating there. However, by this time, demersal stocks in the area, and other trawl grounds in the Philippines, had been depleted (in 1980, estimates of trawlable biomass in San Miguel Bay were only 1600 tonnes, about 20 percent of what the estimate was in 1948) and trawl operations had become economically marginal. No further significant growth of the industrial trawl fishery therefore occurred although trawling from dugouts, using very small nets, expanded gradually from the 1950s onwards and helped in maintaining a small trawl fishery for demersal species in the Philippines, which continues today.

Japanese fishing companies were also active in developing offshore pair- and otter-trawl fisheries in the 1930s in other areas of Southeast Asia, particularly in the waters around Taiwan, the South China Sea and off the coast of Viet Nam, including the Gulf of Tonkin where between 1935 and 1937 these trawlers caught an average of 11000 tonnes per year, mainly of species such as yellowback bream *(Taius tumifrons)* and other bream species. In addition, Japanese trawlers operated as far south as Sarawak and were also based in Singapore, apparently fishing in areas as far south as the northwest coast of Australia.

In contrast to most other fishing activities in the region at the time, these Japanese trawlers did not land their catches in the countries where they were taken but, rather, landed the frozen product to markets in Japan and Taiwan. These Japanese trawlers, together with Japanese operations in the Philippines constituted, therefore, the main trawling activities in Southeast Asia by the late 1930s since none of the surveys by European Governments or entrepreneurs had resulted in a viable trawl fishery using European-type trawlers.

Following the Second World War, demersal fish landings in the region recovered quickly to pre-war levels, despite the problems of the limited supply of vessels, fishing gear and other equipment. By 1950, demersal fish landings had reached around 166000 tonnes (in addition to some 43000 tonnes of shrimp) of which perhaps half came from trawling activities. These landings then increased rapidly, reaching about 1.7 million tonnes by 2002 in addition to about 600000 tonnes of shrimp. Although data on landings by fishing methods has not been consistently collected in the region, by far the majority of this increase in demersal landings has come from the expansion of trawling activities for demersal fish species, with the rate of increase having accelerated a little in the period after 1990.

This increase in landings from trawling activities resulted from a number of developments in different countries. Japanese pair-trawling expertise was used to successfully develop both fish and shrimp trawl fisheries in the Gulf of Thailand in 1959 and, in 1961, a joint German-Thai Government initiative to introduce small-scale, inshore trawling in Thailand was hugely successful with the number of trawlers operating in Thailand increasing from 99 in 1960 to 2700 in 1966. Catches from these vessels correspondingly increased from around 59 000 to 36 000 tonnes (representing about 57 percent of total Thai landings and about 64 percent of total regional demersal landings) during the same period. Interestingly, these large increases in landings, particularly for species not suitable for human consumption (which represented about 40 percent of total trawl landings), helped support and develop ancillary industries such as pelletized feed and duck production. Without a market for these so called "trash" fish, the profitability of this fledgling industry would have been a lot less than it otherwise was.

As the number of trawl vessels in the Gulf of Thailand increased rapidly and catch rates (and profits) declined, the fleet looked for other opportunities. Thai trawlers moved further afield and, by 1974, had begun fishing on the west coast of Viet Nam, Burma, Sarawak, the east coast of Malaysia and Java. The number of Thai-registered trawlers continued to grow with the exploitation of these new fishing grounds and, by 1977, had reached 6300 with landings from these vessels totalling some 1.1 million tonnes.

The impact in the region of trawling by Thai vessels was profound. In Malaysia, despite a government rejection in 1958 of trawling as a potential direction for the fishing industry, trawling accounted for 48 percent of total landings of 440000 tonnes by 1974. The introduction of inshore trawling as a fishing method in the Straits of Malacca occurred in the early 1960s and was a direct result of the development and success of the Thai trawl industry although it is uncertain whether the initial impetus was provided by Thai trawlers operating in Malay waters or Malay operators visiting Thailand to learn trawling. As a result of this osmosis, the techniques and net design for otter trawling used in the Straits of Malacca was identical to that developed by the German-Thai fisheries project and used by the Thai vessels.

The introduction of trawling to the Straits of Malacca was, however, fraught with conflict and violence with other fishers, particularly since the trawlers essentially ignored a ban on trawling operations within 12 miles of the coast and in waters less than 15 fathoms. As the industry followed the development pattern of the Thai trawl industry, and the fishery was essentially unregulated, the number of vessels increased rapidly and catch rates declined. On the east coast of the Malay Peninsula, catch rates fell from 520 to 160 kg/hour between 1970 and 1981 while in the northern part of the Straits of Malacca, catch rates fell from 130 to 55 kg/hour during the same period. In both areas, Thai trawlers as well as Malay vessels contributed to the depletion of fish populations.

The success of the initial development of trawling in the Straits of Malacca prompted the development in 1966, by Chinese fishers based in Bagan Si Api Api, of a similar trawl fishery on the western shores of the Straits, in Indonesia. With supporting government investment incentives, the industry expanded rapidly, driven by investment by Japanese fishing companies and, from the start, targeted shrimp for the Japanese market (see Section V below) although significant quantities of demersal fish were also taken. However, unlike Thailand, there was not an immediate market for this "trash" fish and much of it was dumped at sea after sorting out the shrimp and valuable edible fish species. In 1969, the Government stipulated that foreign companies operating in the industry had to enter into a joint venture arrangement with local companies and, again, it was the Japanese companies that provided the capital for these joint ventures with local companies providing labour, capital and political connections. This development of a large trawl industry in Indonesia had profoundly transformed the Indonesian fishing industry in a few years.

Supporting infrastructure of freezing and cold storage facilities, harbours etc. followed the development of the fishery and, by the end of 1976, foreign investment in the Indonesian shrimp fishery totalled US$46 million with 51 cold storage facilities being operational. Exports of frozen shrimp increased from around 5600 tonnes in 1969 to over 35000 tonnes in 1979.

However, already by 1970-71, trawlers were having to move to new fishing grounds as catch rates declined in areas such as the Straits of Malacca. In 1971, 50 trawlers moved from Sumatra to the north coast of Java because of dwindling catch rates; trawlers moved for the first time to the south coast of Irian Jaya and a Japanese company moved its entire operations to east Kalimantan. Soon, however, these new areas also experienced dwindling catch rates: catch rates in the Arafura Sea approximately halved between 1973 and 1976, and total landings decreased in the area even though the number of trawlers had increased by over 30 percent. In 1980, it was reported that the size of shrimp in the Straits of Malacca, south and east Kalimantan, Cilacap and the

Arafura Sea "had decreased tremendously". By the late 1970s, there were no more new areas to which the fleet could move and so, after reaching a peak of some 132000 tonnes in 1979, total landings of shrimp from Indonesia began to decline, partly a result of a ban on large trawlers implemented in 1980/81 (see below). It was to be another decade before Indonesian shrimp landings again reached that level of production.

Impacts of the trawl fishery were also felt in the declining abundance of demersal fish species in the areas where trawlers operated (particularly the Arafura Sea), made even more critical by the common habit of dumping "trash" fish at sea rather than landing and utilizing them, as was the case in Thailand. This led to several violent clashes between traditional fishers and trawlers and, between 1964 and 1976, according to official records, 62 vessels were sunk and 34 fishers killed in clashes between trawlers and inshore fishers.

In 1980, in response to these increasingly violent clashes and continuing complaints from inshore fishers, industrialized trawling was banned in all waters surrounding Java and Bali and in 1981 this ban was extended to the waters surrounding Sumatra. Trawling was still permitted in other areas, including the Arafura Sea where a requirement for the installation of by-catch reduction devices was also implemented, although probably not effectively enforced. Both shrimp and fish stocks recovered quickly as a result of the ban (the density of demersal fish in the Straits of Malacca, for example, more than doubled from 1.2 tonnes/km^2 to 3 tonnes//km^2 between 1983 and 1985) and, with government assistance, small-scale fishers moved to fill the void left by the trawlers. In some areas, the number of small motorized vessels more than doubled in the early 1980s and total shrimp landings rebounded to pre-1980 levels by the late 1980s.

However, the ban on industrialized trawling was, like regulations controlling mesh sizes etc. in areas such as the Arafura Sea, never fully effective and, by the early 1990s, there was a resurgence of trawling, with many vessels operating illegally and also many being "licensed" by local authorities despite the supposed ban. In 1996, small-scale fishers in Jakarta claimed that more than 200 industrialized trawlers were operating within a kilometre of the coast and, inevitably, violent clashes between small-scale fishers and trawlers once again became common. By the mid-to-late 1990s, the trawl ban had ceased to be effective (except in areas where small-scale fishers were able to enforce it themselves by violence) and landings of shrimp and demersal fish species again increased, reaching over 280000 tonnes by 2002.

In other countries of the region, as well as Indonesia, the declaration of national Exclusive Economic Zones (EEZ) under the UN Law of the Sea Convention (UNCLOS) during the 1980s had a profound impact on the development of trawling activities in the region. Much of the waters that had previously been international waters (and in which Thai trawlers in particular had operated) now came under the jurisdiction of one or other of the countries of the region. The largest EEZs were those of the archipelago states of Indonesia and the Philippines. According to UNCLOS, the fishing fleets of those countries which had traditionally fished in the EEZ of another country should continue to be given access to those waters so long as the coastal state lacked the capacity to exploit the fisheries resources within its EEZ.

This prompted a flurry of development of national fishing industries and the setting of conditions for foreign access to demersal resources, particularly in those states such as Indonesia which had a huge EEZ, and terms of access for foreign fishing vessels became a useful bargaining chip in other diplomatic negotiations. These conditions often included a requirement to land the catch in the coastal state (which impacted the reporting of national landings statistics), employment of local labour and payment of access fees. However, in Indonesia, the enforcement of the conditions of foreign vessel access was again difficult as local authorities issued "permits" and lacked the required resources such as patrol vessels to effectively monitor foreign fishing activity.

Of the countries in the region, it was the Thai trawlers that had the capacity to fish extensively in other countries' EEZs and they continued to do this, often illegally, following the declaration of EEZs. Thai vessels operating within the EEZ of other countries often simply entered the EEZ without permission to seek fish. This led to numerous arrests of Thai trawlers in Viet Nam, Burma, Philippines, Indonesia and Malaysia but these arrests were only a tiny proportion of the Thai fleet which, in any case, had invested in faster vessels, detection equipment and weapons so as to avoid arrest. Many violent clashes occurred between national fishers and Thai trawlers in Burma, Viet Nam, Indonesia and other countries through the 1980s and 1990s in response to these illegal activities. Catches were most often shipped directly to Thailand or other markets by transport vessels and were not landed in the coastal state. During the late 1990s, Thailand began to enter into joint venture arrangements with a few countries to allow their fleet to operate legally in other countries' EEZs. Such arrangements were entered into with Indonesia and Myanmar within the region and with other countries around the Indian Ocean rim. However, illegal fishing in foreign waters continued to be common and was exacerbated by the inability of Thai authorities to control the number of vessels in its own national waters, thereby providing incentives for these vessels to look further afield for their catches.

Despite early attempts at developing a trawl industry in the first few decades of the twentieth century, the history of industrialized trawling in Southeast Asia has therefore been one of unregulated, sequential expansion beginning initially with the development of the Thai trawl industry in the early 1960s. The successful expansion of the Thai trawlers to other areas within the region prompted parallel industrial-scale developments in other countries, most notably Indonesia and the Malay Peninsula although this expansion has been characterized by often violent conflicts with small-scale fishers in a number of areas. Throughout its development, landings of demersal fish and shrimp from industrial trawling activities have been dominated by three countries: Indonesia, Thailand and Malaysia, with these countries contributing 73 percent of total regional shrimp landings in 2002 and 80 percent of total regional demersal fish landings (FAO, 2004).

As Butcher (2004) notes, the development of trawling in the region occurred by the sequential exploitation of new areas with vessels maintaining and increasing landings by moving to new areas as stocks were depleted. Such sequential depletion has also impacted significantly on traditional fishers, often resulting in violent clashes as demersal stocks have, in many areas, been effectively transferred from small-scale fishers to the industrial trawl fleet. Attempts at regulating and controlling this industrial trawl development, where it occurred, were universally weak and ineffective.

In the 1970s, with the declaration by most countries of Exclusive Economic Zones through the UNCLOS process, the existing trawler fleet (which was mainly of Thai vessels) continued to operate and expand into other countries' EEZs while several national governments looked at ways of developing their own national fleets. With Thai authorities unable to control the number of vessels in their own waters, the Thai fleet has not only continued to expand but has also looked for opportunities beyond their own waters. This has led to a major issue of illegal fishing activities in many countries of the region, which has proved difficult to control.

Despite, or perhaps because of, this essentially unregulated development of industrial trawling in the region, landings of demersal fish and shrimp species have increased dramatically and are currently in excess of 1.7 million tonnes of demersal fish and 600 000 tonnes of shrimp. Although detailed statistics are often not available, most of the increases in these shrimp and demersal fish landings have come from the activities of industrial trawling, except in the Philippines where small-scale fisheries dominate and where demersal fish and shrimp landings have only increased marginally over the past three decades. In 1950, prior to the development of industrial trawling, the Philippines was the major contributor to demersal fish landings in the region, accounting for 76 percent of total regional demersal fish landings. By 2002, its contribution had shrunk to less than 20 percent (FAO, 2004).

With no more new fishing areas for the trawlers to exploit, the challenge for the region for the future is to not only bring illegal fishing under control but, in parallel with this, to develop and implement strategies that will limit the region's industrial trawl fleet to levels which will ensure long-term, sustainable demersal resources.

PUSH NETTING

Industrial push netting developed from traditional, small hand-operated push-nets and small boat-operated nets (dugouts, rafts and sailing boats) in the region. Fishing with traditional push-nets involves scooping or seining, usually along the bottom or just off the bottom in relatively shallow waters in estuarine areas, mangrove creeks, shallow bays and littoral areas. A bag net connected to poles is pushed forward through the water by hand to catch coastal marine animals such as shrimp, crabs and fish. Traditional push-net fishing operations of different scales are reported from Indonesia, Malaysia, Myanmar, the Philippines, Singapore and Thailand. The most visible push-net fisheries in the region are those off the Gulf of Thailand covering the Thai and the northern Malaysia (Terengganu) coastlines.

In the wake of fishery industrialization, some push-net fisheries have developed beyond the non-motorized or hand-held operations and, since 1970, the efficiency of this traditional equipment has increased by using motors rather than manpower (in the Manila Bay, Philippines [Silvestre *et al.*, 1987] and Gulf of Thailand [Nagalaksana, 1987]). This change allowed for push-net fishing farther from the shore and a larger sized net. Push nets are non-selective and it is believed that motorized push-net fishing boats are causing the deterioration of marine animal resources and the coastal ecology in shallow, near-shore areas.

In Thailand, the Department of Fisheries imposed a 3 km near-shore fishery limit to exclude trawling and push netting but the number of push-net boats has increased and there have been warnings from many local communities regarding push-net fishing boats operating illegally within the 3 km near-shore limit. The rapid development of the commercial trawling and purse seining fleet resulted in economic hardships for small-scale, coastal fishers who became less competitive, forcing them into these illegal fishing activities, which is particularly damaging to the resource because of the high percentage of juvenile shrimp and fish species captured with this gear (Nagalaksana, 1987). Controlling push-net activities in the near-shore zone has proven difficult (Suvapepun, 1996). The use of artificial reefs in these shallow waters has been recommended as a means to deter both push-net fishing and trawling (Pramokchutima and Vadhanakul, 1987).

In Thailand, a total of 354 push-net fishing boats were registered in 1970, the first year of registration. In 1974 there were 740 registered push netters with a length of between 14 and 18 m (out of a total fleet of 3241 vessels, representing 22 percent of fishing vessels) operating mainly on the Gulf of Thailand seaboard (Everett, 1974). In 1984, a total number of 16006 fishing boats were registered to the Department of Fisheries of which 960 were push netters. (Pramokchutima and Vadhanakul, 1987). By 1989, the number of boats had increased to 1907. A census of marine fishing in 1995 counted about 4000 push-net boats, of which 1142 were large boats, and noted a trend toward even more such boats. Large boat push-net poles are about 28 to 44 m long with a net mesh size of between 0.5 and 1.5 cm. The push-net poles of small push-net boats are 6 to 15 m long, with approximately the same size of net mesh as large push-net boats. Push-net boats are still operating in many areas such as Prachuapkhirikhan, Chumpon, Suratthani and Pattani provinces and in some extreme cases the legs of the push-net have been extended to allow push netting in deeper waters beyond the near-shore zone up to depths of around 30 m.

Push-net boats harvest both large and small marine animals. In Thailand, those with economic importance such as shrimp make up about 40 to 45 percent of the total catch; the balance, some 60 percent which are classified together as trash fish, include juveniles of economic marine animals such as sardines, spider crabs and drum fish. These juvenile economic fish constitute some 65 to 70 percent of the trash fish total. The remaining 30 to 35 percent are true trash fish. It has been estimated that in one year the total push-net harvest from boats of all sizes is 26289 tonnes, of which 15–16 percent are large shrimp, 8–9 percent are spider crabs, 7 percent are fish, 4–5 percent are squid/cuttlefish, and the balance a mixture of other species.

PURSE SEINING

Although simple purse seining for pelagic species had been carried out in the region since the nineteenth century, the impetus for the development of an industrial-scale purse seine industry was, perversely, often the serial declines in a number of areas of demersal fish species which were taken by trawl fishing, which has been discussed above. In many cases, which will be further elaborated below, declining demersal fish stocks stimulated the search for new fisheries and, with mechanized vessels available, purse seining of pelagic fisheries was an obvious choice.

In the nineteenth century, various surrounding nets came to be used like purse seines, with the ability to close the lower end of the net by pulling a rope that passed through lead rings hanging from the lower edge of the net. Such nets were used, for example, in the Mollucas to catch a variety of pelagic fish and were often used in conjunction with fish aggregating devices, locally known as *rumpon*. In Cebu, fishers modified traditional floating nets to act as purse seines and these were extensively used by the 1930s to take flying fish. In the Philippines, a traditional purse-shaped net known as *sapyaw* was used prior to the 1920s to take large quantities of *Sardinella* although this net did not have a closing mechanism and needed to be positioned beneath the fish school, rather than surrounding them. After the 1920s, some operators in the Philippines adopted a net locally known as a *kubkuban* which was a small purse seine net (240 m long, 20 to 40 m deep and with a very large mesh) operated from a single large double-outrigger vessel. Because of the large mesh, larger pelagics such as mackerel were targeted.

By the early 1900s, sail-powered Chinese junks based on Hainan Island and on the Chinese mainland were operating purse seine nets (as well as trawl nets) in the Gulf of Tonkin. In 1910, between 600 and 700 such junks paid for a fishing permit at Cac Ba Island and many others were apparently fishing illegally. Butcher (2004) estimates that these vessels took 20000–25000 tonnes of prepared fish back to their home ports annually . Similar vessels (operated by Chinese from Hainan and each supported by three smaller tenders) were later used to develop purse seining in the Gulf of Thailand and also for Indian mackerel in Malayan waters in the Straits of Malacca during the 1930s, using nets that were about 310 m long, 50 m deep and with a 1.27 cm. Contemporary records show that catches varied enormously, and ranged from about 300 kg to 12 tonnes in a single haul.

A dramatic development occurred in the Straits of Malacca fishery in 1937 with the introduction of motorized vessels in place of the sail-powered junks. As a result of this development, landings of Indian mackerel at Pangkor increased dramatically, rising from 860 tonnes in 1931 to 5700 tonnes in 1938. The success of the venture stimulated local Malays to also begin purse seining, although the nets they used had larger mesh sizes than those of the Chinese purse seiners to enable them to be handled from their existing vessels. This resulted in landings of larger size mackerel, including, it is presumed, of Spanish mackerel.

Although developments of these traditional fishing methods resulted in increased landings, the increases were modest when compared with the dramatic increase in demand for fish and fish products, the increase in production from both aquaculture and from the developing trawling industry, and the increase in imports of fish products.

By the late 1960s, however, there were emerging problems with the large number of trawlers that were operating in areas such as the Gulf of Thailand and vessels were looking for new trawl grounds in the region. Drastic declines in trawl catch rates in the Gulf of Thailand and soaring oil prices prompted fishers to either modify existing vessels or have new vessels built for taking pelagic species, instead of trawl species. There were large stocks of pelagic species in the Gulf (particularly Indian mackerel) and methods such as purse seining required much less fuel than trawling. The total pelagic catch in the Gulf of Thailand therefore increased dramatically from 63000 tonnes in 1971 to 480000 tonnes in 1977, a result not only of an increasing number of purse seine vessels but also because of the use of light lures and the move to new fishing areas within the Gulf. This latter factor resulted in the landing of species such as scads and sardines that previously had not been a significant part of the pelagic catch.

Also, during the 1970s and early 1980s, the Government of Thailand promoted the development of a canning industry by encouraging foreign investment. The first tuna cannery was established in 1972 as a joint venture between an Australian company (Safcol Holdings) and Thai and Hong Kong investors and by 1983 there were 30–35 canneries in operation. This demand for tuna from the canneries led to purse seine vessels targeting the abundant stock of small tuna such as longtail (*Thunnus tongil*), kawakawa (*Euthynnus affinis*) and frigate (*Auxis thazard*) tuna. However, the fleet by 1991 had to rely on tuna catches from foreign waters (including Malaysia and the Natuna Islands) since the stocks in the Gulf of Thailand had diminished significantly. The development of the canning, particularly tuna canning, industry in Thailand during the 1980s (which made Thailand the world's largest exporter of fish products by 1989, with 51 percent of global exports) was so rapid that canning capacity outstripped the ability of the fleet to supply raw product. This resulted not only in the Thai purse seine fleet seeking additional supplies in other waters of Southeast Asia, but, perhaps more importantly, also led to a rapid rise in the imports of frozen raw tuna, and other fish, for their canneries. By 1991, 79 percent of the 630000 tonnes of tuna that was canned in Thailand was derived from imported raw product. This demand for raw tuna for the Thai canneries therefore helped, in large part, to drive the development of tuna industries in other countries of the region, particularly the Philippines. The vast majority of this imported tuna originated from purse seine operations throughout the region, and, although a small quantity of tuna from pole-and-line and longline vessels was supplied to the Thai canneries, much of the tuna from these fisheries increasingly went to the Japanese sashimi market.

As the fishery in the Gulf of Thailand developed without significant regulation, overexploitation of some pelagic fish species in the Gulf became evident and total landings in the Gulf fell steadily to 290000 tonnes in 1980.

In Indonesia, the development of the purse seine fishery was also influenced by the development, and subsequent problems with, the industrial trawl fishery. Although landings of pelagic species had been increasing substantially since the early 1900s (reaching 154000 tonnes by 1950 and 620000 tonnes by 1978 as both Chinese and Indonesian-owned purse seine vessels supplied newly built canneries and became the dominant fishing gear in Indonesia), the ban on trawl fishing in the 1980s accelerated the development of the purse seine fishery, particularly in the Java Sea. The Government, when banning trawling in the western part of the country, provided financial incentives for vessels to convert to purse seining, with the result that the number of purse seiners increased from an average of 810 during the period 1975–79 to 2100 in 1984–87. At this time, the larger purse seiners extended their operations into the eastern part of the Java Sea, with the result that landings by the Java Sea purse seine fleet increased from 49000 tonnes in 1975–79 to 140000 tonnes in 1984–87. After 1985, total landings (as well as annual landings per vessel) fell significantly, a result of overexploitation of the major species, particularly the small pelagics. Fortunately, the price of these fish increased at this time which enabled the purse seine fleet not only to survive economically but also expand to new areas in the southern part of the Makassar Strait and the waters between the Malay Peninsula and Borneo. The purse seiners also improved their technology, using light to attract fish and hence increase their efficiency. However, by 1995, total catches of pelagic species in the Java Sea had stagnated at around 150000 tonnes, roughly the same level as the early 1980s.

The catch by industrial purse seine vessels accelerated again after 1995, reaching 8 percent of the total marine catch of Indonesia by 1997 (FAO, 2000) as the vessels continued the expansion of their area of operations into the eastern areas of Indonesia, a process that had begun in the 1980s. In total, small-scale purse seine operations and industrial purse seine vessels together contributed approximately 17.6 percent of total marine production in Indonesia in 1997 (FAO, 2000) with the majority of this still coming from the small-scale sector, which continues to dominate the industry. However, the larger industrial purse seine vessels contribute much more in terms of value of the catch than the small-scale sector because they focus on high-value species such as tuna and other large pelagics whereas the small-scale fishers concentrate on inshore small pelagics in the western part of the country.

This expansion of industrial purse seiners into eastern Indonesian waters has been supported by the increased development of infrastructure such as tuna canneries and ports which also provide services to foreign fishing vessels. Purse seine vessels in the west of Indonesia fish for small pelagic species and are concentrated primarily in the Java Sea, South China Sea, Malacca Strait and Mollucas Sea. In general, these seiners range from 10 to 30Gross Registered Tonnage (GRT)[2] , although in the last decade larger ones have been built, exceeding 100GR T. Purse seine vessels operating in the east of the country tend to be larger vessels, in excess of 100 GRT.

During the late 1970s, Japanese purse seiners were also expanding their operations in Southeast Asia and, in 1980, at least 14 vessels were operating off the north coast of Irian Jaya and Papua New Guinea, each taking about 15 tonnes of fish per day. As part of this operation, the Japanese vessels also captured large quantities of tuna in and around Indonesian waters.

In the Philippines, the traditional *kubkuban* purse seine net, in use since the 1920s, has continued to be used by small-scale, inshore fishers to take mackerel. In addition, in the 1950s, large-scale purse seining was introduced to the Philippines, probably by American tuna seiners operating in the eastern Pacific. The introduction included the use of nylon nets and power blocks for hauling the net. As the new fishing method was taken up enthusiastically, with trawlers being converted to seiners and secondhand Japanese purse seine vessels being imported, the move to purse seining was further supported by government incentives and assistance from a United Nations Special Fund project in importing nylon nets and other equipment.

At first, the increasing number of purse seine vessels (there were already 48 operating by 1966) targeted small pelagic species but, because of the large quantities of fish being landed and the lack of onshore processing facilities to handle the catch, prices collapsed in the late 1960s. With this price collapse, together with warnings that increasing fishing on small pelagic species may lead to a reduction in the quantity of fish available, vessels began to turn their attention to tuna. By 1975, purse seining for tuna in the Philippines had increased dramatically, aided by the development of fish aggregating devices, locally called *payaw*, around which the purse seiners as well as handline fishers operated. The *payaw* is particularly effective for aggregating skipjack and yellowfin tuna. Recorded tuna landings in the Philippines exploded from about 23 000 tonnes in 1973 to 220000 tonnes in 1977 although statistics are imprecise because of factors such as unrecorded foreign catches and the practice of Filipino vessels selling their catch to foreign vessels at sea.

Since the late 1970s, catches from tuna purse seining in the waters of the Philippines have increased only slowly, with recorded landings reaching about 300000 tonnes by 1997 and 400000 tonnes by 2002. However , during this time, Filipino operators of tuna purse seiners have expanded their operations considerably to other areas in the Indian and Pacific Oceans and these increases in recorded landings partly reflect this expanded fishing area as well as the targeting of other, smaller tuna species. Purse seining remains, however, the most common form of commercial fishing gear in the Philippines with 61 percent of operators using this gear, 15.7 percent using ring-nets and 12.4 percent using bag nets (FAO, 2005a). By contrast, only 3.7 percent of small-scale fishers use the small traditional purse seine or *kubkuban.* The purse seines, ringnets and handlines usually account for over 80 percent of the annual tuna catch, with nearly half the commercial tuna catch in 1995 taken by purse seine.

In addition to tuna, commercial purse seiners target small pelagic species, particularly roundscad, sardines and Indian mackerel. Together, these small pelagic species accounted for 47 percent by weight of overall commercial landings in 2003 (FAO, 2005a) from all gear types with tunas comprising the remainder. However, the proportion derived only from purse seine operations has not been reported. Because of their lower value, the small pelagic species comprise a much smaller proportion by value of the total commercial catch.

The shift in emphasis in a number of countries such as Indonesia and the Philippines in the 1960s and 1970s from demersal trawling to purse seining of small pelagics and, later, tuna, has also prompted other countries of the region to examine purse seining. In Viet Nam, some purse seining was undertaken early in the twentieth century by Chinese junks operating in the Gulf of Tonkin, as noted above. However, Viet Nam has not developed its own offshore purse seine fleet to any great extent although small purse seine vessels have, for some decades, taken small pelagic species in inshore waters. Although the inshore fishery is dominated by small trawlers, the offshore fleet of some 20000 vessels includes only about 100 vessels (with engines of 400–500 horsepower) which have the capacity for deep-sea fishing. This fleet comprises either trawlers or purse seiners. Trawlers are used in waters 35–80 m deep in southeastern waters, whereas purse seiners fish pelagic species in deep waters, mainly off the central region. The estimated percentage of the total catch from major types of fishing gear (FAO, 2005b) are; trawling 30 percent, purse seine 26 percent, gillnet 18 percent, lift net 5 percent, longline 6 percent and others (fixed net, push-net etc.) 15 percent. However, the development of offshore fisheries (including purse seining for tuna) has been vigorously promoted by the Government and has been included in a recent long-term strategic plan for the fisheries sector (FAO/Fishcode, 2004).

The expansion of purse seining by Thai vessels in particular also impacted the waters of Cambodia. Although Cambodia has a traditional, small-scale purse seine fishery, which operates in inshore waters to take Indian mackerel and anchovies (FAO, 2005c) together with small quantities of tuna, it has not developed a national industrial-scale purse seine fleet. Foreign purse seine operations in the waters of Cambodia, using industrial scale vessels, has, however, long taken place, often by Thai and Japanese vessels and this currently includes illegal operations. No data are available on the number of vessels involved or their catches.

While small-scale purse seine fisheries have a long tradition in many countries of the region, the development of industrialized purse seine fisheries in Southeast Asia accelerated following the initial decline in demersal fish stocks in the late 1960s. This development led to a search for new fisheries and, most importantly, for employment for the vessels and crew that were engaged in demersal trawling. Subsequent support of the boatbuilding industry in several countries and the increase in oil price in the 1970s also added to the attractiveness of vessels moving into the purse seine fishery.

With the decline in small pelagic stocks and reduced prices, the purse seine vessels turned their attention to tuna fishing in the early 1970s, particularly in the Philippines where this development was assisted by the use of fish aggregating devices. In addition, most of the purse seine fleets expanded out of their national waters in search of tuna (and also, to a lesser extent, small pelagic species) and it was this expansion and the move to tuna fishing that supported continued expansion both of the purse seine fleet and their catches. However, since the purse seine fleets were operating both inside and outside their national waters (both legally and illegally) and landing their catch in various places, the statistics on landings, the place of capture and the number of vessels operating are notoriously unreliable.

While the expansion of the tuna fisheries (and, to a lesser extent, small pelagics) is still occurring in some areas, and countries such as Viet Nam are still looking to expand their industrial purse seine fleet, most stocks of small and large pelagic species within the national waters of countries of the region are considered to have reached their peak production. Examining the region's large-scale marine ecosystems (LMEs), Sugiyama *et al.* (2004) concluded that small pelagic stocks in the region had either peaked or were fluctuating in all areas except within the Sulu-Celebes Sea, the Indonesian Sea and the South China Sea LMEs where they were still increasing while large pelagics had either peaked or were fluctuating in all areas except the South China Sea LME. They also noted that the small and large pelagic resources in all areas generally had peaked after the demersal stocks, which is consistent with the known development of the trawl and purse seine fisheries in the region.

In the Philippines, recent studies on pelagic fisheries indicate overfishing and declining catch per unit effort (CPUE). Exceptions are in lightly fished areas in waters off Palawan, parts of the country's Pacific coast and some parts of Mindanao. Such findings are supported by an observed change in species composition, i.e. anchovies have partially replaced sardines, scads and mackerels in the catch, an indication of gradual stock collapse (Green *et al.*, 2003).

Like the demersal resources, the potential for expanding landings of small and large pelagic species by purse seining in the region therefore appears limited and the challenge for national governments is to move to long-term control and management of their existing fishing fleets. There are some encouraging signs that this is happening. Several countries (e.g. Viet Nam and the Philippines) have recently introduced new fisheries laws and, in the Philippines, the Government has made a significant policy shift by introducing joint management mechanisms of the fisheries sector, involving both the central government and the municipalities, and the fishers, through Fisheries and Aquatic Resources Management Councils. However, much remains to be done in bringing long-term, sustainable management to purse seine operations in the region.

SHRIMP TRAWLING

The development of shrimp trawling in the region paralleled the development of demersal fish trawling and, in many areas, shrimp were taken as a by-catch to demersal fishing. However, in Indonesia, the development of trawling in the 1960s was, from the beginning, specifically targeted at catching shrimp and Gulf of Mexico-type shrimp nets, rather than demersal fish trawls, were used.

The increasing interest in shrimp in the Indonesian trawl fishery, as well as in other areas, coincided with a growing demand for shrimp in Japan. It is therefore not surprising that Japanese companies were involved in the development of the Indonesian shrimp fishery, initially by themselves and, after 1969, as partners in joint venture arrangements with Indonesian fishing companies. Between 1967 and 1971, one wholly owned Japanese company and about 10 joint ventures began operating shrimp trawlers in the Straits of Malacca, the waters off Kalimantan and the Arafura Sea.

Supported by Japanese capital investment, these joint ventures were vertically integrated undertakings, operating a range of trawlers which delivered the catch to their own freezing and cold storage facilities and exporting the product. Exports of frozen shrimp from Indonesia rose from 5600 tonnes in 1969 (valued at US$873000) to 35000 tonnes in 1979, valued at over US$200 million. As the prices paid for shrimp increased substantially and additional freezing and cold storage facilities were added, landings and exports continued to increase dramatically as small-scale fishers and independent trawlers sold their product to the cold storage and export companies, and vessels travelled further to find new fishing grounds.

During the 1980s, the declaration of Exclusive Economic Zones also had a profound impact on shrimp trawling in the region. Countries with extensive EEZs were able to continue to expand their shrimp trawling operations (supported by onshore cold storage facilities and onboard freezing) while countries with smaller EEZs had greater difficulty in accessing shrimp grounds beyond their own EEZ. Because of this, the shrimp catches of Indonesia continued to increase throughout the 1980s and 1990s (rising from 117000 tonnes in 1980 to 288000 tonnes in 2002) while those of Malaysia stagnated, declining from 84000 to 76000 tonnes during the same period.

As the price of shrimp increased dramatically in the late 1960s and early 1970s, trawl fisheries that had been established in other countries, particularly Thailand and Malaysia, targeted areas where good shrimp catches could be taken, although they continued catching and landing demersal fish. For example, between 1965 and 1972, the proportion by weight of shrimp to demersal fish landed in Malaysia increased from 38 to 59 percent and in Thailand it increased from 54 to 71 percent. However, shrimp stocks in most areas were soon under pressure and the focus returned to demersal fish species, particularly since the price of shrimp started to decline with the introduction in the early 1970s of shrimp culture in the region and its subsequent explosive growth over the next two decades. In Thailand, for example, the proportion by weight of shrimp to demersal fish in the landings declined from 71 percent in 1972 to 35 percent in 1992.

In 2002, 73 percent of total regional shrimp landings of about 623 000 tonnes came from just three countries: Indonesia, Thailand and Malaysia — a similar percentage (72 percent) to that from the same three countries in 1970. However, in 2002, Indonesia's landings had increased to 287 990 tonnes or about 46 percent of total regional landings compared with only 50 200 tonnes or 22 percent of regional landings in 1970. By contrast, Malaysia's share of total regional landings fell from 22 percent in 1970 to 12 percent in 2002, as landings there increased only slightly over the 32 year period.

With the possible exception of Indonesia, shrimp trawling in the region is inextricably linked to a more general, multi-species demersal trawl industry that takes fish, shrimp and other species. Its development and future direction therefore very much depends on the relative prices for shrimp and other species of the demersal trawl catch (and their relative abundance) since these relative prices will, in large part, determine the species that are targeted by trawl vessels. In this regard, the development of shrimp aquaculture in the region, and in other parts of the world, is a major factor since it has led to a long-term decline in world shrimp prices. These declining shrimp prices have probably eased the pressure on shrimp stocks and, throughout the region, shrimp now comprise a smaller proportion of demersal catches than at any other time. Whether this is a result of fewer shrimp, because of overexploitation or habitat degradation, or an active targeting of other species, it is not possible to judge from the little data and analyses that are available.

TUNA LONGLINING, POLING AND PURSE SEINING

As noted in Section IV above, purse seining activities in the region, although initially targeting small pelagic species, had, by the early 1980s, begun to target various tuna species and also expanded their operations to the eastern part of Indonesia, the coasts of Irian Jaya and further afield. Initially, Japanese purse seine vessels led this expansion although vessels from the Philippines and Indonesia quickly followed.

The taking of tuna in the area, however, was a traditional fishery practice in many countries. In the nineteenth century, trawl-shaped nets (locally called *payang*), trolling using lures made from feathers and longlining (locally called *rawai*) were all common fishing methods in the western islands area of Indonesia, Singapore and Malaya (Butcher, 2004) and took not only small tuna species but also other large pelagics and, in the case of longlining, demersal species such as sharks and rays. In the Mollucas, pole-and-line fishing for skipjack tuna was also a common fishing method and involved the use of live bait and barbless hooks with a piece of feather as a lure. By the early 1900s, Japanese fishing vessels had begun fishing in a number of countries of Southeast Asia. Japanese trollers, driftnetters and *muro ami* (a net for specifically taking fusiliers, family *Caesionidae*) fishers had established themselves in Singapore by the 1920s and, in the 1930s were taking, in addition to fusiliers, shad, small sharks and other species, both skipjack tuna (*Katsuwonus pelamis*) and bigeye tuna (*Thunnus obesus*) by trolling. Although the catches of these species were not large (about 100 tonnes were landed in 1932), the development is significant in that it introduced deepwater trolling for these species to the region.

The Japanese were also active in developing the pole-and-line fishery for skipjack tuna (although, as noted above, there was a traditional pole-and-line fishery for tuna in the Mollucas), which was mainly caught for the Japanese market and formed part of a broader skipjack pole-and-line fishery that extended beyond Southeast Asia into the Pacific coast of Japan and the western Pacific Ocean. Beginning in about 1910 the Japanese started developing bases in the region, and by the 1930s they had them established in a number of countries including at Ambon, Manado, Ternato, Davao, Zamboanga, Si Amil Island and Aertembaga. These bases were used as receiving, processing and exporting depots and produced not only dried tuna stick (known to the Japanese as *kasuobushi*) but also canned product. The pole-and-line technique used was similar to that used in the Mollucas and involved bamboo poles, live bait and barbless hooks. However, the Japanese also introduced the technique of spraying water on the sea surface, giving the illusion of even more small fish. While accurate statistics on this fishery are scarce, one company based at Zamboanga landed 1100 tonnes of skipjack and 260 tonnes of immature yellowfin tuna in 1938, with the fleet fishing over a wide area that included the Sulu Sea, Moro Gulf, Celebes Sea and the Davao Gulf. The pole-and-line fishery seems to have been favourably received and, as one researcher in the Philippines commented in 1940 (quoted by Butcher, 2004, p.158), the pole-and-line fishery is "not conducive to depleting the tuna fishing grounds" although the use of purse seines for catching tuna "should be discouraged as much as possible in Philippines tuna grounds since the purse seine was far less selective in what it caught than the pole and line".

During this period, the Japanese were also exploring the development of a deep water longline fishery for tuna and, by 1932, had factory ships operating in Sumatran waters that processed and canned yellowfin tuna on board for the Japanese market. By 1941, the Japanese had conducted longlining activities in the South China, Sulu, Celebes, Mollucas and Banda Seas as well as the Pacific Ocean between New Guinea and Mindanao and the Indian Ocean.

In the year after the Second World War, Japanese activity in tuna fishing in Southeast Asia declined dramatically. However, the potential of tuna stocks in the region was well recognized. In 1950, in recognition of the virtually unexploited status of tuna in the Philippines, a company began operating longliners that had been brought from Taiwan. However, the venture failed. By 1970, however, companies that operated freezing and processing plants began supplying fishers with small vessels and hand troll lines to take large yellowfin tuna for export to Japan. By the late 1970s, the fishers based at General Santos City were landing about 40 tonnes of yellowfin tuna per day. A major development in the tuna fishery in the Philippines came in 1975 with the development of a fish aggregating device, locally known as a *payaw*. This floating fish lure was used by both the purse seiners (described in Section IV) who targeted skipjack and juvenile yellowfin tuna and by the hand-line fishers who targeted large yellowfin and bigeye tuna. This combination of purse seine and hand-line catches brought about a spectacular increase in tuna catches in the Philippines, which rose from 23000 tonnes in 1973 to 220000 tonnes in 1977.

By the early 1950s, however, Japanese vessels had begun to return to longlining and pole-and-line fishing for tuna, including in waters around Indonesia and the Philippines, as well as the Indian and Pacific Oceans. The catching vessels were supported by mother ships, taking their catch directly back to Japan. The nature of this fishery meant that landings statistics for tuna in the region are certainly underestimated with the extent of underestimation being related to the extent of this type of foreign fishing.

The Japanese longliners involved with mothership operations varied in size from 20-50 tonnes to over 200 tonnes but, according to a 1963 report, were typically 100-200 GRT[3]. These longliners targeted yellowfin tuna but also took significant quantities of bigeye tuna and operated initially in the western areas of the Banda, Celebes and Mollucas Seas (which were international waters in the 1950s) but quickly spread their operations westwards into the Indian Ocean. In 1968, and in response to Indonesia's territorial seas claims, Indonesia and Japan signed the Banda Sea Agreement which provided access for Japanese tuna longliners to areas of the Banda Sea and to Indonesian ports for payment of an annual fee. This Agreement lasted until 1975, when the Indonesian Government attempted to establish its own tuna longlining company, Perikan Samodra Besar (PSB), although this company then entered into a new agreement with the Japanese to allow continued access to the tuna fishing areas in the Banda Sea, but under much stricter conditions than before.

With a move away from canned tuna and towards sashimi product in the 1970s, the Japanese longline fleet in Southeast Asia declined as longliners began targeting species such as southern bluefin tuna in the Indian Ocean and the vessels remaining in Southeast Asia shifted their emphasis away from yellowfin to species that were more suitable for sashimi product, such as bigeye tuna. In the Banda Sea area, yellowfin tuna comprised about 75 percent of total tuna catches in 1974, but by 1980 bigeye tuna made up 50-75 percent of the catch. The better targeting of bigeye tuna was achieved by changing the method of longlining from surface to deep longlines, set at 100-300 m below the surface. This development of "deep longlining" therefore extended the area available for fishing deeper into the water column and led to continued expansion of landings throughout the region during the 1980s. The Japanese pole-and-line fishery has always been more important in the areas around the Philippines and the eastern seas of Southeast

Asia than around the western areas and, in 1970, their main area of operation was the Philippines and the northern tip of Borneo. Because of their reliance on live, small baitfish (which are generally found in inshore waters), the pole-and-line vessels are not able to fish in areas remote from land. This reliance on land-based operations also meant that Japanese pole-and-line vessels, unlike purse seine vessels or longliners, could not operate without close relationships with the coastal states and therefore, Japanese operations in places like the eastern areas of Indonesia and the Philippines were more often under joint-venture arrangements.

However, by the mid-to-late 1970s, Japan was taking steps to replace its pole-and-line vessels with purse seiners, which were proving a much more efficient and profitable method of taking tuna. This also coincided with the Japanese longliners move from canned product to sashimi product (and the consequent shift in targeted species) and increased fishing by Japanese vessels in the Indian Ocean. These two developments resulted in an overall decline of Japanese tuna fishing activity in Southeast Asian waters and allowed the fledgling pole-and-line and longline industries in countries such as Indonesia and the Philippines to further develop. As noted above, purse seining and trolling, using the *payaw* fish aggregating device, developed rapidly in the Philippines after 1975 and by 1980 in Indonesia the PSB company, established in 1975, was operating seventeen 111 GRT[4] tuna longline vessels off Bali and Sumatra although they had reverted to targeting yellowfin tuna by sub-surface longlines rather than bigeye tuna with deep longlines. Three pole-and-line tuna companies were also formed and operated 29 vessels off Irian Jaya (in areas where the Japanese had formally fished) by the early 1980s. At that time, the Government of Indonesia was anxious to support a local tuna industry and supported these, and other, tuna longlining and pole-and-line companies financially, enabling them to expand their operations during the 1990s.In 2002, Indonesia and the Philippines were the dominant tuna fishing nations in the region, accounting for more than 85 percent of regional tuna landings (Figure 4). While the majority of these came from purse seining (see Section IV above), trolling, pole-and-line and longline vessels were major contributors to tuna landings, and were particularly important in the small-scale fisheries of both countries. The statistics on tuna landings for the region, however, highly questionable because of the nature of the tuna industry and the nature of the national reporting systems. For example, tuna taken in the Philippines by Japanese vessels and landed in Japan are unlikely to appear in the national statistics of the Philippines and, likewise, tuna taken by Thai vessels in Indonesia are likely to appear in the national statistics of Thailand, not Indonesia. These issues need to be taken into account when considering tuna landing and production statistics for the region, although the overall upward trend in landings for the region may not be influenced as much by these factors.

DRIFTNETTING

Driftnetting has a long history in Southeast Asia, with the nets originally being made from coconut or ramie fibre imported from China. In areas such as the Straits of Malacca, Borneo, the Mollucas and Java, the landings from driftnets probably accounted for the majority of the catch in some areas during the nineteenth century. The traditional use of such nets were to set them in the evening and haul them in the morning with catches consisting of species such as shad, Spanish mackerel, wolf herring and small sharks, depending on the area fished and the mesh size of the net. The fishery in these early years was undertaken exclusively by small-scale fishers operating nets that were typically 110-400 m in length.

However, by the late 1920s, Japanese fishers based in Singapore had begun using driftnets in the Straits of Malacca and, by the early 1930s, there were two Japanese companies specializing in driftnetting there. These fishers undertook driftnetting on a much larger scale than the Malays and Chinese fishing in the Straits, using a 25 tonne vessel[5] with a 50 horsepower engine to tow several smaller sail-powered fishing vessels from Singapore. Each of these smaller vessels operated nets that were some 900 m long and the catch was iced and returned to Singapore on a regular basis by a transport vessel. The fishing vessels therefore were able to stay fishing for long periods of time without returning to port. Catch rates were about 90 kg per vessel per day, compared with the Chinese and Malay vessels' catches of about 9 kg per day. In 1932, the Japanese driftnetters landed 1400 tonnes of fish, mainly of Spanish mackerel, wolf herring, small sharks and shad, which comprised some 13 percent of total landings in Singapore.

By the end of the Second World War, the Japanese driftnetters, like other Japanese fishing fleets, no longer operated in the Straits of Malacca. However, their methods of using motorized vessels to tow smaller vessels to the fishing grounds and to transport the catch to market were soon adopted by local fishers. By the 1950s, outboard motors were becoming readily available and one of their first uses was to power existing craft that were used for driftnetting, particularly in the Straits of Malacca and the Malay Peninsula. The pace of mechanization of fishing vessels, and the impact that this had, cannot be overestimated - in 1947, about 1 percent of vessels in the Malay Peninsula were mechanized while by 1965, 55 percent of vessels had engines.

This increasing mechanization not only allowed catches to be transported from the fishing grounds to the market but also allowed vessels to follow fish schools, thus extending the area which was fished. At the same time, nylon nets began to replace the traditional fibre or cotton nets and, in 1958, it was noted that "drift net catches in the Malacca Straits have doubled with the replacement of cotton by synthetic fibre resulting in an increased supply of Tenggiri [Spanish mackerel] and Parang [wolf herring] to the west coast markets" (Anon, 1958).

In Indonesia, driftnetting for the same species as taken on the Malay Peninsula had also had a long history and the Japanese driftnetters based in Singapore in the 1930s also operated near the east coast of Sumatra within the Straits of Malacca. Indonesian fishers, however, continued to use small nets and sail-powered craft both on the east and west coast of Sumatra, Java and Borneo and the contribution to total catches from driftnetting remained small. In the 1950s, the number of vessels and fishers in Indonesia began to increase dramatically, from 80000 vessels in 1951 to 200000 in 1961, an increase of 120000. However , much of this increase was in non-motorised, traditional craft, which increased by 115000 vessels. In contrast to the 55 percent of the fishing fleet in Malaya that was motorized by 1965, in Indonesia only 1.4 percent of the fleet was motorized by 1967. Driftnet fishing in Indonesia, therefore, continued using traditional small nets and sail-powered craft, although the number of such craft evidently increased substantially during the 1950s and 1960s. When motorization of the fleet came to Indonesia in the late 1960s, it spurred the development of the trawl fishery but was adopted more slowly by other sectors such as the driftnet fishers. As a result, the importance of the driftnet fishery in Indonesia declined as a percentage of total landings as the landings from the trawl fishery increased rapidly.

After the trawl ban imposed by Indonesia in 1980 and 1981 in western parts of the country, there was a rapid recovery in inshore demersal and pelagic fish stocks, despite the trawl ban being only partly effective. At the same time, the Government provided easy credit for the building of new vessels and imposed no restrictions on other forms of fishing, apart from trawling. This resulted in both an upgrading and mechanization of vessels (the number of motors about doubling during the early 1980s and the number of fishers increasing by a third) and an increase in both the number of motorized and non-motorised vessels. Although it is not known how the driftnet fishery was impacted by such changes, it seems reasonable to assume that driftnet fishers also took advantage of this situation to upgrade vessels and fishing gear so they could better target the increased abundance of fish in inshore waters. In 1998, the number of fishing vessels in Indonesia had reached about 334000 with 57 percent of them still without motors. Most of these were involved in small-scale traditional and subsistence fishing and, in 1998, this small-scale sector contributed 94.6 percent of total marine landings of 3.27 million tonnes (but total landings data apparently show a typographical error and therefore have been corrected in accordance with FAO, 2004). The purse seine fishery (17.64 percent), lift net fishery (8.26 percent), trammel net (5.02 percent) and the skipjack and yellowfin tuna pole-and-line fishery (3.08 percent) were the most important fisheries with driftnetting remaining a very minor component of overall landings.

Driftnet fishing also remains the preserve of small-scale fishers in most other countries of the region. In the Philippines, small-scale (or "Municipal") fishers took about 922000 tonnes of fish in 2003 (Anon, 2005a), which represented about 45 percent of total landings. Although the most common fishing method used by these Municipal fisheries is hook and line, a fixed or floating gillnet contributed around 45.5 percent of total Municipal small pelagic landings in 1995 (Zaragosa *et al.*, 2004). Small pelagic species are by far the most important component of the Municipal landings and these are also caught by other fishing methods (Zaragosa *et al.*, 2004) such as hook-and-line (15.3 percent of total Municipal landings), ringnet (11.5 percent), beach seine (8.3 percent), purse seine (3.7 percent), fish corral (2.9 percent) and bag net (2.9 percent).

In Viet Nam, fixed and floating gillnets are also significant contributors to the landings from the inshore small-scale sector, with 18 percent of total landings in 2003 coming from these nets. However, no distinction is made in the landings data between the types of net although at least some of these gillnets are operated as small driftnets. Drift gillnetting is, and always has been, more important in the northern parts of Viet Nam (including Ha Long Bay and the Gulf of Tonkin) than in the south although current statistical data (Anon, 2005b) does not allow the separation of landings and other data by fishing method.

TROLLING

Trolling was a well established fishing method in many areas of Southeast Asia (particularly the Straits of Malacca, the Philippines and the western islands of Indonesia) by the nineteenth century with unbaited hooks, and a lure made from chicken feathers being towed behind sail-powered vessels to take small tunas and Spanish mackerel.

Like driftnetting, the Japanese that who were based in Singapore from the 1920s transformed the way in which trolling was conducted in the region and, in the 1930s, were taking both skipjack tuna (*Katsuwonus pelamis*) and bigeye tuna (*Thunnus obesus*) by trolling. Although the catches of these species were not large when compared with the driftnet fishery (about 100 tonnes were landed by trolling in 1932), the development is significant in that it appears that it introduced deepwater trolling for these species to the region. Skipjack inhabit deep coastal and oceanic water while bigeye tuna seldom appear at the surface, but are abundant at thermocline depths and therefore the landing of quantities of these species would indicate that the Japanese trollers had developed techniques to fish in deep offshore waters. In 1932, it was reported that these fishers, using motorized vessels, were working in areas remote from Singapore as far as the Anambas and Natuna Islands, the northern entrance to the Straits of Malacca, the Mergui Archipelago and the coasts of Borneo.

With the cessation of the activities of the Japanese troll fishers after the Second World War, trolling in the Straits of Malacca and other areas reverted to the operations of small, local, sail-powered vessels and further development of this sector was intimately tied to the rate of mechanization of the small-scale fishing fleet. As discussed in Malaysia and also in Singapore, this mechanization occurred rapidly during the 1950s and 1960s whereas in Indonesia and the Philippines, it occurred more slowly. As a result, a return to the use of mechanized vessels for trolling, and the exploitation of waters remote from the vessel's home base, pioneered by the Japanese, occurred more quickly in Malaysia and Singapore than in other countries. Malaysia and Singapore, therefore, were able to sustain a small dedicated troll fishery, mainly for tuna, whereas in other areas trolling was often undertaken by small-scale fishers as an additional activity (often as they made their way to and from fishing grounds) to demersal hand-lining, gillnetting and other methods. In no area, however, was trolling a dominant activity.

In the Philippines, the development in 1975 of a fish aggregating device, locally known as a *payaw,* impacted significantly not only on the purse seine industry but also on fishers who were taking tuna by hand-trolling. The tuna *payaw* was a larger version of a similar lure that inshore fishers had traditionally used for small pelagic species, except the tuna *payaw* was placed between 35 and 110 km offshore, about 11 km apart from each other and in waters up to 3000 m deep. The rafts were "harvested" every 5 or 6 days. The cooperation between the two groups of fishers was significant with trollers and hand-line fishers targeting the larger tuna species that were attracted by the smaller prey fish but which swam at depths out of reach of the purse seine net. The hand-line and troll fishers watched over the *payaw* in return for the privilege of fishing there. This combination of purse seine and hand-line catches brought about a spectacular increase in tuna catches in the Philippines, which rose from 23000 tonnes in 1973 to 220000 tonnes in 1977.

Apart from this positive interaction between purse seine and troll fishers, the development of the tuna purse seine industry in the region (and, to a lesser extent, the pole-and-line fishery) also impacted negatively on vessels that were using trolling to take tunas.

As the appetite of Thailand's tuna canneries grew through the 1980s and the Thai purse seine fleet moved into new waters to meet the demand of the canneries, the total catch by the Thai fleet of small tuna species suitable for canning jumped from 20000 tonnes in 1981 to 170000 tonnes in 1992, but then, as they ran out of new areas to exploit, the catch began to decline. One of the impacts of this intensified fishing on small tunas by the Thai trawlers was that catches by Malaysian trollers operating off the east coast of the Malaysian Peninsula collapsed.

Trolling, like driftnetting, remains primarily an activity of the small-scale fisheries sector in Southeast Asia, particularly in Indonesia, Malaysia and the Philippines.

However, unlike driftnetting, trolling for tuna and other pelagic species is generally undertaken as an adjunct, and often opportunistic, activity to other fishing operations. Because of this, and because of its relative small importance in most areas, statistics specific to this fishery are usually not available.

OTHER INDUSTRIAL FISHING OPERATIONS, INCLUDING FAILED TYPES OF INDUSTRIAL FISHING

While much of the large-scale industrial fishing technology in the region, such as purse seining and trawling, has been introduced by expansion from other areas of existing fishing methods, there are a number of large-scale production technologies that have developed from existing techniques used by small-scale fishers. Perhaps the most important of these is the technology of fixed stake nets used in various parts of the region, and particularly the *muro ami* net that was first introduced by Japanese fishers to Manila and Singapore in 1919 and later into Batavia in 1925. These nets, which were portable fixed nets secured to coral reefs, were used to take fusiliers (Family *Caesionidae)* around the reef areas and quickly became so important that, for example, between 27 and 42 percent of all fish landings in Singapore between 1931 and 1938 were fusiliers from *muro ami* nets. Similar developments occurred in Batavia (where, in the period 1935-38, 25 percent of all fish sales were fusiliers from *muro ami* fishing) and in the Philippines where a single *muro ami* team typically landed 70-80 tonnes of fish per month in the late 1930s.

The technique, however, was so effective that it not only quickly resulted in declines of the stocks of reef fish but also impacted severely on the coral reefs where the nets were used. This was particularly so during the period 1945-1960 where the technique was used on a vastly increased scale in the Philippines with mother vessels, large nets and very large teams of divers and fishers being used to serially deplete coral reef areas in the region. However, by the 1980s there was an increasing concern about not only the heavy fishing pressure on coral reef fish stocks, but also on the physical damage that was being done to coral reefs in the Philippines and the South China Sea and the employment of children in the dangerous work of diving.

The technique was first banned in the late 1980s in the Philippines but later permitted using a modified *moru ami* net (called *pa-aling* fishing) which did lesser damage to the coral reefs. However, the technique was finally banned under Section 92 of the new Philippines Fisheries Code in 1998 because of the continued destruction of coral reefs and a study which concluded that stocks of reef fish, particularly on isolated reefs in the South China Sea, had been severely depleted. In the transition from subsistence fishing using traditional techniques to the development of industrial fishing techniques to supply a rapidly increasing regional population, there were a number of other ventures that were tried but were not successful.

Some of these, such as the attempted introduction of diving bell technology into the pearl shell industry in the 1870s, failed because they were inappropriate technologies while others (such as the early attempts at demersal trawling and purse seining for small pelagics) failed because they were pioneering attempts at introducing new industrial fishing methods and therefore, although failing, provided the experience for others to later successfully introduce similar technology. Throughout the history of fishing in the region, fishers in Southeast Asia have been characterized by their ingenuity in developing innovative ways of catching fish using local materials or materials available at the time. For example, items such as marine engines and munitions were abundant after the Second World War and were used to power fishing vessels and, particularly in the Philippines, to capture fish using explosives. However, this tradition of innovation has often been restricted to small-scale fishers where the costs of experimenting with innovation were minimal.

Innovation in the industrial fishing sector has also been entrepreneurial and opportunistic (and often assisted by government financial incentives) rather than the result of any detailed analysis of the long-term risks and rewards of investment in the fishing industry. Some of these government financial incentives were spectacularly successful (such as the promotion of a fish canning industry in Thailand in the 1970s) while others were less so. In several instances, development of new fisheries production methods occurred rapidly despite government policies, such as in Malaysia where, despite a government rejection in 1958 of trawling as a potential direction for the fishing industry, trawling accounted for 48 percent of total landings of 440000 tonnes by 1974. However , the common factor that unites both successful and unsuccessful government intervention and incentives for investment has been the often scant regard that has been paid to the capacity of the fisheries resource to support the proposed development. The region is littered with examples ranging from national government support for the unregulated development of the trawl industry in Thailand and Indonesia in the 1960s to the support, up to 1998, of large-scale *moru ami* fishing discussed above.

CONCLUSIONS

The study by Butcher (2004) highlights the boom-and-bust nature of development of industrial marine fisheries in the region over the past century or so as, one by one, stocks and habitats were exploited in an often uncontrolled, unregulated manner and, when these were depleted, the fleet moved on to the next area or stock. This sequential plunder also occurred across fisheries as the declining economic performance of one fishery spurred the transfer of vessels and fishers to a new, developing fishery (very often with government assistance) which in its turn also declined. However, the point was reached in about the 1980s where there were very few new, underexploited areas for fleets to move to within the region and very few new types of fisheries that fleets could transfer to. This remains the situation in the region today.

This boom-and-bust nature of development of industrial fishing has severely impacted on the small-scale fisheries in the region, which still account for the vast majority of landings (up to 94 percent of total landings for example, in Indonesia) and this led in the past, and continues to lead to, violent clashes between industrial and small-scale fishers.

Another issue highlighted by the analysis of Butcher (2004) is the poor state of even basic statistics on landings, fishing methods and fishing effort. This lack of statistics from the past has made the analysis by Butcher (2004) on the development of fisheries in the region very difficult and often reliant on isolated, qualitative information which, nevertheless, Butcher has assembled from an impressive range of sources. There has never been and there remain today virtually no statistics that are collected on a regional basis (an important gap since many stocks cross national boundaries and are fished by fleets from a number of nations) and there is no consistent regional approach to the type and methodology of statistics collection. In addition, most national statistics are poor both in the extent of their coverage and precision. The basic data upon which to assess the impact of fishing on fish stocks and to make informed fisheries development and management decisions was, therefore, never collected in the past and this important gap in knowledge remains today.

2

Low-cost Equipment and Facilities in Large Urban Areas of Asia

INTRODUCTION

Scope and Purpose of the Paper

This chapter is addressed primarily to those concerned with the planning, development and administration of urban fish marketing operations and its supporting infrastructure in Southeast Asia. It may be useful to those concerned with fish marketing systems such as itinerant vending and formal and informal street markets; in particular, urban fish distribution and marketing and development of consumer demand for fish and fishery products. It may also be found useful by persons involved in the planning, development and expansion of the retail trade of fresh fish in municipal governments, as well as those engaged with the design of trade policies, legislation and administration.

Urban marketing of live and fresh fish, as well as some examples of low-cost fish retailing equipment and facilities used in four large urban centres of Southeast Asia (Manila, Kuala Lumpur, Singapore and Bangkok) are described as case studies. In addition, some considerations regarding the design and operations of low-cost fish retailing equipment used in fresh and live fish trade are outlined.

Products Covered

For the purposes of this study, the main products considered were live and fresh fish and shellfish. Fresh fish and shellfish are defined as products that have not been subjected to any process of preservation, except chilling, which reduces temperatures close to the temperature of melting ice (0°C).

Fresh fish was marketed in diverse forms according to consumer preferences, such as:

- Whole
- Headed
- Gutted
- Headed and gutted
- Split
- Fillets (skin on or skinless)
- Double fillets
- Steaks
- Portions
- Minced and minced fish-based products.

Shellfish consisted of molluscs and crustaceans as well as cephalopods, which are frequently marketed as:

- Live
- Whole
- Headed
- Shucked (molluscs)
- Headed and gutted
- Peeled and deheaded
- Peeled and deveined
- Cooked (tails, claws/legs)
- Minced seafood (one or more species of fish, squid, shrimp) as well as surimi-based products

In addition, for the benefit of those concerned with planning and investment in retail equipment for perishable fishery products, a brief description of low-cost equipment for street vending of ready-to-eat fish balls, squid balls and fish sausages is included.

Methodology

The main research objective was to collect information on low-cost retailing equipment and facilities suitable for fish marketing in large urban areas of Southeast Asia, as well as current legislation and improvement programmes for street vending operations. Figure 1 illustrates the steps involved in this marketing research process. In

Southeast Asia, the main urban centres have grown at an accelerated rate. The development of informal street food market outlets is due to several factors, such as the lack of an adequate number of other food market outlets, unemployment, and socio-economic conditions of the urban population as well as influx of rural residents into main cities. Street fish vending supplies fish to low-income earners and is a source of income for many others, including women, who otherwise would be unemployed.

Where possible, secondary data compiled by national statistics agencies and FAO sources is used. Primarily, however, this paper relies heavily on information gathered on a firsthand basis through market surveys and interviews with street seafood vendors, public market seafood retailers, super-market staff, officials from national fish marketing agencies and local governments, and visits to wholesale and retail markets in Manila, Singapore, Kuala Lumpur and Bangkok. In addition, INFOFISH, MFRD/SEAFDEC and the FAO Representative office in the Philippines provided data and liaison with local counterpart institutions.

Table: Counterpart Institutions, by Country

Country	Counterpart Institutions
Philippines	Bureau of Fisheries and Aquatic Resources (BFAR)Philippines Fisheries Development Authority (PFDA)
Malaysia	Fisheries Development Authority of Malaysia (LKIM)INFOFISH
Singapore	Marine Fisheries Research Department (MFRD), SEAFDECPrimary Production Department, Ministry of National Development
Thailand	Department of Fisheries (DOF), Ministry of Agriculture and Cooperatives

It is important to note that fish prices, like those of other commodities, are subject to fluctuation. The prices found in this study were current at the time of the market surveys.

Primary and Secondary Data Collection

Table below shows the schedule of field work; the surveys were conducted from 13th February to 7th March 2000. Of the 165 respondents interviewed during the surveys, about 68 percent were either street vendors, retailers or wholesalers/traders and 32 percent were national government officials, local government officials and consumers at street fish markets.

Table: Schedule of Field Work

City	Starting Date	Completion Date
Manila	13/2/00	20/2/00
Kuala Lumpur	20/2/00	24/2/00
Singapore	24/2/00	29/2/00
Bangkok	29/2/00	7/3/00

On the field and before the start of the surveys and interviews, a certain amount of preparatory work was required to co-ordinate with national counterparts including the preparation of a detailed schedule of visits and interviews planned. Questionnaires were e-mailed to counterpart agencies in advance, to be distributed particularly to personnel with access to data, regarding training programmes, national legislation and improvement programmes related to urban street fish vending and infrastructure. In most instances, background data on fish marketing, street vending operations and street ready-to-eat food vending was collected from various sources. Compilation, assembly and analysis of these background data in most cases was of particular importance to reveal the most conspicuous gaps in information and to identify areas which needed particular attention.

Among the essential requisites in the preparation of the field surveys were the collection of detailed and reliable city maps. In addition, all survey questionnaires were prepared in advance, tested and modified accordingly. Weights, currencies and measures actually used in each city were employed and care was taken that the unit used was clearly indicated on the questionnaires. Most questionnaires were, as a rule, completed by the person conducting the interview in the local language or in English, and at the end of the day, were translated when required. Questionnaires used in connection with background data were filled out by responsible officials from local governments or concerned agencies during the survey work and later checked by the interviewer.

In some cases, the interviewer collected the questionnaires at a later date and checked the information with the responsible officer to clear up doubtful points. Fundamentally, purposive/judgement sampling (based on the researcher's judgement, to select population members who are good prospects for accurate information) was used in the selection of fish vendors for interviews, in accordance with the enumerator's experience and knowledge of the local behaviour as well as the availability of time. The survey teams aimed at obtaining specific information on improved fish retailing equipment and facilities, *modus operandi* of street fish vendors, operational costs and fish prices; therefore, in most cases, street fish markets were chosen intentionally according to the needs of the study. The number of fish vendors interviewed varied from location to location, but represented about 10-20 percent of the total street fish vendors in each site and provided a representative sample of the various types of stalls/equipment available and fish and fishery products offered. The time schedule for collection of primary data was set up so as to coincide with the street fish vendors' working hours at the marketplace.

It was important for interviewers to make a good presentation to avoid creating a doubt in the respondent's mind as to the confidential nature of the survey. In order to avoid answers that came about as a result of the respondent wishing to mislead the interviewer, several fish vendors operating in the same marketplace and offering the same type of products were interviewed. Where the interviewer suspected that he/she was given misleading answers, he noted this under "remarks" and sought to verify the suspected information with other fish vendors in the same marketplace. In some cases, follow-up interviews were required to clear up some points or in cases where incomplete answers have been given.

Additional statistical information on retail prices of some fishery products, red meats/poultry and wholesale prices of live fish, were also collected by national counterparts through follow-up surveys, and are included accordingly.

METRO MANILA

Manila supports a substantial market for live, fresh, frozen, cured fish and canned fishery products. The Metropolitan Manila Area (MMA) was established in 1975 through Presidential Decree 824 and amended by Presidential Decree 1396, which established this geographical area as the National Capital Region (NCR). Under the administration of the Metropolitan Manila Development Authority, the NCR comprises the following cities: Manila, Quezon City, Caloocan, Pasay, Mandaluyong, Pasig, Makati, Muntinlupa, Marikina, and Las Piñas. Currently the NCR is administratively divided into seven municipalities, namely: Malabon, Navotas, Parañaque, Pateros, San Juan, Taguig and Valenzuela, with an estimated population of 10.4 million in 2000, which represents about 12.8 percent of the country's total population. According to latest estimates, the total projected population of the Philippines for 2000 is about 81 million. Under the 1991 Local Government Code, the City Council of Metro Manila was granted local autonomy and regulatory powers concerning basic city services, and enforcement of inspection of food products and urban sanitation. It is also in charge of policy formulation and supervision of retail food markets and street food vending.

In 1997, FAO fisheries statistics reported an apparent annual per capita fish supply of 31.7 kg in the Philippines. Currently the Philippines, Malaysia and Singapore have the highest per capita supply of fish in the ASEAN region. A breakdown of the annual per capita supply of fish for the Philippines in 1997 is shown in Table 3.

Table 3: The Philippines: Fish per Capita Supply (1997)

Food Item	Annual per Capita Supply(kg/year)
Freshwater fish	4.2
Demersal fish	4.4
Pelagic fish	17.9
Marine fish, other	0.2
Crustaceans	2.0
Cephalopods	0.9
Molluscs, other	2.0
Total Fish	31.7

Source: FAO Food balance sheets, 1994-97

ASEAN countries, particularly the Philippines, Singapore and Malaysia, offer a strong regional fish and fishery products market with significant fish imports. The Philippines is by far the major importer of small pelagics, either frozen (sardine, sardinella, mackerel and round scad), fish meal (mainly sardine, anchovy and mackerels) or canned (mainly sardines in tomato sauce). Japan and Russia are the main suppliers of frozen small pelagics and over 80 percent of the fishmeal comes from Chile and Peru. In 1997, the total imports of fishery products were 295,015 metric tonnes with a FOB value of US$ 138.1 million. The total exports of fishery products for the same period were 173,887 metric tonnes with a FOB value of US$ 549.8 million. In 1999, official statistics[4] showed that the country's total fish catches were 2.86 million metric tonnes, with 34.2 percent coming from aquaculture production, 33.3 percent from commercial fishing and 32.5 percent from small-scale fishing.

Fish Distribution Channels

The domestic market for fish and fishery products is distinguished principally by the dependence on supplies from aquaculture, small-scale fisheries and commercial fisheries. It should be noted that a significant proportion of aquaculture produce, particularly shrimp, is exported. Both freshwater and marine fish and fishery products are regularly being traded in Metro Manila's domestic seafood market. Fish and fishery products are staple foods in the Filipino diet, and constitute the main source of animal protein. Chilled and live seafood is landed at the main Metro Manila fishing port, namely Navotas Fishing Port Complex (NFPC), which handles about 260,000 to 280,000 metric tonnes of fish annually. The Philippines Fisheries Development Authority (PFDA) is in charge of the management and operation of NFPC and of monitoring and compilation of fishery statistics and related fish marketing information. Average daily volumes of seafood landed in Navotas FPC vary according to the fishing season from about 430 to 980 metric tonnes.

Navotas FPC is equipped with two main trading halls with a market floor area of 8,320 m2, on which the brokers or commission agents display and trade fish. Fish at the wholesale marketing halls is sold mainly by secret bidding (whispering) in a public auction conducted by brokers, who sell to retailers, institutional buyers, processors and seafood traders. The wholesale market halls operate regularly at night from about 20:00 hours to 03:00 hours. During 10:00 hours to 13:00 hours, wholesale/retail marketing operations are also conducted at Navotas auction halls for fish coming from small-scale fisheries and aquaculture farms. However, some of the fish and shellfish coming from other landing places or fish farms, do not go through the Navotas auction halls, but are sold through wholesale trade at the Divisoria Central Market, Metro Manila's major food wholesale market, and Pasig wholesale market (mainly dealing with cultured brackishwater fish coming from the Laguna de Bay area).

Live Fish

There is a significant domestic live fish trade, a portion of which does not go through the auction, but are handled by private wholesalers. These wholesalers usually operate small live fish carrier trucks (with tanks and aeration systems), collecting live milkfish (*Chanos chanos*), groupers and freshwater fish (tilapia, catfish, snakehead) produced by aquaculture farms. Domestic live shellfish trade comprises molluscs such as cultivated green mussel (*Perna viridis*) and oyster (*Crassostrea* spp.); crustaceans include mangrove crabs (*Scylla* spp.). These live shellfish are regularly distributed in the Philippines using air, sea and road transport; supplies come from brackishwater ponds and small-scale fisheries. Most of the production of oysters and green mussels are sold alive and a relatively limited proportion is sold as shucked flesh, either fresh or salted. There is a very limited export trade of frozen, chilled and dried oysters to Hong Kong and Singapore. Oysters and green mussel farm operators usually sell their production either through middlemen wholesalers or to a lesser extent, by direct retailing. Mussels and oysters are generally packed and distributed in woven plastic bags (usually holding about 30 kg) and traditional vegetable fibre baskets (locally known as *kaing*), holding about 20 - 25 kg.

There is also a significant export trade of live reef fish, particularly groupers, with supplies coming from capture fisheries. Export markets for live groupers include Hong Kong and Singapore. The domestic market is growing, but is limited mainly to Chinese restaurants. Current ex-farm prices for marine cage and brackishwater pond-cultivated live groupers are about US$ 7.5 - 9/kg.

Crabs

Four species of crabs are of commercial importance in Metro Manila; these are pelagic swimming crab (*Portunus pelagicus*), mangrove crab (*Scylla serrata*), peregrine crab (*Varuna litterata*) and horned ghost crab (*Ocypode spp*). Mangrove crabs are considered a delicacy and are always marketed alive. The Metro Manila market is characterised by consumer preference for live mangrove crabs which command high prices; in particular, ripe females fetch premium prices. The domestic market is supplied with mangrove crab the year-round, with a peak season from May to September. During the Christmas period, there is an increased demand and prices of live mangrove crab are relatively higher.

Table 4: Commercial Grading of Live Mangrove Crab

Grading	Size (g/piece)
Small	250 -300
Medium	300 -500
Large	500-850
Extra large	850 -1,000

Source: Crab traders at Seaside Fish Market, Metro Manila.

There is a significant export trade of live mangrove crab to Taiwan and Singapore; Table 4 shows the size grading of live mangrove crabs for export markets. With the increasing demand both from export and domestic markets, the current production has increased significantly to about 4,000 metric tonnes annually. Size requirements of live mangrove crab in the domestic market vary from market to market. The catering sector, particularly restaurant chains and specialised seafood restaurants, prefer small, medium and large sizes; in the retail markets the most common sizes available are small and medium. The minimum commercial size for export purposes is more than 200 g/piece; however, market requirements are oriented toward medium to large sizes, with strong preference for ripe females which fetch premium prices. The relatively high survival rates (5 - 7 days) of mangrove crabs out of the water may be explained based on the fact that they have gill structures that allow adequate levels of oxygen uptake in air. Therefore, local handling methods based on a practical understanding of the crab's physiology are used to minimise capture and transport stress and to cover the overall logistics of export marketing as well as for the domestic trade. Main preventive handling practices for live mangrove crabs include the control of temperature, humidity and careful handling to avoid injuries.

Dried Fish

There is an important dried fish market in Metro Manila for products such as dried anchovies, dried-salted and salted mackerel, shrimp, squid, cuttlefish and oyster. Small sardines and anchovies are usually brine-salted and dried whole; larger fish are split open, cleaned, salted and sun-dried. Traditional smoked fish products, in particular sardines, mackerel and milkfish are also sold at retail markets in Metro Manila. Speciality cured fishery products such as boneless smoked milkfish are usually sold under several commercial brands well packed in plastic bags; marinated split open and dried milkfish (with garlic, ginger, black pepper, vinegar and salt) is also sold at retail level, especially in the public markets. The domestic dried fish production is significant and the country's per capita apparent consumption of cured fish (including dried-salted fish) is one of the highest in the region. In addition, locally produced fresh as well as dried seaweed products are also offered in the market. Fresh *Caulerpa* and *Gracilaria* seaweeds are usually consumed raw or blanched as the main ingredient in traditional salad dishes or as garnishes for other seafood dishes.

Table 5 shows the average retail prices of dried fish in Metro Manila during 1999. The most expensive products were dried squid at US$ 9.4/kg, followed by dried anchovies and dried-salted groupers at US$ 3.2/kg and US$ 2.96 respectively. The cheapest products were dried whole sardines, split dried-salted bigeye scads and Indian mackerel at US$ 2.1/kg, US$ 2.2/kg and US$ 2.3/kg respectively.

Table 5: Average Retail Prices of Dried Fish in Metro Manila

Period: January - December 1999

Dried- salted Fishery Products (P. Peso/kg)	Retail Price
Split Indian Mackerel (*Rastrelliger kanagurta*)	95
Whole Dried Sergestidae Shrimp (*Acetes indicus*)	114
Split Fusilier (*Caesio spp.*)	97
Split Rabbit Fish (*Siganus spp.*)	108
Split Bigeye Scad (*Selar crumenopthalmus*)	91
Split Trevally (*Caranx spp.*)	115
Split Groupers (*Epinephelus spp.*)	120
Split Squid (*Loligo spp.*)	384
Whole Fringescale Sardinella (*Sardinella fimbriata*)	106
Whole Indian oil Sardine (*Sardinella longiceps*)	86
Whole Commerson's Anchovy (*Stolephorus commersonii*)	131

Source: Philippines Fisheries Development Authority (PFDA)

Canned Products

With population rising and coastal fishery stocks declining, the Philippines is becoming increasingly reliant on imports of frozen fish to satisfy local fish canning industry demand. Canned fish, in particular canned tuna and sardine products, are locally manufactured, while imported canned sardines in tomato sauce are very popular in supermarket chains, public markets and small grocery retail outlets. Metro Manila still boasts a large number of small-scale independent grocery/food retail shops locally known as *sari sari* stores, that serve mostly neighbourhood clientele and which proliferate in every urban area. Many of these retail outlets sell a wide variety of canned seafood and some cured and fermented fishery products. *Sari sari* stores and supermarket chains have the largest share of the canned seafood retail market. Popular canned seafood packs include the following:

- Sardines in tomato sauce, in cylindrical cans with net contents of 155 g
- Mackerel in tomato sauce or in vegetable oil, in round cans with net contents of 180 g to 250 g
- Tuna in oil, solid, chunk and grated packs, in round cans with net contents of 180 g
- Squid in natural ink, in round cans with net contents of 400 g
- Tuna with vegetables & seasonings, mechado, afritada, caldereta and hot & spicy packs, in cylindrical cans with net contents of 155g
- Milkfish in oil, tomato sauce and in brine (salmon style)

The consumption habits in Metro Manila vary according to the consumer's socio-economic level, with upper and middle income homes buying more high value tuna packs and lower income homes buying low-priced sardine products. The most frequent practice of consuming canned tuna products is either as a salad or with bread (sandwiches); canned sardines and milkfish are usually served with cooked rice or bread as a snack, as well as sautéed with garlic, onions and vegetables.

Table 6 shows the average retail prices of canned seafood products in Metro Manila during 1999. In general, canned squid and tuna in oil packs were the most expensive products; the cheapest canned products were sardine in tomato sauce and mackerel in tomato sauce or in oil.

Table 6: Average Retail Prices of Canned Seafood Products in Metro Manila

Product Form	Retail Price (P. Peso/can) (155 g.) Net Contents	Retail Price (P. Peso/can) (180 - 250 g.) Net Contents	Retail Price (P. Peso/can) (400 g.) Net Contents
Sardine in tomato sauce	6.35 - 9.50	10.05 - 11.45	15.50 - 20.30
Mackerel in tomato sauce/oil	6.35 - 9.05	9.50 - 12.50	14.25 - 25.30
Squid in natural ink	8.25 - 15.65	14.25 - 25.50	22.55 - 39.50
Tuna in oil, chunks	10.75 - 14.75	17.65 - 22.00	n/a

Source: Philippines Fisheries Development Authority (PFDA)

Seafood reaches Metro Manila consumers through a multi-level system, which may involve at least three to four transactions before a fish or fishery product is purchased by a consumer in a public fish market, or supermarket, or eaten in a restaurant/food stall. The channels of distribution incorporate locally caught and processed seafood, live and chilled cultured species and frozen imported items from the region and around the world, which can be processed locally. A long chain of traders/middlemen usually distinguishes the seafood distribution chain in Metro Manila, starting from Navotas FPC to the final consumer. Supermarket chains often obtain supplies from direct importers or distributors of frozen and canned seafood products, which makes possible a shorter distribution chain.

Metro Manila's Retail Fish Market

Metro Manila's urban area is home to a variety of retail establishments offering live, fresh, frozen, cured and canned seafood to consumers. The range of shopping options include public retail markets, supermarkets and street hawkers which offer a wide selection of live fish, fresh fish, frozen and canned fishery products as well as cured and fermented fish. Public markets currently hold a significant share of the retail trade of chilled, live fish, fermented and cured fishery products.

Large supermarket chains and medium-sized independent supermarkets offer mainly chilled, frozen, cured and canned seafood. Supermarkets are currently handling a less significant portion of the retail market share for chilled fish and fishery products. The sales of chilled fish in supermarkets are still not significant, because housewives associate fresh/chilled fish with public markets and only grocery goods/ canned fish with supermarkets. Despite the fact that most supermarkets are low-cost, low-margin, high volume, self-service operations designed to provide the consumer's total needs for food and household-maintenance products, there is still a strong preference to shop for chilled/fresh seafood in the public retail markets, and to a lesser extent at street hawker stalls. Most supermarkets have well-defined seafood product sales strategies, including adequate product mix and a variety of frozen, fermented fish products, fish sauce, and canned seafood products. The most popular product form is whole fresh fish and preferred species of seafood are: milkfish, Spanish mackerel, Indian mackerel, all tunas, *Loligo* squid, round scad, slipmouth, red snapper, groupers, anchovies, sardines, golden *Caesio*, lizardfish, tilapia, shrimps and mangrove crabs. Recent trends indicate that tilapia (hybrid strains) is increasingly becoming popular in the domestic market, and is now considered as a substitute for milkfish, which is regarded as first-class fish. When comparing retail prices of fresh tilapia with milkfish, currently tilapia is sold at lower price levels, with average retail prices of about US$ 1.7 - 1.9 per kg and US$ 2.57 - 2.69 per kg respectively. Some fish retailers indicated that sometimes both species are sold at the same price level.

Table 7: Comparative Retail Prices of Fresh Fish at Selected Street Seafood Markets and Public Markets in Metro Manila

Species	Street Seafood Market Price (P. Peso/kg)	Public Market Price (P. Peso/kg)
Milkfish	90 - 120	100 - 120
Tilapia	65 - 75	70 - 85
Squid	100 - 130	110 - 130
Bullet & frigate tuna	60 - 70	65 - 74
Yellowfin tuna	110 - 130	120 - 130
Catfish	60 - 70	65 - 75
Snakehead	110 - 120	100 - 125
Anchovy	60 - 65	60 - 65
Indian mackerel	85 - 90	80 - 90
Mackerel (imported)	50 - 55	n/a
Round scad	60 - 70	65 - 75
Trevallys (*Carangoides* spp.)	120 - 150	125 - 155
Hairy shrimp (small size) (*Metapenaeus* spp.)	140	135 - 145

Source: Data from field market surveys carried out by the author and counterparts in February 2000.

Table 7 shows the comparative retail prices for fresh fish at selected street seafood markets and public markets in Metro Manila. In general, retail prices at street seafood markets were slightly lower than public markets with a price difference of 4.3 to 12%, however some products like Indian mackerel and hairy shrimp were at the same price level. Taking into consideration that most supermarkets have similar or slightly higher prices than public markets, we can conclude from this relatively limited data that street seafood markets are currently offering slightly lower retail prices for fresh seafood in Metro Manila.

Table 8 shows a comparison of average wholesale and retail prices for selected fish species in Metro Manila for 1999. The estimated market margins for chilled fish ranged from 11.8 to 136 percent, with an average marketing margin of 57.6 percent. Based on the relatively limited data obtained from the field surveys in general, the results obtained were in line with the above marketing margins.

At most public markets, there are full-service seafood stalls in charge of taking and preparing orders from consumers. Preparation may include weighing a specific quantity of fish or shellfish, gutting, cleaning or cutting a whole fish to the desired size or product form. Orders are then wrapped for the consumer in plastic bags. This service is considered as a marketing tool used to maintain the loyalty of regular clientele and attract new customers.

Live fish and shellfish, including mangrove crab, oysters, mussels, catfish, snakehead and tilapia, are well-established products in the domestic market. They are sold in simple water tubs, bamboo baskets or cages. Live crab retailers interviewed at the Seaside private fish market indicated that their daily sales range from P. Peso 6,000 to 12,000 and during Christmas, sales could reach up to P. Peso 36,000/day. These specialised shellfish retailers usually operate from 4:00 hours to 23:00 hours, seven days per week. They indicated that their average daily sales comprised 40 to 50 kg of live crab, with an estimated 3 - 5 kg sold in chilled form at reduced prices. The catering sector is also an important outlet for mangrove crab, oyster, mussels, catfish, and tilapia, and recently for giant freshwater prawn. Some restaurateurs indicated strong consumer preference for mangrove crabs, oysters and mussels, traditionally cooked grilled, steamed or fried with vegetables (with coconut milk). Giant freshwater prawn are sold through the catering sector in specialised restaurants including some Thai restaurants operating in Metro Manila. The species is well accepted by local consumers, but there is a need to develop the market and create regular demand. However, supplies of giant freshwater prawn are limited, coming mainly from a few freshwater ponds within Central Luzon.

Seasonal variations in supplies and prices of fresh fish are currently affecting demand for fresh/chilled fish and its substitute products. At the retail level, the main substitute product to fresh fish is dressed chicken, followed by pork. When prices of preferred species such as fresh milkfish increase, consumers may shift to dressed chicken or to low-cost species such as fresh sardines, Indian mackerel or round scad, if available. Retail prices of fresh cultivated milkfish and dressed chicken have not increased significantly since 1998 and this trend is basically market-determined. In 1999, a PFDA study of the milkfish industry indicated that relatively lower domestic wholesale and retail prices for milkfish had aggravated the already delicate situation of milkfish producers, who were facing significant increases in the costs of inputs (mainly imported feeds and feed components) and declining demand caused by a drop in consumer buying power. Local production of cultivated milkfish is highly dependent on imported fish meal and other feed ingredients; therefore any significant currency fluctuation or price rise could result in a cost-revenue squeeze with declining profits.

Table 8: Average Wholesale & Retail Prices of Selected Fresh Fish in Metro Manila

Period: January - December 1999

Species	Wholesale Price (P. Peso/kg)	Retail Prices (P. Peso/kg)	Marketing Margin (%)
Indian Mackerel (*Rastrelliger kanagurta*)	61.86	78.32	26.61
Milkfish (*Chanos chanos*)	62.54	81.32	30.03
Threadfin (*Nemipterus spp.*)	53.24	86.96	63.34
Fusilier (*Caesio spp.*)	70.83	86.64	22.32
Round Scad (*Decapterus spp.*)	48.62	65.22	34.14
Bigeye Scad (*Selar Crumenopthalmus*)	60.85	76.60	25.88
Squid (*Loligo spp.*)	70.99	103.61	45.95
Trevally (*Caranx spp.*)	55.97	77.40	38.29
Ponyfish (*Leiognathus spp.*)	29.83	70.39	135.97
Goatfish (*Upeneus spp.*)	29.88	67.91	127.28
Trevally (*Caranx spp.*)	67.63	117.84	74.24
Indian Oil Sardine (*Sardinella longiceps*)	20.27	43.23	113.27
Bullet & Frigate Tuna (*Auxis spp.*)	59.29	66.33	11.87
			Average margin: 57.60%

Source: Philippines Fisheries Development Authority (*PFDA*)

Table 9 shows a comparison between available fresh meat, poultry and small pelagics offered in the Metro Manila retail food market in February 2000.

Table 9: Comparative Average Retail Prices of Meat, Poultry and Fish in Metro Manila

Period: February 2000

Product	Average Retail Price (P. Peso/kg)
Red Meats:	
Lean pork	110
Pork loin	112
Beef loin	140
Beef tender chuck	141
Poultry:	
Dressed chicken (chilled)	80
Chicken breast/chilled)	88
Chicken drumstick (chilled)	95
Eggs	62
Product	**Average Retail Price (P. Peso/kg)**
Small Pelagics (whole):	
Anchovy	63
Sardines	50
Round scad	70
Indian mackerel	85
Other fish species (whole)	
Bullet & frigate tuna	67
Catfish	68
Tilapia	74
Milkfish	108

Source: Data from field market surveys carried out by the author and counterparts in February 2000.

Beef was the most expensive animal protein source, with an average retail price of US$ 3.5/kg, followed by pork with an average retail price of US$ 1.75/kg, and chicken with an average retail price of US$ 2.1/kg. Small pelagics such as sardines and anchovy, with an average retail price of US$ 1.2/kg and US$ 1.5/kg respectively, were the cheapest protein source.

Public retail markets and supermarkets currently offer a variety of traditional minced fish products and surimi-based products. These products include fish balls, squid/cuttlefish balls, native fish sausages, fish burgers, and surimi analogues. In addition, minced fish-based dried fish/shrimp crackers (locally processed and imported) are also offered. Traditional fish & squid balls and native fish sausages (fish *quekiam*), and snack type foods, which are consumed mainly deep fried and dipped in sweet and sour sauce, are very popular among consumers. The average wholesale prices of squid balls and native fish sausages varied from P. Peso 78 to 80 per kg (US$1.71 - 1.96 per kg) and P. Peso 60 to 64 per kg (US$1.46 - 1.56 per kg) respectively. The main sources of raw material are from by-catch, market surpluses and some low-cost freshwater species.

Besides the above-mentioned minced fish products, value-added products such as cuttlefish/squid/fish/shrimp nuggets and patties and shrimp tempura are locally processed and marketed. Some supermarket chains are also offering pre-packed chilled and frozen imported seafood, including Japanese-style sushi products (e.g. shrimp roe, tuna *tekka maki*, minced tuna & chilli, crab stick roll).

Imported frozen fish (mainly low-cost small pelagics and cuttlefish) are increasingly being distributed in Manila's retail markets at relatively lower prices than locally caught species. During field surveys, it was noticed that imported frozen fish blocks were regularly traded in both the Navotas FPC and Divisoria wholesale markets. This market trend apparently is in response to the increased domestic demand for fish, particularly during the lean fishing season. Therefore, consumers' attitudes toward frozen fish are gradually changing; it now appears that frozen fish is considered more desirable, but still not superior to its fresh/chilled counterpart, particularly in terms of its texture. This is a significant change from previous years, when most consumers strongly preferred fresh/chilled fish; frozen fish was not well accepted even if they were the same, or fresh fish prices are relatively too high. In general, these imported frozen fish are currently retailed at prices 15 to 35 percent lower than similar fresh/chilled species.

Street Food Hawkers in Metro Manila

Street food hawkers in Metro Manila, in particular those selling fresh seafood and ready-to-eat seafood, are considered to be catering to middle and low-income consumers. Current data on the total number of street food hawkers indicates an estimate of some 15,000 (about 5,000 are licensed), according to the Manila Hawkers Permit Services, Bureau of Permits, Office of the Mayor.

This number includes those vending ready-to-eat foods and beverages, raw food (fruits, vegetables, seafood, poultry) and native sweets and delicacies. Street seafood hawkers currently play a significant role as fresh/chilled seafood suppliers in Metro Manila; however, there is no detailed data on the number of hawkers operating in the city. The main characteristics of fresh/chilled fish street hawkers include the following:

- Setting up temporary stalls on busy streets during certain times of the day. This is the simplest market system, making use of existing road infrastructure and with a low level of investment. In general, it is easy to relocate facilities/equipment to another site, which often causes street congestion and traffic management problems. They are usually not allowed to operate in areas surrounding public markets as they compete with the permanent fish retailers;
- Carrying fresh seafood in baskets, metal/plastic tubs or insulated boxes from the wholesale markets to the street marketing areas using either motorcycles, taxis, public transportation and private cars and vans (jeepneys);
- Limited provision of adequate potable water supplies and waste disposal systems to ensure appropriate sanitary conditions;
- In general, street food markets, when compared with public markets or supermarket chains, offer significantly less variety of fishery products, but with the advantage of being less expensive. In most street food markets visited, besides fish and fishery products, vegetables, fruits and other items such as charcoal, noodles, pork meat and fresh dressed chicken, were also offered;
- In addition to the regular practice of selling by weight, a kind of "pantry" service was also available, where fish and fishery

products are sold in extremely small quantities and in fractions of the most common units of sale, e.g. sales by small dishes or small heaps.

Retail sales of raw food, in particular fresh fruits and vegetables, and fresh cured seafood at busy streets or around public markets by informal vendors in Metro Manila, are an integral part of the Filipino marketplace. These market outlets are locally known as *talipapas* and according to municipal legislations, are not permitted to operate within a radius of 200 meters from the public markets. However, itinerant street fish vendors peddling from place to place and carrying two baskets for fish display/transport on shoulder poles were not common in urban areas.

In the past, Metro Manila was besieged by the problem of street hawkers, sidewalk vendors and ambulant peddlers. Municipal authorities were then authorised to establish flea markets (*tiangge*) or vending areas in selected streets, roads and open spaces.

The municipal ordinance No. 79 - 2 of 1/5/79, issued by the Metropolitan Manila Commission, indicated that the Mayors of the cities and municipalities in Metro Manila were in charge of the design, measurements and specifications of the structures and equipment to be used in these flea markets or vending areas; the allowable distances; the days and times allowed for conduct of the business authorised; the rates of fees or charges to be imposed, levied or collected; the kinds of merchandise, goods and commodities sold and service rendered; and other matters and activities related to the establishment, maintenance, management and operation of the flea markets and vending areas. However, the establishment of such flea markets and vending areas under such terms and conditions was subject to the final approval of the Metropolitan Manila Commission.

With the implementation of the Presidential Decree 856, Code of Sanitation of the Philippines, hawkers are no longer allowed to sell food on the streets. The City Council of Metro Manila formulates and implements policies on the operation, licensing and control of hawkers. The Bureau of Permits under the City Council of Metro Manila, Office of the Mayor, is directly in charge of licensing street hawkers and enforcing local regulations. Street food vending is considered illegal under the following local legislation:

Offence/Violation	Legislation
(i) Traffic obstruction	Police Manual Provisions
(ii) Prohibition in the use of utensils for ambulant vendors	Code of Sanitation

Nevertheless, street food hawkers are still operating in Metro Manila and current trends indicate that their number is increasing in the more commercial areas. Currently, a municipal fine (P.Peso 5) is levied on all street vendors found plying their trade within a 200-metre distance from public markets for the use and occupancy of city property, in accordance with Executive Order No. 41. The main factors for this growth in street food vending can be explained as follows:

(i) Local eating habits, the cultural significance of street food hawkers, socio-economic environment, high unemployment rates, rapid urbanisation and urban population growth;

(ii) Loyal patronage by a growing clientele; street food vending has emerged in response to a socio-cultural need for inexpensive nutritious foods. In the particular case of fresh seafood, informal street markets operating at strategic locations during the busy hours of the day save customers time and/or money;

(iii) The effects of the Asian financial crisis, which dragged the country's economic growth down, had severely hit the urban poor population. Therefore, street food vending activities flourished;

(iv) The change in the role of the Metro Manila municipal authorities, which is operating under difficult conditions, including the negative effects of the economic crisis on the urban poor population. The implementation of a participatory approach and education programmes in street food business, public information campaigns and the recognition of street food marketing as an important informal activity were necessary changes in policy, which helped to clarify the benefits and disadvantages of unregulated street food vending. However, specific interventions (such as adequate training, credit, improved food safety, hygiene and inspection, equipment/infra-structure development programmes and policy formulation to support regulated street food vending) are still confronted by financial problems and lack of adequate manpower for law enforcement.

In most cases, it will require some time to gradually implement the necessary changes.

Currently the City Council of Metropolitan Manila is planning to regulate street food vending to include the designation of specific areas in the city for vending as well as provision of support to vendors through the construction of inexpensive food stalls (with sanitary facilities).

It was observed during field surveys that the fish offered by street hawkers was of acceptable to good quality. Most consumers interviewed at informal street fish markets mentioned that they had a good to acceptable experience with fish purchased there. In addition, it appeared that consumers appreciated the convenience of obtaining readily available seafood at street fish markets. Based on observations, most street fish markets visited were well accepted by consumers and provided personalised services. It was evident that consumers appreciate seafood hawkers, who were in general, knowledgeable about seafood and who cared about the needs of the consumers. Most street fish market outlets surveyed catered to middle and low-income consumers on busy corners of Metro Manila. Low-income families may purchase fish in small lots (heaps/dishes). Based on direct observation and limited survey data, we recognise that convenience, strategic location and affordable prices directly influence repeat purchase of street vended fish, rather than solely customer satisfaction and loyalty.

At most street food markets outlets visited, acceptable to fair conditions were observed regarding fish handling practices. Usually, seafood was displayed without ice; however some small pelagics, shrimp and squid were kept in plastic tubs or trays in a slush of ice and water. Most street fish vendors had at least one insulated box to keep chilled fish with crushed ice and one (1) 10 - 15 litres capacity plastic bucket or container with a cover for storage of potable water for fish cleaning. Regarding the variety of fish and fishery products at street markets, most stalls had between four to eight fresh/chilled fish species or 2 - 4 fishery products (mainly cured fish and fermented) on display. Fresh/chilled fish stalls offered only fresh fish, while specialised stalls displayed only cured fish (smoked and dried-salted fish). Most fish hawkers indicated that they handled inventories of fresh fish for one working day, while a few indicated that they kept fresh fish on ice for two days. On average, street seafood vendors operated about 6 to 8 hours daily;

most indicated that the average number of working days is about 7 days per week. The average daily sales per stall are about 50 kg of fresh fish and shellfish, 5 - 7 kg of dried fish and 4 - 5 kg of smoked fish.

Provision for solid waste to be deposited in bins was inadequate to fair in most street fish market outlets. However in most of the street markets visited, there was not much solid wastes in evidence. Most vendors indicated that they manage solid waste collection and disposal by themselves. The most common procedure was to store wastes in a woven fibre basket or plastic bag which stood without a lid until full. Hygienic conditions could be greatly improved, if adequate potable water supplies (tap water) and solid waste bins with lids could be made available to street fish markets.

The use of simple dial metallic thermometers is suggested to regularly measure the temperature of fish on display at street fish markets. Dial thermometers can easily be calibrated to a known temperature by adjusting a hex nut located under the dial. These thermometers were available at some supermarkets and specialised shops. This basic tool could be included as part of the training kit for street fish vendors.

In addition, the provision of an adequate wastewater drainage system to street fish market outlets is greatly needed. Water is used extensively in fish markets not only for fish cleaning, but also to flush offal and blood from equipment and floors, and to flume wastewater to floor drains and collection sumps. The first step for the implementation of potable water supplies (tap water) to individual stalls at street fish markets should be to analyse water use patterns, install water meters and regularly record water consumption.

The next step should be to undertake a survey of all market area and ancillary operations to identify wasteful practices and undertake corrective actions. Each street fish vendor should pay according to their water consumption and proportionally for the provision of wastewater drainage systems.

Although street vending may be a family business, the survey indicated that women were the main operators. This reflects the need of most poor women to balance income generation with household responsibilities. A limited gender analysis showed that most women and men run street vending as a family business. Other observations with regard to women engaged in street seafood vending were:

- Women were more personal when it comes to dealing with consumers. In general, they were careful with words and more patient in handling business problems;
- Consumers, fish wholesalers/middlemen, local government inspectors and police officers tended to be more patient and friendly when dealing with women;
- Some women indicated the difficulty in balancing the demands of business and family. However, most women interviewed indicated that street fish vending gave them greater time flexibility than other types of jobs/businesses, with the advantage that it does not need as much capital or skills;
- Taking into consideration women's predominant role in street fish marketing, greater female participation in training activities in the fields of small business management, fish handling and marketing should be encouraged.

The principal challenges with regard to informal street fish vending in Metro Manila are therefore the need for effective and sustainable interventions and the formulation of a comprehensive policy. To be effective, statutory requirements (including licensing), should be properly linked to training, monitoring, supervision and equipment/infrastructure development programmes. In particular, seafood street vending should have adequate provision of basic facilities for handling, chilled storage, preparation and waste disposal which can be provided in the street areas where seafood vendors regularly operate. In addition, depending on the type of seafood prepared and sold (e.g. chilled raw fish and cooked fish/squid balls), working hours, working places, and *modus operandi* (with fixed stalls or itinerant vendors with push carts), vendors may require other equipment and facilities. They may also have different views regarding proposed improvements of their services and facilities. The views of street fish vendors and their clientele should be taken into account during the formulation of statutory requirements and legislation applicable to street fish vending. Sanitary regulations and codes of practice for street seafood vending should be drafted using simple non-technical language, and if possible, well illustrated versions of these regulations in both English and Tagalog should be prepared for training purposes and the information disseminated.

Regular training courses on fresh/chilled seafood handling and hygiene should be part of any development programme for street fish vendors organised by the City Council of Metro Manila or Metro Manila Development Authority in co-ordination with the relevant government agencies. This training should be aimed at providing adequate guidance and technical assistance to fish hawkers on proper seafood handling and personal hygiene practices. All stall holders and their assistants who are involved in the preparation and sale of seafood should be required to attend and pass this training course.

Basic technical fields, which may be relevant for training courses intended for street fresh fish vendors, are as follows:

- Introduction to the concepts of freshness, quality, wholesomeness and nutritive value.
- The care of live and fresh fish, handling methods, use of ice, receiving deliveries, quality inspection, storage of live and chilled fish; hygiene and sanitation for fish retailers, selection and application of detergents and disinfectants.
- Quality of fish and quality aspects at retail level; assuring seafood safety at street fish markets; retail display of fish; promotion of fish sales techniques. Avoiding bad marketing practices.
- National and municipal regulations and codes of practice for seafood vending.
- Introduction to business planning and simple economics in fish retailing.
- Equipment and facilities development programmes for street fish vending.

In addition, ready-to-eat seafood vending is a flourishing small-scale business in Metro Manila, which requires adequate training for vendors to improve safety and reduce the risk to public health from poor quality products. Training programmes should focus on improving hygienic conditions at the point of sale, use of potable water, and assuring overall safety of popular street-vended snacks/dishes.

Based on field surveys carried out in Metro Manila, the following street-vended fish snacks/dishes were very popular:

- Fish/squid balls
- Native fish sausage (*quekiam*)
- Mussel soup
- Rice noodles with vegetables and pre-cooked shrimps (*shrimp pansit*)

- Fish/shrimp soup with vegetables (*fish/shrimp sinigang*)
- Deep-fried fish
- Cooked fish with ginger and vinegar (*paksiw na isda*).

Examples of Street Market Outlets in Metro Manila

In most raw food market outlets (*talipapas*) surveyed, the following food items were offered:

- Fresh fish and live shellfish (live mussels and oysters)
- Cured fish (traditional smoked small pelagics and milkfish; dried fish)
- Fermented fish sauce and paste (*patis* and *bagong*)
- Squid/fish balls
- Noodles and rice
- Dressed chicken
- Fresh pork and beef; traditional sausages & frankfurters
- Fresh fruits and vegetables
- Ready-to-eat food and beverages (quail eggs, fish *quekiam*, pineapple juice, *sago gulaman,* roasted peanuts, fish balls)
- Common salt
- Charcoal.

Most fresh and live fish stalls were concentrated in the 15th Avenue area and a few were along First Camarilla Street. Considering the significant area occupied by this street market and the variety of food items offered, we can conclude that it is an important outlet in comparison to other markets visited. The layout of another typical street food market outlet (*talipapa*) located in Project 3, Quezon City. About 18 stalls were there, of which 12 were selling either fresh or live fish and shellfish or smoked fish. Most stalls were concentrated in Molave Street, with some chicken and fresh pork and meat vendors operating in Narra Street. This appears to be a medium size market outlet (with few food items offered) in comparison to other street markets visited. Most vendors interviewed in both street markets indicated that their daily sales were about 50 kg of fresh and/or live fish, 5 - 6 kg of dried-salted fish and 5 - 8 kg of smoked fish. The preferred source of fresh fish in both street markets was the Farmer's Market in Cubao, and the main source of cured fish and minced fish products was the Divisoria wholesale market.

The street markets in Manila are usually located around public markets or busy corners of main streets. According to all street fish vendors interviewed in the Quezon City area, there is no fixed opening time for street markets, taking into account that they are considered as illegal vendors. However, in most of the markets visited, vendors indicated that they usually operate from 13.00 hours to 20.00 hours, seven days per week. The solid wastes were regularly collected by the street vendors and placed in plastic bags for further disposal. Street vendors were in charge of the cleaning of their working area after market hours.

The basic equipment of a street fish vendor consisted of small wooden tables, a wooden cutting board, trash bin, umbrella, water for washing fish and cleaning the stall area, insulated boxes, weighing scale and plastic display dishes. Most of the smaller stalls were equipped with only secondhand wooden packaging crates as a framework for wooden tops, or round flat bamboo/rattan trays for fish display, weighing scale and cutting boards. The typical sales or table area per seafood retailer would be in the range of 1.5 to 3 m^2. The larger stalls use up more space to keep insulated boxes that may not fit below the wooden tables. The most common material used for manufacturing the round display trays was rattan. In most locations visited, retailers displayed their fish on wooden tops lined with plastic sheets; in some stalls, whole *Acetes* shrimp, small pelagics or squids were displayed in small plastic dishes (on top of the tables) and sold by the dish (volume).

Some vendors, operating in the outskirts of Metro Manila, were offering live freshwater fish and shellfish, mainly snakehead, catfish, mussels and oysters. Basic equipment for live fish sales consisted of metal tubs or plastic bins filled with water, weighing scale, round display trays (rattan) and chopping boards. Mussels and oysters were displayed on round display trays and kept moist with regular sprinkles of seawater. Snakehead and catfish were displayed in metal tubs or plastic bins filled with freshwater. In general, green mussel was the predominant species offered in live form; this was available in most of the street markets visited. According to most vendors, the sales of mussels and oysters are regularly affected by red tide. As a result, the Government sometimes imposes a complete ban on the harvesting and sales of these bivalves in the interest of public safety. These bans negatively affect marketing operations and the livelihood of street fish vendors specialised in live shellfish vending.

Improved Equipment and Technologies for Street Seafood Vending

In contrast to the considerable emphasis on modern food vending equipment in outlets which cater to the middle/high income consumers, very little consistent effort is directed for the benefit of low-income consumers. It remains a fact that much technology and expertise exists locally today, which, if adapted to the needs of the low-income sector, could play an important role in improving and streamlining the safety and quality of ready-to-eat street seafood. Among the major deficiencies observed during field surveys of traditional street fish/squid balls vendors in selected areas of Metro Manila, were the lack of basic facilities (running potable water for hand washing, cleaning worktops and utensils), and limited access to refrigerated/chilled storage for their daily stock of fish balls.

A successful pilot scheme on food carts for street food vending sponsored by the Food and Nutrition Research Institute in co-ordination with other local agencies/institutions was implemented in San Juan, Metro Manila and Los Baños, Laguna during 1996. It provided improved food cart prototypes to selected street food vendors on a "rent-to own" basis and a flexible payment scheme which considered the prevailing street vendor's payment capabilities. The prototypes were locally constructed and the cost ranged from P. Peso 3,500 to 4,200. This scheme was aimed at field testing two models for integrating the street food system into feeding operations in selected urban schools. However, during the field work, there was insufficient technical information available on the design and materials used for the construction of these improved food cart prototypes to allow a proper analysis.

Improved Pushcart for Retailing Fish/Squid Balls and Native Fish Sausage

A good example of improved equipment locally developed for the retail of fish/squid balls and native fish sausage (*fish quekiam*) was identified by the field survey team in Quezon City area. This improved pushcart (locally known as *carreton*) was an initial attempt by a local propane gas company to focus attention on development of low-cost equipment (see next section). It was technologically-based and motivated by a desire to improve the traditional preparation and retailing habits of local vendors and as well as promote the safe use of propane gas. In Metro Manila, street vendors of fish balls traditionally prepare and retail their products using poorly designed wooden pushcarts. According to the improved pushcart operator, the fish balls and *fish quekiam* stock is kept in a home refrigerator. During trading hours she uses an insulated box to store the fish/squid balls and *fish quekiam.*

Street vendors should be advised not to store fish balls for more than three (3) days under chilled storage conditions and to cook them thoroughly before selling them to their clientele. A research study suggested that fish balls were included among the ready-to-eat food items sold by Metro Manila's street food vendors, which were associated with the risks of cholera infection. However, that research study concluded that only *pansit* (rice noodles with shrimp, meat and vegetables), mussel soup and the absence of piped water at home remained as risk factors associated with cholera transmission in Metro Manila. Infrastructure requirements for fish balls vending to ensure that they are hygienic and safe, will depend on whether the fish balls were prepared at the vendor's home or purchased semi-prepared (ready-to-fry) for completion at the point of sale.

According to the results of the field surveys, most of the fish/squid balls were processed elsewhere and purchased at wholesale markets by vendors. At wholesale level, it was observed that most fish/squid balls and *quekiam* were adequately packed in plastic bags, and kept either chilled or frozen. Therefore, the main concerns were the storage conditions of fish/squid balls after purchase and during the time of storage. Refrigeration/chilled facilities for traditional street seafood vendors were very limited and were not normally encountered among these vendors during field surveys. However, block ice was very accessible in Metro Manila; it is widely used by street vendors to cool soft drinks and for preparation of a traditional delicacy called *halo halo* (crushed ice mixed with chopped fruits, milk and ice cream).

Operation of the Improved Pushcart

The improved pushcart prototype was constructed locally by a propane gas company, using stainless steel sheets for the body and a stainless steel angle frame. The heating system consisted of one cooking stove, constructed of angle iron frame and fitted with one burner and gas storage tank with a manual safety on-off valve. The main body was attached to a bicycle with one turnable and two fixed wheels. A canvas cover with a metallic pipe frame was fixed to the main body for protection against rain and sunshine. This pushcart has significant advantages over the traditional *carreton*, which uses kerosene-cooking stoves for frying fish balls and are considered more prone to accidents due to malfunction. It had a well-designed gas cooking stove with a protective surface against strong draughts, thus avoiding disturbed combustion. The manufacturer has paid particular attention to the necessity for regular inspection and maintenance of this equipment, particularly of safety devices, in order that they may be relied upon to give adequate service to the user. The gas storage tank was located far away from the heated area of the pushcart and it was easy to detect any possible gas leaks. It also included adequate storage space below the worktop which was used to keep an insulated box for chilled storage of fish balls/squid balls during the trading day.

Traditional pushcarts are constructed in wood, without adequate chilled storage facilities (insulated boxes), as well as lacking a suitable worktop area which can be easily cleaned and sanitised. During the trading day, fish balls are kept at ambient temperature and, as a result, they deteriorate in quality and value. The use of improved pushcarts, it was suggested, would improve returns and reduce financial risks to the fish balls vendor by:

(i) Increasing marketing range

(ii) Maintaining the fish balls in high value condition longer, thus reducing losses and spoilage.

(iii) Reducing the risk to public health from poor quality products; improving hygienic conditions at the point of sale; improving the safety of street-vended fish/squid balls and native fish sausage (*fish quekiam*).

(iv) Improving clientele loyalty and encouraging repeat purchases.

This street seafood enterprise can be characterised as small-scale, requiring relatively simple cooking and administrative skills, a small amount of initial capital to start the business and only basic facilities at home for storage of raw materials and preparation of sauces. The main capital input required comprised the purchase of the improved pushcart; this was done through a special credit arrangement with the propane gas company, with a small down payment and regular monthly instalments. This scheme was initially aimed at assisting the development of small-scale fish balls businesses among family members of the propane gas company's employees, thus ensuring adequate repayment. The interviewed owner and operator of the improved pushcart can be characterised as a casual street vendor selling fish balls as a supplement to other activities.

The operations of this small-scale street seafood business include the following:

(i) Forecasting and planning the daily operations. From the forecasting (based on the experience of the vendors) comes the planning regarding the number of raw fish/squid balls and native fish sausages (*fish quekiam*) to carry daily; how much freshly made sweet and sour sauce to prepare; how many staff will be needed and when;

(ii) Organising all needs including regular wholesale purchases of fish/squid balls, native fish sausages (*fish quekiam*), ingredients for sauce preparation and non-returnable packaging materials at Divisoria wholesale market or making arrangements with a wholesaler for regular deliveries of purchase orders (the squid balls & *quekiam* vendor interviewed indicated that she had an arrangement with a wholesaler for deliveries twice a week). Organising for adequate chilled storage of raw materials to avoid spoilage. Arranging practical training in the use of equipment and cooking techniques. Cleaning schedules for all kitchen utensils and the pushcart.

(iii) Controlling of staff and products and preventing pilferage as well as improving performance. It is important to check that fish/squid balls and *fish quekiam* is of the right standard, (that is to say the correct quality and quantity); checking to prevent waste and that the staff operates the cooking stove properly. Checking that the cooking times are correct, avoiding undercooking or excessive shrinkage due to overheating. In general, vendors start preparing fish/squid balls or *quekiam* once the clientele has placed their orders; tried products are normally not kept on display. Sweet and sour seasoned vinegar and traditional sauces are prepared at home at least every two days. For each trading day, small quantities of fresh sauces are placed in plastic dispensers or glass bottles and the leftovers are removed at the end of the day.

(iv) Understanding the preferences, eating habits, purchasing behaviour and needs of the consumers to encourage repeat purchases. Therefore, lastly and perhaps most important, a good knowledge of the target market is a great asset, to be able to formulate simple marketing tactics. A brief analysis of the competition, namely small low-cost restaurants (locally known as *carinderia*) and fast food chains is of some importance. For example, the apparent declining sales in restaurants and fast food chains in Metro Manila since 1998 (due to the economic crisis and consequently lower consumer demand) had positive effects on the sales of street food. As we can easily figure out, the main target market comprises the younger sector of the population, including students and workers looking for low-cost, tasty and convenience snacks. We must realise that lower income consumers (D and E socio-economic class) represent about 65 - 70 percent of the population in Metro Manila and they may be looking for low-cost seafood products. Small-scale enterprises offering inexpensive seafood products should consider marketing strategy clearly identifying their seafood products as meant for price-conscious consumers.

(v) As a marketing tool, the sales of soft drinks and the traditional delicacy locally known as *halo halo*, helps to provide consumers with a wider variety of products, which combine well with the main seafood products offered. In the case of the improved pushcart operator interviewed, she mentioned that she could offer these additional products, considering the fact that she currently places her selling point in front of her home, placing some wooden benches for consumers to sit and enjoy her products. The *halo halo* snack is prepared at her kitchen, under good hygienic conditions using her domestic refrigerator (with a freezing compartment to keep ice) to store all ingredients. The operator's home had a well-designed kitchen with potable water supply and suitable facilities for hand washing, and washing dishes and utensils. In addition, suitable sanitation and waste management facilities were observed at her selling point. Disposable paper plates and bamboo sticks were used for retailing fish/squid balls and *quekiam*; returnable glass cups used for retailing *halo halo* were well cleaned with running water and detergent and looked tidy and clean.

The estimated investment costs of the improved pushcart prototype for street vending fish/squid balls and *quekiam* are shown in Table 10.

The major investment cost consists of the pushcart itself which is about US$ 367, representing 95 percent of the total investment cost. The operator of this improved pushcart indicated that her daily gross sales was on average, P. Peso 500 to 600 and a daily gross income of P. Peso 300; currently she was only operating 4 - 5 hours/day and 5 days/week. A daily gross income when operating 8 hours/day was estimated to be about P. Peso 350 to 480. Average retail prices of squid balls and *quekiam* were P. Peso 2 and P. Peso 1 per piece respectively. The average daily sales were 2 - 3 kg of fish balls and 3 - 4 kg of *quekiam.* Her target market consisted of mainly middle class consumers (but also included some D class consumers), in particular, students and housewives, as well as government workers.

Table 10: Investment Costs for Imported Pushcart

Description of Item	Quantity	Cost (P. Peso)
Improved pushcart, with stainless steel body, including propane gas stove.	1	15,000
Frying pan	1	350
Plastic container with lid (trash bin)	1	50
Plastic dispensers for sauces	2	40
Disposable paper plates:		
Small size	1 pack (50 pieces)	14
Medium size	1 pack (50 pieces)	27
Raw materials (stock for 1 day):		
Squid balls	3 kg	
Quekiam	4 kg	240
Vegetable oil	5 litres	125
Propane gas (for 10 days)	5 kg	85
Bamboo sticks	50 pieces	20
Small insulated box (expanded polystyrene)	1	84
		Total: 16,035

Based on the assumption of an average daily gross income of P. Peso 400/day and operating 7 days/week, the expected monthly gross income would be P. Peso 11,200. After accounting for labour costs, electricity, propane gas, ice, raw materials and equipment depreciation at P. Peso 4,800, it is expected that monthly net revenues of the improved pushcart would be about P. Peso 6,400. Assuming that a loan is taken for capital expenditure on the improved pushcart, the repayment period would be about 10 months, with monthly instalments of P. Peso 1,500. Challenging conventional wisdom about the informal sector, this example documents street fish and fishery products vending as an economic activity that produces an income ranging from minimum wage to higher than average income depending on the ownership, working schedules and market strategies used. It is important to note that most successful street ready-to-eat fish/squid balls vendors work in the trade for a lifetime, but there are also a few casual street vendors selling as a supplement to other activities.

The critical factors affecting the acceptability of the improved pushcart prototypes in gaining acceptance among street seafood vendors include the following:

(i) Provision of adequate credit and flexible/affordable payment terms, considering the limited financial capabilities of street seafood vendors. These schemes should also emphasise the specific benefits of improved technologies and equipment. In simple words, it should explain what the vendors would miss if they don't own the improved equipment

(ii) Development of improved prototypes suitable for the different type of seafood snacks/dishes being offered regularly; these would need to be simple, cost effective and suitable to local conditions

(iii) Provision of training programmes to street seafood vendors on improved hygienic conditions and safety of ready-to-eat seafood products

(iv) Provision of adequate programmes to formalise and monitor the commercial activities of street seafood vendors aimed at orderly integration and development of street seafood vending

(v) Provision of consumer education programmes to create awareness on the nutritional quality and safety of street seafood vending under the proposed improved scheme.

Although the use of traditional pushcarts will probably continue amongst the poorer street fish balls vendors, greater local research and adaptation would be required to result in the introduction of improved designs, alternative materials and better features to upgrade food safety and sanitation. For example, an alternative form of pedal-powered equipment known as the Oxtrike could be considered as a possible improvement. Its three-speed gearbox and differential drive overcomes some of the design deficiencies of traditional tricycles. This modern tricycle is specifically designed for carrying loads (150 - 300 kg) and could be adapted to improve traditional pushcarts retailing fish balls. Benefits that would result from using improved pedal-powered equipment and pushcarts include the following:

- Less time and effort may be required to move a mobile cart for vending fish balls. In addition, the efficiency of street vending may be improved by making fish balls available to consumers at the right time and place
- Domestic manufacturers, using local resources and materials can make low-cost improved pedal-powered equipment and pushcarts. In addition, the manufacture and maintenance of this low-cost equipment can provide employment and their use will provide safer ready-to-eat fishery products at a low investment cost.

KUALA LUMPUR

Kuala Lumpur supports a substantial market for live, fresh, frozen and cured fish and canned fishery products. Under the administration of the Kuala Lumpur City Council, the capital city of the country is centrally located on the West Coast of peninsular Malaysia. Covering an area of 243 square km, in 2000, Kuala Lumpur City has an estimated population of 1.6 million (according to latest estimates, the total projected population of Malaysia[9] for 2000 is about 22 million). Table 11 shows the distribution of Kuala Lumpur's population by ethnicity. Under the Local Government Act 1976 (Act 171), all laws related to local government were revised and consolidated. In February 1972, Kuala Lumpur was granted local autonomy, conferred city status and declared a Federal Territory in 1974. Under Parts VII and IX, Public Places, Food, Markets, Sanitation and Nuisances (Local Government Act 1976) the Kuala Lumpur City Hall is in charge of basic city sanitary services, enforcement of inspection of food products and urban sanitation. It is also in charge of policy formulation and supervision of wholesale and retail food markets and street food vending.

Table 11: Kuala Lumpur's Population, by Ethnicity, 1998

Ethnic Group	Percentage (%)
Malay	38.4
Chinese	44.7
Indian	11.8
Others	1.3
Non-Citizens	3.8

Source: Kuala Lumpur City Hall

ASEAN countries, particularly the Philippines, Singapore and Malaysia, offer a strong regional seafood market with significant imports. In 1997, FAO reported an apparent annual per capita fish supply of 52.5 kg for Malaysia. Currently Malaysia, the Philippines and Singapore have the highest per capita supply of fish in the ASEAN[10] region. A breakdown of the annual per capita supply of fish for Malaysia in 1997 is shown in Table 12, with pelagic fish constituting the biggest portion, followed by other marine fish. The total fish production was 1,276,282 metric tonnes, including aquaculture production. Malaysia is by far a net importer of seafood although exports are substantial. The main export products are high value items such as chilled, cured, canned and frozen fish, molluscs, shrimp and cephalopods. In 1997, total exports and imports of seafood were about 236,643 metric tonnes and 374,893 metric tonnes, respectively. Main import products included pelagic fish (70.3 percent), other marine fish (12.7 percent) and crustaceans (12 percent). Much of the imported pelagic fish was used as raw material for the local canning industry.

In 1998, Malaysia had an average per capita gross domestic product (GDP) of US$ 3,304. Only Singapore and Brunei Darussalam had higher per capita GDP among Southeast Asian countries. However, the recent Asian financial crisis caused a deceleration in GDP growth, increases in unemployment, lower income levels and weakening of trade accounts. The Federal Government has imposed capital controls to protect the national currency while cutting interest rates to stimulate the economy. In addition, several economic adjustments have been made to combat rising unemployment. Financial recovery has begun.

Table 12: Fish per Capita Supply (1997)

Food Item	Annual per Capita Supply (kg/year)
Freshwater fish	1.6
Demersal fish	7.5
Pelagic fish	20.1
Marine fish, other	13.7
Crustaceans	5.2
Cephalopods	2.0
Molluscs, other	2.4
Total fish	52.5

Source: FAO Food Balance Sheets, 1994-97

Table 13 shows the national meat and eggs per capita supply for 1997. When comparing meats with seafood products, the highest per capita supply item was poultry meat (including chicken, duck and other birds) with 34.78 kg/year, followed by pelagic fish with 20.1 kg/year.

Table 13: Meats and Eggs, per Capita Supply (1997)

Food Item	**Annual Per Capita Supply**
(kg/year)	
Beef and Veal	5.23
Mutton and Goat Meat	0.62
Pork	11.23
Poultry	34.78
Other meat	0.02
Eggs	13.97

Source: FAO Food Balance Sheets, 1994-97

Fish Distribution Channels

Current apparent consumption/supply levels of about 52.5 kg per capita place Malaysia among the highest seafood consuming nations in the world. Both freshwater and marine fish and fishery products are regularly traded in Kuala Lumpur's domestic seafood market. Fish and fishery products are staple foods, and are the main source of animal protein for virtually all ethnic and income groups.

Fresh seafood is landed at several centres along the coastline of Peninsular Malaysia and is marketed by private fish traders/wholesalers. Much of it is traded through private contracts at negotiated prices and to a lesser extent, public auction. In addition, supplies originating from Thailand are transported by road to urban centres on the West Coast of Peninsular Malaysia. The distribution of fresh seafood in peninsular Malaysia shows a strong flow southward to main urban centres, in particular to Kuala Lumpur and Singapore. Seafood reaches consumers in Kuala Lumpur through a multi-level system, which may involve at least four transactions before the fish or fishery product is purchased by consumers in a public fish market or supermarket, or eaten at a restaurant/food stall. The channels of distribution incorporate locally caught and processed seafood, live and chilled cultured species and frozen locally processed and imported items from the region. Figure 3 illustrates the marketing channels for fresh seafood in Peninsular Malaysia. Kuala Lumpur's supermarket chains often obtain supplies from direct importers or distributors of frozen and canned seafood products, which makes possible a shorter distribution chain.

The Fisheries Development Authority of Malaysia (LKIM) is in charge of the following functions:

- Management and operation of fish marketing landing complexes
- The promotion and development of fishery enterprises and fish marketing
- The registration and supervision of Fishermen's Associations and Co-operatives
- The promotion and development of activities to upgrade the socio-economic status of fishermen and the provision of credit facilities for fish production.

There is a significant domestic live fish trade which is handled by mainly private wholesalers, who operate small trucks (with tanks and aeration systems), collecting live freshwater fish (tilapia, catfish, snakehead) produced by aquaculture farms. Domestic live shellfish trade comprises molluscs such as cultivated green mussel (*Perna viridis*), cockles/clams (*Anadara spp.* and *Arca spp.*), in particular blood cockle (*Anadara granosa*) and oyster (*Crassostrea spp.*); crustaceans include mangrove crabs (*Scylla spp.*). These live shellfish are regularly distributed in Malaysia using sea and road transport; supplies come from mariculture enterprises and small-scale fisheries. Most of the production of oysters, blood cockles/clams and green mussels are sold alive and a relatively limited proportion is sold as shucked flesh.

There is also a significant domestic and export trade of live cultivated seabass (*Lates calcarifer*) and to a lesser extent, groupers, with supplies coming mainly from cage culture. Singapore is the main export market for live seabass, which is transported by road in trucks equipped with tanks and aeration. Current ex-farm prices of pond-cultivated live seabass are about US$ 2.6 to 3.9/kg according to size; average market size of cultured seabass is about 500 to 700 g/piece. The most important domestic market channel for cultured seabass is the catering sector; according to latest estimates, about 3,000 tonnes of cultured seabass are consumed in Malaysia annually. Chilled/fresh cultured seabass is regularly offered through supermarket chains and public food retail markets. Table 14 shows the price range and average wholesale prices of selected seafood at the Kuala Lumpur wholesale market during February/March 2000. Of the fresh/chilled fish species, white pomfret and threadfin fetched the highest prices. Fish is usually size- graded in three categories (large, medium and small). Shrimp species were among the most expensive seafood traded; and were graded according to the number of pieces per kg; most common sizes were 35 - 40 pieces/kg, 40 - 60 pieces/kg and > 60 pieces/kg.

Malaysia has becoming increasingly reliant on imports of frozen fish to satisfy the local fish canning industry demand. Canned fish, in particular mackerel and sardines, which are locally manufactured, are easily found in supermarkets, public markets and small grocery retail outlets. Some canned fish products from Thailand are also offered in the domestic market. Many of the retail outlets sell a wide variety of canned seafood, fish/squid snacks and cured fish. Supermarket chains are considered to have the largest share of the canned seafood retail market. Popular canned seafood packs include the following:

- Sardines in tomato sauce, in cylindrical cans.
- Mackerel in tomato sauce or in vegetable oil, in round cans.
- Tuna in oil, solid, chunk and grated packs, in round cans with net contents of 180 g.
- Cuttlefish/squid in sauces, in round cans.

• Anchovy in *sambal* (chilli) sauce, in cylindrical cans.

Table 14: Average Wholesale Prices of Selected Seafood in Kuala Lumpur

Period: February/March 2000

Species	Wholesale Price (M. Ringgit[13]/Kg)
Indian Mackerel	3.6 - 7.2
(*Rastrelliger kanagurta*)	(5.3)
Spanish Mackerel	7.0 - 12.5
(*Scomberomorus spp.*)	(10)
Threadfin	7.3 - 23.0
(*Nemipterus spp*)	(19)
Seabass	7.6 - 13.5
(*Lates calcarifer*)	(10.5)
Red snapper	8.3 - 14.0
(*Lutjanus spp.*)	(10.8)
Brown spotted Grouper	7.3 - 17.0
(*Epinephelus chlorostigma*)	(11.6)
Red Grouper	8.5 - 23.5
(*Cephalopholis sonnerati*)	(14.8)
Black Pomfret	7.5 - 13.0
(*Formio niger*)	(10.3)
White Pomfret	14.0 - 36.5
(*Pampus argenteus*)	(25.5)
Black Tiger Shrimp	23.5 - 45.5
(*Penaeus monodon*)	(35)
White Shrimp	24.5 - 47.0
(*Penaeus indicus*)	(36)

Source: INFOFISH Trade News

Kuala Lumpur's Retail Fish Market Sector

There are 78 public food markets, the Selayang food wholesale market being one of Kuala Lumpur's main sources of fresh produce, including seafood.

The Kuala Lumpur urban area is home to a variety of retail establishments offering live, fresh, frozen, cured and canned seafood to consumers. The range of shopping options include public retail markets, supermarkets and street outlets, which offer a wide selection of live fish, fresh fish, frozen and canned fishery products as well as cured and fermented fish.

Public markets and street fish hawkers currently hold a significant share of the retail market of chilled and live fish, as well as fermented and cured fishery products. Large supermarket chains offer mainly canned and processed seafood (including fish/shrimp crackers, shrimp paste, fish sauce, fish snacks, boiled-dried anchovy and dried fish). There is a strong preference by consumers to regularly shop for chilled/fresh fish at public retail markets and to a lesser extent, at street hawker stalls.

Boiled-dried anchovies is a well-established product in the domestic market and was available in most retail outlets visited; according to some retailers, its demand is strong and steady the year-round.

The most popular product form is whole fresh fish and the species most in demand are Spanish mackerel, Indian mackerel, squid, threadfin bream, red snapper, grouper, sardine and shrimp. In a market where culinary traditions regard intrinsic characteristics of fresh fish as important, frozen products have to overcome consumer resistance. Usually, unsold fish is frozen and offered for sale the next day, at which time it fetches lower prices in comparison with fresh fish.

However, frozen imported seafood (including hoki fillets and shucked mussels) is sold at some fast food restaurants; according to the restaurant management, improved availability and advertising campaigns have raised acceptance levels for frozen products among consumers in the catering sector. Cultured fish such as seabass, snakehead and catfish are well accepted by most ethnic and income groups.

Table 15 shows comparative retail prices for fresh fish at selected street seafood markets and public markets in Kuala Lumpur.

In general, retail prices at street seafood markets were slightly lower than public markets with a price difference range of RM (Malaysian Ringgit) 0.5 to 3 per kg. However some products like Spanish mackerel, round scad, threadfin bream and sand velvet shrimp were at the same price level.

Table 15: Comparative Retail Prices of Fresh Fish at Selected Street Seafood Markets and Public Markets in Kuala Lumpur

Species	Street Seafood Market Price (M. Ringgit/kg)	Public Market Price (M. Ringgit/kg)	Price Difference (%)
Red Snapper	8 - 12	13.0	+3
Mangrove Snapper	8.0	8 - 9	+0.5
Squid	6 - 9	8 - 10	+1
Spanish Mackerel	13 - 15	14.0	0
Round Scad	5.0	4 - 6	0
Catfish (Live)	n/a	4.0	-
Hardtail Scad	4 - 5	5.0	+0.5
Yellow Striped Trevally	4 - 5	5.0	+0.5
Indian Mackerel	5 - 6	7.0	+1.5
Skipjack (small size)	3.0	3.0	-
Silver Pomfret	16.0	15 - 16	- 0.5
Black Pomfret	15.0	15 - 17	+1
Chinese Pomfret (small)	9.0	n/a	-
Tilapia (small)	3.0	n/a	-
Tilapia (medium)	3.5	n/a	-
Carps	7.0	n/a	-
Threadfin Bream	7.5	7.5	0
Mangrove Crab	13.0	13.5	+0.5
Sand Velvet Shrimp	25.0	25.0	0
Giant Freshwater Prawn	19.5	20.0	

Source: data from field market surveys carried out by the author and counterparts.

At most public markets, there are full-service seafood stalls in charge of taking and preparing orders from consumers. The preparation may include weighing a specific quantity of fish or shellfish, gutting, cleaning or cutting a whole fish to the desired size or product form. Orders are then wrapped in plastic bags.

Live fish and shellfish, including catfish, snakehead and blood cockles, are well-established products in the domestic market. The fish are kept in aerated tanks/aquaria, or simple water tubs or display baskets (for blood cockles) - this is a traditional and attractive marketing approach found in many public retail markets. Live catfish retailers indicated that average sales range from 60 - 70 kg/day; however one retailer indicated an average sales volume of 150 kg/day. Average retail prices of live catfish and eel were RM 4 and 15 per kg respectively. The basic equipment of a typical live catfish retailer consisted of one (1) plastic tank with a storage capacity of 500 kg of live catfish, weighing scales, chopping boards, plastic containers and one display table. Reportedly, the catfish can be kept alive for up to 7 days and with about 2 percent losses. Sales through the catering sector are also an important outlet for seabass, catfish and snakehead. Some restaurateurs indicated strong consumer preference for catfish, seabass and snakehead, either traditionally steamed or fried with vegetables. Blood cockles are also very popular in restaurants, steamed or sautéed in curry sauces.

The retail market for minced fish-based products includes fish balls, squid/cuttlefish balls, fish cakes, fish fingers and surimi analogues. In some street markets it was noticed that traditional small-scale production of minced fish paste was carried out regularly. This product was offered at some street markets, in particular those catering to the ethnic Chinese population. In addition, minced fish-based dried fish/shrimp crackers (locally processed and imported) were also offered. Public retail markets and supermarkets currently offer a variety of traditional minced fish products and surimi-based products. Traditional fish and squid balls are consumed in soups, mixed with vegetables or deep-fried.

Besides the above-mentioned minced fish products, value-added fishery products such as breaded shrimp and fish fillets are locally processed and marketed. In addition, dried squid and soaked/processed squid (*sotong*) are popular with consumers. Despite substantial local production of squid, some fresh/chilled squid/cuttlefish and dried squid is imported to meet domestic demand.

Street Food Hawkers in Kuala Lumpur

Street food hawkers in Kuala Lumpur, in particular those selling fresh and ready-to-eat seafood, are considered to be catering to the low-income consumers. According to current data from the City Hall, Department of Hawkers and Petty Traders, the total number of licensed street hawkers is about 34,593. However, it is recognised that about 12,000 unlicensed street hawkers are currently operating in the city. Some 35 percent of the total number of street hawkers are involved in retailing ready-to-eat foods and beverages, raw food (fruits, vegetables, seafood, poultry) and native sweets and delicacies. According to the type of stall, hawkers in general are categorised as follows:

(a) With static stalls
(b) With stalls in marketplace
(c) With stalls in hawker centres/food centres
(d) Locked-up stalls
(e) With stalls in open market place/night markets
(f) With kiosks
(g) With stalls in office buildings
(h) Seasonal hawkers (festivals/cultural events).

Since the formulation of the National Action Plan on Hawkers in 1990, a comprehensive policy has been in effect to tackle the social and economic problems associated with street hawkers both at rural and urban levels. Its implementation includes the provision of funds to support credit schemes and training programmes for street hawkers to improve their facilities. In addition, the sanitary aspects of street food trading were to be addressed. Unfortunately, during the survey work, it was not possible to collect any available data on the level of implementation.

The main legislations formulated by the Federal and municipal authorities related to street food vending included regulations/laws which required hawkers to apply for registration/licensing, follow codes of practices, undergo periodic medical examinations, and follow training and inspection procedures. In addition, City Hall has implemented measures to try to control the number of hawker licenses; since 1996, a complete freeze in the issue of new licences began. However, this drastic measure apparently has not been totally effective, as more street hawkers have appeared. The authories acknowledge the following problems associated with the increase of the street hawker population:

(a) Inappropriate location and poorly designed/non-uniform stalls
(b) Inadequate basic amenities; wastes are not properly disposed of
(c) Poor management and low personal hygiene habits
(d) Improper food handling practices; lack of adequate health awareness.

Street fish hawkers currently play a significant role as fresh/chilled seafood suppliers in Kuala Lumpur; however, there is no detailed data on the number of such hawkers operating in the city. The main characteristics of fresh/chilled seafood street hawkers include the following:

- Temporary stalls are set up in busy streets/around public markets during certain times of the day. It is the simplest type of market available, making use of existing road infrastructure and with a low level of investment. In general, it is easy to relocate facilities/equipment to another site. When operating in areas surrounding public/private markets, they compete with the permanent fish retailers. These vendors usually operate at fixed and regular locations, mainly using portable equipment, umbrellas and tent-type stalls
- Fresh seafood are carried in plastic boxes or insulated boxes from the wholesale markets to the street marketing areas using taxis, public transportation and private cars and vans
- Limited availability of potable water supplies and wastewater disposal systems at the stalls; however, all street food markets visited had an acceptable common solid waste disposal system and a regular cleaning schedule
- In general, fish hawkers at street markets, when compared with public markets or supermarket chains, offered significantly less variety of fishery products per stall, but with the advantage of being comparatively less expensive. In most informal street markets visited, besides fish and fishery products, vegetables, fruits and other items such as noodles, dried fish, traditional food items, fresh chicken, pork and beef were also offered.

Retail sales of raw food, in particular fresh fruits, vegetables and fresh and cured fish at busy streets or around public markets by informal vendors in Kuala Lumpur are an integral part of the local market place. These market outlets are regulated and supervised by the municipal authorities.

The main factors for this growth of street food vending in Kuala Lumpur can be explained as follows:

(i) Local eating habits, cultural significance of street food hawkers, socio-economic environment, unemployment rates, and urban population growth
(ii) Loyal patronage of a growing clientele; street food vending has emerged in response to a socio-cultural need for inexpensive

nutritious foods. In the particular case of fresh raw seafood, informal street markets operating from strategic locations at busy hours of the day save customers time and/or money which might otherwise be spent in search of public markets or supermarkets

(iii) The Asian financial crisis had severely hit the urban poor population. Therefore, street food vending activities flourished.

Currently Kuala Lumpur City Hall is planning to regulate street food vending to include the designation of specific street areas as well as provision of support to vendors through the construction of adequate food stalls and related facilities. Joint plans with the Hawkers Association include the design of adequate vans for mobile food vending. Also a survey is being planned to collect updated information on the socio-economic characteristics of the street hawkers and petty traders.

In general, it was noticed during field surveys that fish and fishery products offered by street hawkers were of acceptable to good quality. It appeared that consumers felt satisfaction and convenience with readily available fresh fish at street seafood markets. Based on observations, it is concluded that street fish markets were well accepted by consumers and in general, provide personalised services with adequate seafood expertise. However, it is important to note that Asian consumers, in particular the Chinese, are less likely to complain when dissatisfied with a purchase due to cultural factors (face saving behaviour). Based on direct observation and limited survey data, it appears that convenience, strategic location and affordable prices directly influence repeat purchases of street vended fish, rather than customer satisfaction and loyalty.

At most street food markets visited, adequate to fair conditions were observed regarding fish handling practices. At most stalls, fresh seafood was displayed without ice, except some high value finfish, shrimp, prawn and squids which were kept with crushed ice. However, most street fish vendors had at least one insulated box to keep chilled fish in crushed ice and one (1) 15 - 20 litres capacity plastic bucket for storage of potable water for fish cleaning. Some large stalls had at least one lined insulated HDPE container to keep fish with ice. Regarding the variety of fish and fishery products at street markets, most stalls had about ten (10) fresh/chilled fish species or six (6) fishery products (mainly minced, cured and fermented) on display. The hawkers indicated that they were holding inventories of fresh fish from one to two working days. On average, street fish vendors operate about 6 to 8 hours daily and most of the vendors interviewed indicated that the average number of working days is about 7 days per week. The average daily sales per stall are about 45 - 60 kg of fresh fish and shellfish.

Our limited street fish retailer's survey indicated that men are the predominant operators of the street seafood retail stalls in Kuala Lumpur. A limited gender analysis showed that most women and men run street vending as a family business.The main challenge is therefore the need to implement effective and sustainable interventions, taking into account the peculiar characteristics of street fish vending in Kuala Lumpur. Statutory requirements, including licensing, should be linked to equipment/infrastructure development programmes. In particular, seafood street vending should have adequate provision of improved facilities for handling, chilled storage and preparation which can be provided by targeting busy street areas where seafood vendors regularly operate. In addition, different seafood vendors, depending on the type of seafood prepared and sold (e.g. chilled raw fish and cooked fish/ squid balls), working hours, working places, *modus operandi* (with fixed stalls or itinerant vendors with pushcarts), have varied requirements in terms of equipment and facilities, as well as different views regarding proposed improvements of their services and facilities.

The use of simple dial metallic thermometers is suggested, to regularly measure temperature of seafood on display at street fish markets. Dial thermometers can easily be calibrated to a known temperature by adjusting a hex nut located under the dial. These thermometers were locally available. This basic tool could be included as part of the training kit for street fish vendors. In addition, adequate supplies of potable water (water taps) as well as suitable wastewater drainage systems should be made available to each street fish stall. Water is used extensively in fish markets not only for fish cleaning, but also to flush offal and blood from equipment and floors, and to flume wastewater to floor drains and collection sumps. The first step for the implementation of potable water supplies in individual stalls at street fish markets should be to analyse water use patterns, install water meters and regularly record water consumption. The next step should be to undertake a survey of all market area and ancillary operations to identify wasteful practices and undertake corrective actions. Each street fish vendor should pay according to their water consumption and proportionally for the provision of wastewater drainage systems.

Regular training courses on fresh/chilled fish handling and hygiene should be part of any development programme for street seafood vendors organised by the Kuala Lumpur City Hall in co-ordination with the relevant government agencies. This training should be aimed at providing adequate guidance and technical assistance to fish hawkers on proper seafood handling and personal hygiene practices. All stall holders and their assistants who are involved in the preparation and sale of seafood should be required to attend and pass this training course.

Basic technical fields, which may be relevant for training courses intended for street fresh fish vendors, are as follows:

(i) Introduction to the concepts of freshness, quality, wholesomeness and nutritive value

(ii) The care of live and fresh fish, handling methods, use of ice, receiving deliveries, quality inspection, storage of live and chilled fish; hygiene and sanitation for fish retailers, selection and application of detergents and disinfectants

(iii) Quality and quality aspects at retail level; display of fish; promotion of fish sales techniques. Avoiding bad marketing practices

(iv) National and municipal regulations and codes of practice for fish vending

(v) Introduction to business planning; simple economics for fish retailing

(vi) Equipment & facilities development programmes in street fish vending.

Typical Street Food Markets in Kuala Lumpur

Municipal authorities license hawkers operating in most street food markets in Kuala Lumpur. In general, hawkers have to pay a monthly stall space fee and an annual license fee. Typical of many urban street markets is their location (usually near public markets) and the use of umbrellas and/or canvas awning which provide shelter and protection from rain and sun.

Seafood stalls are mostly equipped with trestle tables (the table top made of galvanised iron, stainless steel or fibreglass) for display of produce, insulated HDPE containers, chopping boards, weighing scales and price boards. They usually operate 6 - 7 days per week, according to the municipal regulations. The daily cleaning operations and solid waste collection at this street food market is carried out by a specialised private agency under contract with the local authorities. In most street raw food market outlets surveyed, the following food items were offered:

(i) Fresh seafood
(ii) Minced fish (raw)
(iii) Cured fish (dried and dried-salted fish)
(iv) Fermented fish sauce, pickled shrimp/prawn and shrimp/prawn paste
(v) Squid/fish balls
(vi) Noodles and rice/bean curd
(vii) Dressed chicken/eggs
(viii) Fresh goat meat, pork and beef, live frogs
(ix) Fresh fruits and vegetables
(x) Ready-to-eat food and beverages
(xi) Roasted pork/duck
(xii) Charcoal/dry goods/lentils/dried vegetables
(xiii) Cooked food (various)
(xiv) Sweets/cakes
(xv) Traditional medicines
(xvi) Shoes/newspapers/plastic articles/clothes
(xvii) Jade articles/kitchen utensils/joss sticks
(xviii) Garden utensils/seeds/fertiliser.

The total number of hawker stalls operating in the streets surrounding the Pudu retail market was about 1,097, of which 162 stalls were selling fresh seafood (including some also offering fermented and cured fishery products). In addition, 28 hawker stalls were offering fish balls/minced fish and/or bean curd. The seafood stalls were distributed in the five areas allocated in the streets surrounding the Pudu market, without a specific pattern. However, the main concentration of seafood stalls was located in the areas A, B and C. The market hours for street food hawker stalls were from 0600 hours to 1210 hours, immediately after the cleaning operations and solid waste collection were carried out. Some of the stall equipment was kept in nearby areas and the streets used by hawkers were cleared by afternoon. The typical sales or table area per seafood retailer would be in the range of 1.9 to 3 m^2. In addition, some space was taken up for insulated boxes that could not fit below the display table and the chopping board. A typical area for a seafood stall would be in the range of 3 to 4 m^2. Table 16 shows the total distribution of licensed stallholders (including street hawkers) in Pudu market, by ethnicity.

Table 16: Distribution of Licensed Stall Holders in Pudu Market, by Ethnicity (including Street Hawkers)

Ethnic Group	Number of Stall Holders (Percentage)
Chinese	1,316 (81.4%)
Malay	237 (14.6%)
Indian	64 (4%)
Total	1,617 (100%)

Source: Kuala Lumpur City Hall

Table 17 shows details of technical features and estimated costs of basic equipment of a typical street fish hawker in Pudu market.

Table 17: Technical Features and Estimated Costs of Basic Equipment used by a Typical Street Fish Hawker in Pudu Market

Description of Item	Quantity	Unit Cost (M. Ringgit)
Display tabletop (stainless steel); (Dimensions: 120 cm x 164 cm x 6 cm)	1	500
Set of folding trestles (wood)	1	80
Insulated container (expanded polystyrene, 50 mm thick) 50 kg capacity	4	15
Insulated container (HDPE walls and polyurethane foam) 100 kg capacity	1	250
Umbrella (waxed canvas)	1	120
Stand pole for the umbrella	1	50
Plastic trays	12	2
Chopping board (hardwood)	1	65
Filleting knives	1	40

Contd..

Plastic container (for carrying water); 5 gallons capacity	2	8
Price board	1	10
Plastic bin (offal collection)	1	6
Plastic bucket	1	6
Weighing scale (10 kg capacity); platform type	1	75
Portable calculator	1	20
Total Cost of Basic Equipment		1,322

Source: field surveys conducted by the author and counterparts

Improved Equipment for Street Seafood Vending

"Fish on Wheels" Marketing Scheme

A successful seafood marketing scheme known as "Fish on Wheels", based on motorised retail vans and sponsored by the Fisheries Development Authority of Malaysia (LKIM), was initiated in 1997. This marketing scheme was implemented in the Kuala Lumpur area, in co-ordination with other local agencies/institutions, catering to mostly Government employees. A sales officer and driver operate these motorised mobile facilities.

The concept of this scheme is based on the following criteria:

(a) All purchasing is done in bulk at a wholesale market

(b) An adequate market mix can be offered, including appropriate prices, adequate quality products and good product variety (fresh seafood, frozen fish/squid balls, dried fish, and vegetables and poultry products)

(c) Retailing through mobile fresh seafood outlets reduces fixed overhead costs, which is a clear advantage in comparison to conventional fish shops and supermarkets

(d) The concept capitalises on the increasing demand for fresh/chilled seafood of consistently high quality. Fish is a staple food for the local population

(e) The "Fish on Wheels" concept is an innovative marketing scheme which can allow a relatively large volume of sales, as well as consistent standard of operation and product quality

(f) The high level of mobility permits an extensive area of the city and increased number of government agencies to be reached.

However, such motorised retail vans involve comparatively high capital investment and operating costs, which requires careful planning and adequate marketing strategies. Features of the "Fish on Wheels" scheme are as follows:

(a) It comprises a small fleet of four (4) motorised retail vans. Each van is supplied solely from the company's depot (located in Kuala Lumpur) on a daily basis. The central depot also provides facilities including crushed ice supply, engine services and maintenance as well as services for the placing of individual orders for the following day

(b) The retail van has a special purpose-built body, which incorporates a full width platform made in stainless steel, lift-up sides to provide additional protection to seafood and a multiple compartment for storing and displaying other food items such as vegetables, poultry, condiments and dried fish/ shrimp. Insulated fish boxes, HDPE fish boxes, chopping boards and weighing scales are placed on the stainless steel platform. On the lift-up side an attractive price board is placed at the start of sales operations. The vehicle is a standard one (1) tonne van with a 4 - cylinder SOHC engine, 1,400 cc and 78hp/5,500 rpm. The retail price of the van is about RM 38,700 (US$ 10,200) including basic insurance. The total cost of the truck body and display unit is about RM 8,000 (US$ 2,105).

(c) A central buying point (Selayang wholesale market) ensures the best possible availability and price of seafood. However, during the survey period there were some problems with regular supplies of seafood; management personnel indicated that in the previous months, about 60% of the fresh fish was imported from Thailand due to shortage of fish supplies from local landings.

(d) A good variety of seafood is offered regularly (about 10 - 15 species). On average, each retail van sells about 450 - 500 kg of fresh fish daily and serves three (3) Government agencies. There are well-established sales periods in each location namely: a) 09:00 to 11:00 hours; b) 12:30 to 14:30 hours; c) 14:30 to 16:30 hours; operating from Mondays to Saturdays (6 days/ week).

(e) Adequate supervision and motivation of the retail van operators is carried out to improve productivity and services to consumers.

The general profile of consumers served by retail vans could be described as mostly housewives from socio-economic levels B, C and D. They usually purchase food items on a regular basis and to a lesser extent, on impulse. They buy because of assured regular supplies, convenience for them, competitive prices and consistently good quality.

(f) Average daily sales were as follows:

Type of Product	Average Daily Sales (kg)
Fresh/chilled seafood	450-500
Frozen fish/squid balls	25
Dried shrimp	2.5
Dried anchovy/cured squid	2.5
Poultry, beef and vegetable	200

Table 18 shows details of the technical features and estimated costs of basic equipment used by a "Fish on Wheels" unit, based on data provided by LKIM.

Table 18: Technical Features and Estimated Costs of Basic Equipment of "Fish on Wheels"

Description of Item	Quantity	Unit Cost (RM)
Retail van (including special purpose-built body)	1	38,700
Insulated container (HDPE walls and polyurethane foam) 50 kg capacity	1	150
HDPE fish boxes (25-kg capacity)	16	20
HDPE trays (15 kg capacity)	20	5
Chopping board (hardwood)	1	45
Filleting knives	1	40
HDPE baskets	5	6
Price board	1	10
Portable table (HDPE top)	2	35
Weighing scale (30 kg capacity); platform type, digital	1	1,000
Portable calculator	1	35
Total Cost of Basic Equipment		**40,500**

Table 19 shows the retail prices of seafood and meats offered through the "Fish on Wheels" marketing scheme in Kuala Lumpur at the time of the survey.

Table 19: Retail Prices of Seafood and Meats Offered by "Fish on Wheels" Vans in Kuala Lumpur

Products	**Retail Prices (RM/kg)**
Seafood:	
Silver Pomfret	17.0
Black Pomfret	15.0
Spanish Mackerel	14.0
Threadfin	16.0
Wolf-herring	12.0
Mangrove Snapper	15.0
Seabass	17.0
Sand Velvet Shrimp	25.0
Giant Freshwater Prawn	20.0
Mangrove Crab	13.0
Loligo Squid	10.0
Red Snapper	13.0
Threadfin Bream	7.5
Yellow Striped Trevally	6.0
Hardtail Scad	5.0
Indian Mackerel	7.5
Dried Anchovy	15.0
Dried Shrimp	30.0
Meat &Poultry:	
Beef Cutlets	8.0
Dressed Chicken	5.0

Source: Data collected during field surveys conducted by the author and counterparts

Table 20 shows the estimated operational costs of a standard "Fish on Wheels" unit in Kuala Lumpur.

Table 20: Estimated Operational Costs of a "Fish on Wheels" Unit

Cost Item	Daily Expenses (RM)	Days worked per month	Monthly Amount
I) Fixed Costs	68.75	24-30	2,062.50
Depreciation of major equipment:	30.00		(4.50%)
			900.00
Transport van			
Chest freezer			
Weighing scales & fish boxes			
Maintenance of equipment:	6.25		187.50
Transport van			
Chest freezer			
Weighing scales			
Labour costs:	5.00		150.00
Driver			
Assistant			
Transportation costs of fish/fishery products from wholesale market/dealer	10.00		300.00
Miscellaneous expenses:	17.50		525.00
Road taxes			
Insurance			
Rental of premises			
II) Variable Costs	1,451.85	24-30	43,305.90
			(95.45%)
Purchase of fish and fishery products	1,375.00		41,250.00
Ice supplies (4 blocks of ice/day; 70 kg/block)			
Packaging materials:	41.60		998.40
Plastic bags	5.75		172.50
Losses of fishery products	25.00		750.00
Other costs:	4.50		135.00
Water			
Parking charges			
Electricity			
III) Total Operational Costs	1,520.60	24-30	45,368.40
			(100%)

Source: Fisheries Development Authority of Malaysia (LKIM)

"Pasar Tani" (Farmers' Market) Scheme

An interesting marketing scheme known as *Pasar Tani* has as its main objectives to encourage farmers' and fishermen's organisations to participate directly in the marketing of their produce, enabling them to obtain higher prices, expand the market size for agricultural and fisheries produce and provide consumers with a wider choice of foodstuff at reasonable prices.

This marketing scheme is co-ordinated and organised by the Federal Agricultural Marketing Authority (FAMA).

The main characteristics of the *Pasar Tani* scheme are as follows:

(i) This marketing scheme operates usually once a week in selected areas of the city. The retailers can operate in several locations provided that they can assure reasonably regular supply of produce. A selection of strategic locations is done by FAMA in co-ordination with local authorities

(ii) At each *Pasar Tani,* a good variety of fresh vegetables, fruits, seafood, chicken, red meat, dairy products, flowers, traditional medicine and handicrafts is regularly offered.

(iii) FAMA provides the following services:

- Rental of facilities such as umbrellas, tables and baskets
- Market price information
- Promotional campaigns to attract consumers
- Training to upgrade retailers' skills in trading activities
- Supervisory services to manage retailers' requirements, to protect consumers rights and ensure adequate levels of cleanliness
- Conduct feasibility studies on the viability of the business before setting up a new *Pasar Tani.*

(iv) A total of 28 *Pasar Tani* outlets were set up in Kuala Lumpur, with 2 outlets operating every day of the week, 9 on Sundays, 8 on Saturdays, 5 on Thursdays, 3 on Wednesdays and 1 on Fridays. Market hours vary, most operating from 07:00 hours to 13:00 hours and 14:00 hours to 20:00 hours. Retailers are charged a monthly fee (by FAMA) for stall space allocation and an annual license fee (by municipal authorities).

(v) Most seafood retailers operate from vans; fish is displayed on trestle tables with an umbrella to provide protection from rain and sun. They usually carry fish with crushed ice in insulated boxes. This type of stall has the advantage that it can be easily assembled, and after market hours, it can be loaded onto the vans and moved to another market location. The typical sales or table area per retailer would be in the range of 1.7 to 3.4 m^2. The most common material used to manufacture the display tabletops is fibreglass. In most locations visited, retailers displayed their fish on a standard fibreglass tabletop (91.44 cm wide and 182.9 cm long) with folding trestles provided by FAMA. They were equipped with cutting boards, weighing scales, plastic boxes and wash basins for washing fish and cleaning the stall area. After market hours all equipment was washed with clean water, wastes were collected in plastic bags and placed in offal bins and the stall area was rinsed with clean water. The services of the cleaning personnel are included in the monthly stall space fee.

(vi) Seafood supplies in most *Pasar Tani* visited were from Fishermen's Associations. All retailers interviewed indicated that they were not fishermen, but were linked to these Associations; therefore the concept of direct marketing from producers to consumers was somehow met. They also indicated that the frequency of purchases of fresh seafood was 3 - 4 days/week. Average daily sales were about 120 kg of fresh fish. In most cases, the driver was the owner of the business and was in charge of all trading operations. Table 21a shows the technical features and estimated costs of the basic equipment used by a typical *Pasar Tani* fishmonger operating in Kuala Lumpur.

Table 21a: Technical Features and Estimated Costs of Basic Equipment used by* Pasar Tani *Fishmongers

Description of Item	Quantity	Unit Cost (RM)
Van (1.8 tonne) wooden body; secondhand	1	21,000
Insulated container (HDPE walls and polyurethane foam) 50 kg capacity	5	150
Insulated container (HDPE walls and polyurethane foam)		

100 kg capacity	1	250
Display tabletop (fibreglass);		
(Dimensions: 92 cm x 182 cm x 7 cm)	2	170
Set of folding trestles (wood)	2	78
Umbrella	2	120
Plastic trays	12	1.5
Chopping board (hardwood)	1	65
Filleting knives	1	40
Plastic container (for carrying water);		
5 gallons capacity	2	8
Price board	1	10
Plastic bin (offal collection)	1	6
Plastic bucket	1	6
Weighing scale (10 kg capacity); 70 platform type	1	
Portable calculator	1	20
Total Cost of Basic Equipment		22,987

Source: Field surveys conducted by the author and counterparts.

Table 21b shows the estimated operational costs incurred by a typical *Pasar Tani* fishmonger operating in Kuala Lumpur.

Table 21b: Estimated Operational Costs incurred by a* Pasar Tani *Fishmonger (Kuala Lumpur)

Cost Item	Daily Expenses (RM)	Days worked per month	Monthly Amount
I) Fixed Costs	156.90	12	1,882.80 (22.84%)
Depreciation of major equipment:	16.90		202.80
Transport van			
Weighing scales & fish boxes			
Display tables			
Insulated containers			
Maintenance of equipment:	15.00		180.00
Transport van			
Weighing scales			
Folding trestles			
Labour costs (including meals):	90.00	12	1,080.00

Driver			
Assistant			
Transportation costs of fish/			
fishery products from landing places	20.00	12	240.00
Miscellaneous expenses:	15.00	12	180.00
Road taxes			
Insurance			
Rental of premises			
II) Variable Costs	529.80	12	6,357.60 (77.15%)
Purchase of fish and fishery products	480.00		5,760.00
Ice supplies			
(2 blocks of ice/day; 70 kg/block)	20.80		249.60
Packaging materials:	10.00		120.00
Plastic bags			
Losses of fishery products	15.00		180.00
Other costs:	4.00		48.00
Water			
Parking charges			
III) Total Operational Costs	686.70	12	8,240.40 (100%)

Source: Field surveys conducted by the author and counterparts

SINGAPORE

Singapore supports a substantial market for live, fresh, frozen and cured fish and fishery products. Current annual seafood trade data indicate that about S$ 1.2 billion (US$ 696,864,111) was traded in Singapore during 1998 - 1999.

Singapore, due to its strategic location in Southeast Asia, adequate transportation facilities (by sea, air and land) overall economic growth and significant increases in disposable income of the population, has become an important seafood business centre and main distribution hub in the region. It serves as an export market for fish and fishery products from Southeast Asian countries as well as a transhipment base for fishery products from around the world. Singapore has become one of the wealthiest countries in Asia, with an average per capita GDP of US$ 22,205 in 1998; only Japan and Hong Kong had higher per capita GDP among the Asian countries.

However, Singapore's total fish and shellfish catches are relatively small; in 1997, FAO reported a catch volume of 9,250 metric tonnes. Re-exports of seafood from Singapore are increasing; in 1999, re-export figures were estimated at 75,000 metric tonnes.

Official figures for 1998 showed that about 56 percent of imported shrimp and prawns is re-exported to Japan, Hong Kong, the Netherlands and Malaysia, and 91 percent of imported high quality tuna is re-exported to Japan (64 percent), Italy (12 percent) and Thailand (10 percent).

In addition, 57 percent of imported marine fish is re-exported to Malaysia (39 percent), Taiwan (22 percent) and China (20 percent). Re-exports of fish and fishery products from Singapore to ASEAN[15] countries are mainly valued-added or high value fishery products, due to the fact that most of those countries are able to supply fish for their domestic markets as well as for exports markets. Table 22 shows Singapore's imports and exports of fish and fishery products during 1997.

Table 22: Imports and Exports of Fish and Fishery Products (1997)

Fishery Product	Imports (MT)	Exports (MT)
Fish, fresh, chilled or frozen	111,664	83,182
Fish, dried, salted or smoked	3,807	1,389
Crustaceans and molluscs	45,994	22,308
Fish, canned	18,035	2,008
Crustaceans and molluscs, canned	5,039	2,728

Source: FAO Yearbook of Fishery Statistics-Commodities, 1997

Singapore imports more than 90 percent of its fish for domestic consumption; in 1997, FAO fisheries statistics reported an apparent annual per capita fish supply of about 31.2 kg. Table 23 shows the breakdown of food per capita consumption in 1998. It is estimated that in the year 2000, the total population will reach about 4.1 million[16] with an average density of 6,406 people/km^2.

Table 23: Food Per Capita Consumption (1998)

Food Item	Annual Per Capita Consumption (kg/year)
Chicken	32
Fish	26
Pork	23
Beef	3
Duck	3
Mutton	3
Vegetables	77
Fruits	82

Source: The Straits Times (Singapore), 8th March, 2000.

Fish Distribution Channels

The domestic seafood market for fishery products is distinguished principally by the heavy dependence on imports by air from countries such as China, Malaysia, India, Sri Lanka; by sea from Indonesia and by land mainly from Thailand and Malaysia. Both captured and cultured fish and fishery products are regularly traded in the domestic seafood market. Chilled and live seafood is landed at the two main fishing ports, namely the Jurong and Senoko fishing ports and wholesale markets. Jurong and Senoko wholesale markets handle about 100,000 and 20,000 metric tonnes of fish annually, respectively. Jurong is the biggest, with a market floor area of 9,000 m2 and 110 market lots (allotted area on which the agents display and trade seafood). Senoko has a market floor area which currently houses about 36 market lots for trading operations with each agent having an allotted area of 40 m^2 for displaying and selling fish. Fish in both wholesale markets is sold mainly by agreement on price with the buyers, and to a lesser extent through auction by agents, who sell to retailers, institutional buyers, processors and seafood traders. Average daily volumes of seafood traded in the Jurong and Senoko wholesale fish markets are estimated to be about 250 and 45 metric tonnes respectively. The fishing ports and wholesale markets are managed by the Primary Production Department (PPD). Both wholesale markets operate regularly from about 02:00 hours to 07:00 hours.

However, some of the fish landed in Singapore does not go through the auction halls, but are supplied directly to restaurants, hotels and supermarkets; and some chilled fish (particularly tuna and some high value species) is selected and packed for re-export to neighbouring countries.

There is also a significant live fish and shellfish trade, some of which does not go through the auction, but are handled by private wholesalers located at Changi ferry terminal. These wholesalers operate small live fish carriers/vivier boats (with tanks and aeration systems), collecting live marine finfish produced by cage culture farms, air-flown live fish and shellfish, and live fish brought in by fishing vessels operating in Singaporean waters. Indonesian fishing vessels also bring in some live marine fish through Jurong fishing port. High value live finfish and shellfish is transported by importers/traders in carrier trucks equipped with tanks and aeration systems for local distribution to restaurants, hotels, public markets and some supermarkets. A proportion of the live fish is also exported to Hong Kong and China.

The supply of chilled fish from the East Coast of Malaysia is seasonal, with a peak period from March to June and a low supply period during November to February. However, the main influences on market prices and demand for high value chilled fish are the Chinese New Year, the wedding season (August to October) and the country's economy. During the Chinese New Year, rabbitfish (*Siganus canaliculatus*) command high prices (among the ethnic Chinese population, rabbitfish is associated with good luck). Ripe females fetch premium prices, and are traditional holiday delicacies. However, during the rest of the year, rabbitfish has little to moderate demand in the market. During the wedding season, the consumption and demand for high-priced fish and shellfish (shrimp, mud crab and lobster), mainly through restaurants, is very high.

Another important factor that influences prices and demand of high value fish is the level of growth or recession affecting the country's economy. For example, during 1995 to 1998, the domestic market for live marine finfish was price-sensitive (affected by the economic crisis in the region, the number of tourist arrivals, as well as restaurant sales significantly declined) and as a result, imports of live marine fish (mainly seabass, snapper, and grouper) declined by about 35%. The lowered purchasing power of consumers and reduced frequency of dining-out and family celebrations forced the market for live marine fish to look for alternative and cheaper products (such as seabass) or reduce imports significantly. The market for live marine finfish is relatively small in terms of volume and it is estimated that about 1,200 to 1,850 tons were traded annually during the period 1995 to 1998, with an average C&F price of S$ 5.35/kg (US$ 3.097/kg) in 1998. FAO statistics for 1997 reported that Singapore imported a total of 2,954 tonnes of live fish (marine and freshwater). The main suppliers of live marine finfish are Malaysia, and to a lesser extent, Indonesia. Live Indo-Pacific swamp crab or mangrove crab (*Scylla serrata*) has a good demand in Singapore and it is mainly marketed alive. The main suppliers of live mud crab are Sri Lanka, India, the Philippines and Bangladesh. The market size for mangrove crab in Singapore is about 3,300 metric tonnes/year including supplies of chilled crabs (Singapore Trade Statistics do not differentiate product forms for crab). The average C&F price for live mangrove crab in 1999 was about US$ 4 to 5 per kg, but ripe females fetched about US 7 - 8 per kg. During February 2000, the average wholesale prices for live groupers were about S$ 15 to 20 per kg and S$ 8 - 11 per kg for live snappers. Table 24 shows the average wholesale prices of fresh fish at Jurong and Senoko during 1999.

Table 24: Average Wholesale Prices of Fresh Fish at Singapore's Wholesale Markets during 1999

Species	Jurong		Senoko	
	Low Price (S $/kg)	High Price (S $/kg)	Low Price (S$/kg)	High Price (S $/kg)
Red snapper (*Lutjanus sp.*)	3.13	4.29	4.31	5.73
Chinese pomfret (*Pampus chinensis*)	17.67	24.90	17.70	25.91
White/silver pomfret (*Pampus argenteus*)	11.71	14.61	10.39	14.14
Indian mackerel (*Rastrelliger kanagurta*)	3.21	4.42	3.05	4.04
Spanish mackerel (*Scomberomorus sp.*)	4.76	6.67	5.09	6.54
Threadfin (*Polynemus indicus*)	9.80	15.31	10.74	13.29
Yellow-banded scad (*Selaroides leptolepis*)	1.39	3.82	2.61	3.68

Source: Dr. Tan Sen Min, MFRD/SEAFDEC, Singapore.

There is also an important speciality dried fish market for products such as dried anchovies, salted mackerel, sharkfin, fishmaw, sea cucumber, abalone, shrimp, squid, cuttlefish and oyster. The domestic dried fish production is negligible and the country is a net importer of these products. Major suppliers of dried fish to Singapore are Thailand, Malaysia, South Korea, Vietnam, Taiwan and Hong Kong. A portion of the high quality dried fish is re-exported to Hong Kong and China as Singapore's strategic location has made it an important distribution centre of dried fish for Southeast Asia. Table 25 shows the average wholesale prices of dried fishery products in Singapore during February 2000.

Table 25: Average Wholesale Prices of Dried Fishery Products (February, 2000)

Dried Fish Product	Wholesale Price (S $/kg)
Anchovies	
Whole (average quality)	5 - 6
Split open	10
Fillets	9 - 11
Scallops	150
Sea cucumber	
Black lollyfish	23 - 28
Tigerfish	9 - 13
Dried squid (butterfly cut) (6 - 7 pieces/kg)	26 - 28
Sharkfins	
Tiger shark, tails (20 cm/up)	33 - 34
Sharkfin rays (below 10 cm)	64 - 66
Fishmaws	
Jewfish, grade B	
Below 15 pieces/kg	55 - 57
Above 15 pieces/kg	19 - 25

Source: Data obtained during field market surveys by the author and counterparts.

Seafood reaches consumers in Singapore through a multi-level system, which may involve at least two transactions before the fish or fishery product is purchased in a public fish market or supermarket or eaten in a restaurant/food stall. The channels of distribution incorporate locally caught and processed seafood, with live, chilled and frozen imported items from the region and around the world; these items can be re-packed or processed locally and re- exported. The seafood distribution chain is typically very short, in particular for live seafood, with importers acting as distributors and agents directly dealing with retailers and restaurants. Supermarket chains are often direct importers of frozen and canned seafood product. At the two wholesale fish markets, the distribution chain is short, with wholesale agents selling fish to wholesalers, who distribute the products to retailers and institutional buyers. Some wholesalers act as purchasing agents for restaurants, catering organisations, super- markets and large retailers.

Singapore's Retail Fish Market

Singapore is home to a variety of retail establishments offering live, fresh, frozen, cured and canned seafood to consumers. The range of shopping options include public retail markets and licensed hawkers selling through stalls, which offer a wide selection of live fish, fresh fish and fishery products and cured fish. Public markets currently hold about 70% of the retail market share of chilled and live fish and fishery products. Large supermarket chains (such as NTUC Fair Price, Carrefour, Cold Storage, Shop N Save and Prime) and medium-sized independent supermarkets offer fresh, frozen, live, cured and canned seafood. Supermarkets are currently handling about 30 percent of the retail market share of chilled and live fish and fishery products. Despite the fact that most supermarkets are low-cost, low-margin, high volume, self-service operations, which are designed to provide the consumer's total needs for food and household-maintenance products, many still prefer to shop for seafood at public retail markets. The most popular product form is whole fresh fish and preferred species of finfish are: sea bream, Spanish mackerel, yellow-banded scad, red snapper, groupers, black, white & Chinese pomfret, threadfin and horse mackerel. In general, the retail price margin for chilled seafood products is about 25 percent.

There is a steady demand at supermarket level for chilled fillets, steaks and shellfish; consumers are willing to pay a little more for the convenience, dependability, quality and better packaging. Most supermarkets have well-defined seafood product strategies, including adequate product mix and variety. In most supermarkets, there is a full-service seafood section in charge of taking and preparing orders from consumers. The preparation may include weighing a specific quantity of fish or shellfish, gutting, cleaning or cutting a whole fish or fillet to the desired size or product form. Orders are then wrapped and labelled for the consumer. Alternatively seafood may be displayed "pre-packed", when a small number of units, such as 250/500 grams of fish fillets, steaks or shrimp are wrapped in clingfilm on a small tray, and pre-priced. If seafood is to be pre-packaged, it is done at source. Many of the larger supermarkets insist on a high standard of hygiene in the local seafood packhouses. It was also noticed that standards of construction, maintenance, quality control and hygiene were high, which increases the investment incurred by supermarkets. According to some supermarket chains, the true cost of these investments is considered when seafood-selling prices are calculated.

Convenient pre-packed shrimp (head-on, headless, peeled and ready-to-cook) offered in supermarket chains are high value products met with some demand; however, it appears that most shrimp consumption takes place through the catering sector. According to some supermarket personnel, consumers are aware of the difference between shrimp species, but may not know whether the shrimp were cultured or wild-caught. Some supermarket chains are also offering ready-to-eat fish for taking out and consumption at home. The sale of ready-to-eat fish is designed in a similar way to that of traditional Chinese roasted duck, which is very popular at supermarket chains. Table 26 shows the comparative retail prices of live and fresh fish in supermarkets and public markets during February 2000.

The retail market for traditional minced and surimi-based products includes fish balls, squid/cuttlefish balls, shrimp balls, fish cakes, stuffed vegetables with surimi, Foochow fish balls (cooked fish balls with chicken filling), surimi & crab balls, fish/shrimp spring rolls and surimi analogues. In addition, surimi-based dried snack products (locally processed and imported) are also offered; these are popular for parties and celebrations. The domestic market for surimi-based fishery products is expected to grow due to increased production capacity and quality improvement of locally made products, adequate price levels and regular availability of both imported and locally made products. In addition, an increasing number of working housewives and consumers want convenience seafood products, which are easy and quick to prepare at home. Public retail markets and supermarkets currently offer a good variety of traditional and minced, as well as surimi-based products.

Table 26: Comparative Average Retail Prices of Live and Fresh Fish in Singapore (February, 2000)

Species/Type of Product	Price (S $/kg) Supermarkets	Price (S $/kg) Public Markets
Live Fish		
Tilapia (300 g/piece)	9.7	6.0
Grouper	25.8	25.0
Marble goby	28.8	n/a
Snakehead	n/a	10 - 12
Carp	n/a	6.5
Mangrove crab:		
Small size	-	10.0
Medium size	11.5	12.0
Large size	-	14.0
Spiny lobster	48.0	n/a
Giant tiger shrimp	24.9	23.0
Blue swimming crab	13.5 - 15.9	n/a
Crayfish	18.1	n/a
Whole Fresh Fish		
Threadfin bream	4.9	4.7
White pomfret	10.0	10.5
Chinese pomfret	16.9	16.5
Rabbitfish	6.6	6.0
Black pomfret	6.5	6.8
Red grouper	9.5	9.0
Red snapper	14.8	15.0
Spanish mackerel	8.5	8.4
Snobnose pampano (cultured)	13.8	13.5
Hybrid red tilapia (cultured)	3.1	3.5
Seabass (cultured)	9.9	9.5
Slipper lobster	17.9	n/a
Blue swimming crab	6.5	6.0
Giant tiger shrimp:		
Small size		13.0
Medium size	16.9	16.0
Large size		25.0

Source: Data obtained during field market surveys by the author; n/a = not available, meaning that the product form was not available during the market survey.

Table 27: Average Retail Prices of Chilled Value-added Fishery Products

Product	Price (S $/kg)
Dory fillets (trays)	7.7
Salmon fillets (trays)	16.9
Threadfin fillets (trays)	25.9
Cod steaks (trays)	27.9
Red snapper steaks	10.9
Stingray steaks (trays)	6.9
Conger eel steaks (trays)	4.7
Salmon heads/bone/tail (trays)	8.0
King crab legs (trays)	15.9
Cooked mussel meat (trays)	8.7
Squid fillets (skinless)	8.9
Scallops (half shell)	12.0
Scallop flesh	37.9
Oysters (half shell)	13.5
Fresh fish balls (trays)	4.5
Fried fish balls (trays/bags)	5.8 - 6.8
Prawn balls (trays/bags)	6.8
Cuttlefish balls (trays/bags)	6.5
Surimi and crab balls (trays)	7.8
Shrimp balls (trays)	8.5
Foochow fish balls (trays)	7.9
Imitation scallops (trays)	12.9
Softshell crab (4 pieces/tray)	21.0
Seasoned baby octopus (trays)	21.9
Seasoned squid slices (trays)	31.9

Source: Data obtained during field market surveys by the author and counterparts.

In some large public markets, traditional small-scale production of freshly made minced fish paste is a common feature. The main species used are wolf-herring (*Chirocentrus dorab*), conger eel (*Congresox talabonoides*) spotted Spanish mackerel (*Scomberomorus guttatus*) and lizardfish (*Saurida spp.*). Retail prices of fresh minced fish were about S$8 to S$ 12 per kg depending on the fish species used. The shelf life of minced fish paste and surimi-based products ranges from a few days at a temperature of 0 - 5°C to 3 - 12 months when frozen at -18°C. Table 27 shows the retail prices of selected value-added fishery products in Singapore during February 2000.

Table 28 shows the average retail prices of red meats and poultry in Singapore during February 2000.

Table 28: Average Retail Prices of Meat and Poultry Products in Singapore (February, 2000)

Product	Price (S $/kg)
Red Meats:	
Lean pork	8.7
Pork loin	10.5
Beef loin	14.8 - 15
Beef, tender chuck	12.9 - 13
Minced beef	9.9
Lamb leg, chops	15.5
Poultry:	
Dressed chicken (chilled)	3.6
Chicken breast/chilled)	7.8
Chicken, drumstick (chilled)	5.5
Duck, dressed (chilled)	3.7 - 3.8

Source: Data obtained during field market surveys by the author and counterparts.

Street Food Hawkers in Singapore

In 1971, a national programme aimed at building hawker food centres and markets to resettle licensed street hawkers provided basic stall facilities and services such as piped potable water and electricity supplies, waste collection and disposal. By 1996, all street hawkers had been completely resettled into food centres and markets. In 1988, there were about 23,331 hawkers operating in 184 public markets and food centres in Singapore, of which 8,878 were engaged in ready-to-eat vending operations. A total of 42 hawker food centres operated regularly in 1996. Official data on the number of licensed stalls in these hawker food centres is shown in Table 29.

Table 29: Licensed Stalls in Hawker Food Centres in Singapore (1996)

Type of Stalls	Number of stalls
Cooked food retail stalls	2,196
Market retail stalls:	479
(i) Sundry goods	
(ii) Market produce	
(e.g. Seafood, meat, whole fruits)	
(iii) Market produce	
(e.g. Vegetables, eggs, bean cakes, noodles)	
Sub-total	2,398
Total	5,073

Source: Annual Report, 1996. Hawkers Department, Singapore.

The set up and operation of Singapore's hawker food centres was aimed at upgrading the performance of hawkers through appropriate facilities, food control measures, and provision of training and adequate legislation. The Hawkers Department is the Government agency in charge of formulating and implementing policies on the operation, licensing and control of hawkers. This agency also inspects all hawker stalls and enforces the Environmental Public Health Act No. 32 (Chapter 95) of 1968, and its regulations (Environmental Public Health (Hawkers) Regulations, 1969), thus ensuring observance of good food hygiene practices. Regular training courses on food hygiene are part of an on-going programme organised by the Hawkers Department. This training is aimed at providing adequate guidance and technical assistance to food hawkers on proper food and personal hygiene practices. All stall holders and their assistants who are involved in the preparation and sale of food are required to attend and pass this food hygiene course. Since the introduction of this food hygiene course in 1990, up to 1996, the Hawkers Department has trained a total of 10,305 food handlers. About 290 - 300 stallholders and assistants from the hawkers' food centres attend and pass the food hygiene course each year.

Basic design features of market product stalls are mainly fixed type facilities, which resemble those found in the traditional public market retail stall. Potable water, wastewater drainage and electricity is provided to retail stalls, which have glazed tile walls, concrete slopped floors and adequate ventilation and lighting.

Live Fish Marketing and Basic Equipment

It is a well-known fact that live fish and shellfish commands a premium price because of its guaranteed quality, freshness and intrinsic flesh characteristics (better texture and delicate flavour) in comparison with fresh/chilled seafood. Primarily the tastes, traditions and cooking styles of the population (mostly Chinese in orgin) determine Singapore's live seafood market requirements. The consumption of live seafood is a niche market for affluent tourists, the upper class population and businessmen. The negative effects of the financial crisis in Asia are reflected in Singapore's trade of high-value live marine finfish, which has shown a declining trend in the last three years. With the gradual recovery of Singapore's economy, a positive trend in the domestic demand for high-value live marine finfish is expected.

The display of live seafood in aquariums has traditionally been an effective marketing device at restaurants and hotels (main outlets for live seafood sales) as well as in public food markets. Tourist seafood restaurants as well as traditional Singaporean seafood restaurants offer a large selection of live aquatic food, such as lobsters, mangrove crab, shrimp, oysters, snakehead, catfish, carps, seabass, groupers, snappers and other reef fish. For example, for the preparation of the very popular dish known as Singapore chilli crab, (which is offered as a speciality in most seafood restaurants), professional cooks use large live mangrove crabs (preferably ripe females). Most seafood banquet directors interviewed indicated that live fish is an important part of the menu for wedding banquets, company dinners and dances as well as birthday celebrations. Live fish are commonly gutted and either steamed or deep-fried, and generally are served with mixed vegetables and/or sauces. In general, live fish with firm flesh, low fat content, and fine-grained skin are preferred. It should be mentioned that some species of live cultured fish are considered inferior to wild live fish and fetches slightly lower prices; this is particularly evident with groupers. There is a premium price on size, with larger fish (within the range of 1 - 2 kg) often commanding higher prices than smaller fish.

Vivier Boats

Live marine fish is harvested either by scoop net or lifting cage culture nets. The fish is than transported by small vivier boats to the landing centres. The boats are equipped with small fibreglass-reinforced plastic (FRP) containers/tanks and two (2) pure oxygen cylinders. Live marine fish (mainly groupers, tilapia, mullets, snappers and seabass) collected from fish farms are transferred manually to the FRP tanks filled with clean seawater, adequately oxygenated. On average, trips from fish farms to the Changi ferry terminal landing centre last about 1 - 2 hours. The average market size of cultivated marine fish is shown in Table 30.

Table 30: Average Market Size of Cultivated Marine Fish

Species	Market Size (g/piece)
Grouper	600 - 1,000
Seabass	600 - 1,000
Tilapia	400 - 600

Source: data from market surveys conducted by the author and counterparts.

Vivier Trucks

Currently, live marine fish are transported in seawater from the landing centres by vivier trucks. The main features of vivier trucks include aerated seawater tanks mounted on flatbed trucks. The majority of tanks used in Singapore are locally made from fibreglass-reinforced plastic (FRP) or aluminium.

The open transport tanks require aeration to maintain adequate dissolved oxygen levels. For this purpose, the following equipment is used: mechanical water pumping systems to circulate the water and provide aeration to the fish tanks powered by the truck's engine and pure oxygen through oxygen cylinders connected to the tanks through flexible plastic hoses. A typical example of a live marine transportation system is as follows:

(a) Truck: A five tonne payload flatbed truck equipped with six vivier tanks (made of fibreglass reinforced plastic, with aeration fittings and air distributors/diffusers on the bottom, and water drainage)

(b) Small water pump powered by the truck's engine

(c) Oxygen cylinders (two) connected to the tanks through flexible plastic hoses

(d) Scoop nets (stainless steel frames and nylon netting)

(e) Weighing baskets.

On arrival at the landing centre (Changi ferry terminal), the live fish is sorted by species and size and distributed to wholesalers, retail markets and restaurants at mutually agreed prices. Any fish which are not sold are kept in vivier tanks which are equiped with circulatory and aerating systems similar to those installed in the vivier trucks. The fish are normally fed minced fish. During the entire collection, storage and distribution operations, the handling of the live fish is reduced to a minimum to avoid excessive injuries. At the retail or restaurant destination, the fish is transferred to aquariums or portable containers until sold or required for human consumption. Wild-caught live fish such as groupers, snappers, parrotfish and coral fishes are handled in the same way as the live cultured marine fish. In addition, live lobsters, prawns, mud crab and groupers which are air flown from neighbouring countries are also handled and distributed at the Changi ferry terminal. It is estimated that on average, 500 kg/day of live marine fish are landed at the terminal.

Retail Outlets for Live Fish and Shellfish

The main retail outlets for live fish and shellfish are the public markets and some supermarket chains. Retail competition is intense, with a high concentration of sophisticated retailers. There is also substantial foreign investment in this sector, in particular, in supermarkets and shopping malls. However, public markets still play a major role in retailing live seafood.

For example, NTUC Fair Price, which is the largest supermarket chain in Singapore, offers a good variety of live seafood such as spiny lobster, blue swimming crab, mangrove crab, crayfish, giant tiger shrimp and tilapia.

The equipment used for display of live seafood at supermarkets include mainly display tanks. The live seafood distributors supply these units to supermarkets on a loan basis. The largest display unit is equipped as follows:

- Three glass-sided fibreglass display tanks (rectangular in shape)
- One water pump (for water circulation)

- One mechanical filter
- Three-tiered waterfall aerators
- One water chiller.

This large unit can hold about 30 to 50 kg of lobsters or giant tiger shrimp. The display tank units are an important promotional tool in the retail seafood section and an effective assurance to consumers of the good quality of the live seafood being offered. Simple glass aquarium tanks equipped with air pumps are also used for displaying live tilapia and crabs in some smaller supermarkets. These highly visible display units have boosted live seafood sales at most of the NTUC Fair Price supermarkets.

At public markets, the equipment used for display of retail live seafood at supermarkets include mainly aquarium units, portable FRP tanks and plastic containers. Aquarium display units are either metal-framed glass tanks or plexiglass tanks (with silicone rubber adhesive sealed joints), the latter being more commonly used. According to these retailers, most of the display units are equipped with air pumps to maintain adequate oxygen levels. However, mud crabs are either kept in their original packaging boxes or in plastic containers without water. During retail operations, the main control measures for live crabs are to keep them moist and cool all the time and prevent injuries caused by rough handling. Mud crabs survive best in an environment of about 70 -80% relative humidity. Lower temperatures are achieved by the use of chilled moistened materials placed at the bottom of the storage box. Usually, the storage boxes are provided with ventilation holes at the top. On arrival at the public markets, mangrove crabs are carefully examined and weak or dead crabs are removed from the boxes and either chilled or cooked. Live mangrove crabs are tied with raffia; this reduces cannibalism, physical damage and movement during distribution and marketing operations. Live freshwater fish such as carps, catfish and snakehead supplied from Malaysia and Thailand are very popular in public markets. These species are also displayed in aquarium tanks, FRP tanks or plastic containers. Catfish and snakehead can survive for prolonged periods out of water, provided they are kept moist and relatively cool. Adequate preventive measures must be used to avoid injuries due to rough handling.

Daily supplies of live seafood are delivered to public markets to replenish the stocks; on average each retailer holds stocks of live seafood for at least two working days. Our limited seafood retailer's survey indicated that mainly men operate the retail seafood stalls in Singapore. A limited gender analysis showed that most women and men run seafood retail vending as a family business.

Consumer Promotion Tools for Retailing Surimi-based Products

The "*Pick and Choose Yong Tau Foo*" sales promotion scheme is the main consumer promotion tool currently used for surimi-based products at retail level, in particular, supermarkets. This sales promotion scheme consists in offering a wide selection of surimi-based products (including seafood analogues) together with the traditional and very popular Chinese bean curd products at a fixed price of S$ 1.50 for 10 pieces of any of these products. This sales promotion scheme offers consumers savings off the regular price for surimi-based seafood products. It takes the form of a reduced price pack, in which two non-related products (surimi-based products and traditional bean curd products) are banded together. The common use of both types of products in the preparation of traditional Chinese soups makes this sales promotion scheme very effective in stimulating regular sales. Product assortment and quality level are key elements for the success of this sales promotion scheme in a very competitive market. These perishable products are usually displayed chilled; therefore, adequate care needs to be exerted in handling, storage and display to match the target market's expectations. Dealing with a line of highly perishable products, shop managers are supposed to know what consumers want, what products to stock and how much is needed daily, to ensure product freshness. In addition, seafood section staff are supposed to carefully monitor the shelf lives of each product, to ensure that high quality items are displayed.

The following chilled surimi-based and bean curd products were offered in NTUC Fair Price supermarkets during the month of February, 2000.

- Fish balls (*yu yuan*)
- Cuttlefish balls (*xu tong yuan*)
- Fish cake (*yu ping*)
- Fish dumpling with chicken filling (*yu qiao*)
- Imitation scallops (*jia yu zhu*)
- Imitation crab (*jia pang xie ru*)
- Fish rolls (*yu tiao*)

- Shrimp rolls (*xiao tiao*)
- Fresh chillies filled with surimi (*sheng la jiao yu jiang*)
- Fresh ladies' fingers filled with surimi (*jang qiao dou sai yu jiang*)
- Fried dou foo (*ja dou foo*)
- Fresh dou foo (*sheng dou foo*)
- Surimi and crab balls (*yu jiang he pang xie yuan*)
- Fish balls filled with minced chicken (*yu yuan zhan qi ro*).

This self-selection sales promotion scheme operates as follows:

(i) Consumers at the seafood section are encouraged to examine what is on offer and make their own choice of value-added products. With the help of a plastic pincer, the consumer can select the products and place them on a polystyrene tray. The display of products in refrigerated display cabinets is arranged so that consumers can easily examine all type of products

(ii) The seafood section staff checks the contents, wraps the tray with a plastic film, then labels the tray with a sticker

(iii) The consumers include the tray with other grocery items for final payment as they leave the supermarket.

This self-service retailing scheme with limited sales assistance has lower operating expenses because of less staff requirement. The retailer makes up for the reduced profit margin by achieving a high volume of sales. In addition, consumers are willing to carry out their own locate-compare-select process of value-added fishery products, on the understanding that they can save money. In general, traditional bean curd products are bought with little regard to significant brand differences, which can be described as habitual buying behaviour. Therefore, some supermarkets find it effective to use price and sales promotions to stimulate non- branded product trials (in particular, seafood analogues), since buyers are not committed to any brand. This marketing strategy also encourages variety-seeking buying behaviour by offering lower price packs.

Training Activities for Seafood Retailers

Several training courses on fish handling and quality preservation for fish retailers from local supermarket chains have been organised by MFRD, SEAFDEC and PPD since 1986. The trainees included seafood section supervisors, shop-front staff and shop managers. The content of these courses was tailored to suit different levels of staff. Details of the first two training courses are shown in Table 31.

Food Retail Inspection Services

Currently the Food Control Department conducts regular surveillance and enforcement programmes to ensure that safe and wholesome food is sold at retail establishments. Regular food sampling at storage and retail shops is conducted, and samples are checked through physical, microbiological and chemical analysis. Spot-checks at warehouses, supermarkets and public markets include evaluation of food storage condition and quality, labelling requirements and storage temperatures. At present all cooked food vendors are subject to a demerit point system of quality inspection.

BANGKOK

Bangkok was designated as the royal city of the Kingdom of Thailand in 1782, by King Rama I. Since then, Bangkok has grown through the years and the most dramatic growth has occurred since the mid-1900s. Despite Bangkok's modern features and numerous shopping complexes, this fast-growing metropolis still maintains much of its magnificent temples and palaces. Greater Bangkok has an estimated population[19] of 10 million in the year 2000, which represents about 16 percent of the total country's population. According to latest estimates, the total projected population of the Kingdom of Thailand[20] for 2000 is about 61.23 million.

In general economic terms, Thailand was one of the countries in Asia worst hit by the economic crisis in the region. The authorities had to strengthen the social safety net by supporting priority areas in rural and urban sectors in order to augment broader agricultural and fisheries production and industrial restructuring. They accelerated the social investment programme targeted at addressing unemployment. With an average per capita gross domestic product (GDP) of US$ 1,901 in 1998, only Japan, Singapore, Korea, Chinese Taipei, Brunei Darussalam, Malaysia and Hong Kong, China had higher per capita GDP among the Asian countries.

According to the official figures of the Department of Fisheries, in 1997, Thailand exported US$ 5 billion worth of fishery products, therefore maintaining its supremacy as the world's leading exporter of seafood products. Bangkok supports a substantial market for live, fresh, frozen and cured fish and canned fishery products. In 1997, FAO fisheries statistics reported an apparent annual per capita fish supply of 29.5 kg in the Kingdom of Thailand. A breakdown of the data is shown in Table 32, with pelagic fish at the top in terms of per capita supply among seafood, followed by freshwater fish.

Table 32: Fish per Capita Supply (1997)

Food Item	Annual per Capita Supply
(kg/year)	
Freshwater fish	6.43
Demersal fish	2.93
Pelagic fish	12.3
Marine fish, other	0.73
Crustaceans	2.72
Cephalopods	2.05
Molluscs, other	2.36
Total Fish	29.5

Source: FAO Food Balance Sheets, 1994-97.

Table 33 shows the national meat and eggs per capita supply in 1997. When comparing meats with seafood products, the highest per capita supply item was poultry meat (including chicken, duck and other birds) with 15.52 kg/year, followed by pelagic fish with 12.3 kg/year.

Table 33: Meat and Eggs per Capita Supply (1997)

Food Item	Annual per capita Supply (kg/year)
Beef and Veal	4.62
Mutton and Goat Meat	0.01
Pork	6.26
Poultry Meat	15.52
Other meat	-
Eggs	9.00

Source: FAO Food Balance Sheets, 1994-97.

Fish Distribution Channels

The domestic market for fish and fishery products is distinguished principally by the dependence on supplies from commercial fisheries, aquaculture and small-scale fisheries. It should be noted that a significant proportion of aquaculture produce, particularly shrimp, is exported. The strong export orientation of the Thai fisheries sector has limited the supplies available for domestic consumption. To counteract this trend, the development of aquaculture and improved utilisation of fish by-catches for direct human consumption is being encouraged.

Both freshwater and marine fish and fishery products are regularly traded in Bangkok's domestic fish market. Chilled and live fish are landed at the Bangkok wholesale fish market, located on the bank of the Chao Phraya River. The Fish Marketing Organization (FMO), a state-owned enterprise, is in charge of the management and operation of the Bangkok wholesale fish market and of related fish marketing affairs. This wholesale market handles about 105,000 to 157,000 metric tonnes of fish annually. Estimated total daily volumes of fish traded in the Bangkok wholesale fish market vary according to the fishing season, from about 290 to 360 tonnes, of which about 129 tonnes of freshwater fish are traded daily. The wholesale fish market is equipped with two main trading halls, where the fish agents or commission agents display and trade fish. Fish at the wholesale marketing halls is sold mainly by auction or through negotiated prices in public sales conducted by brokers, who sell to retailers, institutional buyers, processors and seafood traders. Fish is usually graded according to different sizes (large, medium and small). Shrimp are often classified into "small", "medium" or "large," while the industry sizing is based on count-per-pound of headless shrimp. During field visits, most head-on black tiger shrimp auctioned at the Bangkok wholesale market were 35 - 40 or 40 - 60 pieces/kg, while smaller shrimp were also available. Table 34 shows the average wholesale prices of selected fish in Bangkok during December 1999 to January 2000.

Domestic shrimp and freshwater prawn consumption has declined after the economic recession. Decreases in the standard of living and disposable incomes typically result in lower high value seafood consumption in most markets. This is reflected in the lower sales of these products reported at public retail markets as well as in the catering sector during the last two years. However, increased domestic demand for shrimp and freshwater prawn is forecast, given that the Thai economy is projected to recover gradually, with a growth rate of 3 percent in terms of the real GDP in 2000.

Table 34: Average Wholesale Prices of Selected Seafood in Bangkok

Period: December 1999 - January 2000

Species	Wholesale Price (Baht/kg)
Indian Mackerel	7 - 35
(*Rastrelliger kanagurta*)	(18)
Spanish Mackerel	8 - 60
(*Scomberomorus spp.*)	(29)
Threadfin	50 - 125
(*Nemipterus spp.*)	(90)
Seabass	60 - 140
(*Lates calcarifer*)	(105)
Red snapper	50 - 115
(*Lutjanus spp.*)	(95)
White Pomfret	120 - 320
(*Pampus argenteus*)	(255)
Black Pomfret	25 - 75
(*Formio niger*)	(65)
Mangrove Crab	85 - 120
(*Scylla serrata*)	(110)
Squid	30 - 100
(*Loligo spp.*)	(65)
Snakehead (live)	40 - 70
(*Ophicephalus striatus*)	(60)
Catfish (Live)	30 - 35
(*Clarias spp.*)	(35)
Striped Catfish (Live)	8 - 18
(*Pangasius sutchi*)	(16)
Eels (Live)	60 - 80

(*Fluta alba*)	(70)
Tilapia	7 - 38
(*Oreochromis spp.*)	(30)
Giant Freshwater Prawn (Live)	Small: 90 - 110
(*Macrobrachium rosenbergii*)	Medium: 220 - 245
	Large: 505 - 540
Black Tiger Shrimp	Small: 125 - 190
(*Penaeus monodon*)	Medium: 250 - 300
	Large: 400 - 450
Banana Shrimp	Small: 120 - 190
(*Penaeus merguiensis*)	Medium: 240 - 270
	Large: 380 - 430

Source: Fish Marketing Organization (FMO), Thailand.

Table 35 shows the distribution pattern for fresh fish from the Bangkok wholesale market, with a significant proportion of supplies distributed to the city's retail markets.

Table 35: Distribution of Fresh Fish from Bangkok Wholesale Market

Period: January - December1998

Destination	Percentage (%)
Retailers:	86.00
Bangkok retail markets	77.40
Provincial retail markets	8.33
Cold storage	0.27
Processing plants & exporters:	10.89
Bangkok	4.12
Provincial	6.77
Others	3.11
Total	100.00

Source: Fish Marketing Organization (FMO) of Thailand.

There is a significant domestic live fish trade, which is handled by private wholesalers. Most traders operate live fish carriers (trucks with tanks and aeration systems), collecting fresh-water fish such as snakehead (*Ophicephalus striatus*), tilapia, carps, catfish, climbing perch, swamp eels and sand goby, as well as seabass (*Lates calcarifer*) produced by aquaculture farms and floating cages. The domestic live shellfish trade comprises molluscs such as cultivated green mussel (*Perna viridis*), cockles (*Arca granulosa*), hard clam (*Meretrix meretrix*) and oysters (*Crassostrea spp.*). Crustaceans include mangrove crabs (*Scylla spp.*), swimming crabs and giant freshwater prawn (*Macrobrachium spp*). Most of the production of giant freshwater prawn, oysters, cockles and mussels are sold in live form while a relatively limited proportion of bivalves is sold as shucked flesh, either fresh or dried.

There is also an important processed seafood market in Bangkok for products such as fish sauce, fermented fish and fermented shrimp paste; steamed, dried-salted fish, shrimp and squid; fish balls, fish fingers, fish noodles, imitation crab meat, value-added shrimp products and surimi-based traditional products.

Thailand has become highly reliant on imports of frozen fish (mainly tuna, which account for over 80 percent of the tuna used for canning) to satisfy the local fish canning industry demand. Canned fish, in particular tuna, mackerel and sardine products, are offered in most super- market chains, public markets and small grocery retail outlets. The overall demand for canned fishery products in Thailand is relatively small, but in Bangkok there is a relatively higher consumption level. Most high-value canned products are packed in two-piece cans with easy-open tops and attractive labels.

The major available canned seafood packs include the following:

- Sardine/scad in tomato & chilli sauces, in round/oval/ rectangular cans
- Mackerel in tomato sauce or in vegetable oil, in round/oval/ rectangular cans
- Tuna in oil, solid, chunk and grated packs, in round cans with net contents of 180 g
- Tuna in either curry with coconut milk or hot and spicy sauces, in round cans
- Squid/cuttlefish/octopus in brine; in round cans
- Baby clams in brine, in round cans
- Crab meat in brine, in round cans

- Shrimp in brine, in round cans

Table 36 shows the average retail prices of selected canned fish packs offered in Bangkok.

The consumption habits in Bangkok vary according to the socio-economic level of the population, with upper and middle class homes showing strong preference for high value tuna, crab, squid, baby clams and shrimp packs. Lower income consumers prefer cheaper sardine and tuna products. Canned tuna, shrimp, baby clams, and squid/cuttlefish products are usually consumed with cooked rice, as a salad or sautéed with vegetables. Canned sardines are frequently served with cooked rice or bread as a snack, as well as sautéed with vegetables.

Table 36: Average Retail Prices of Canned Seafood Products in Bangkok

Period: May - June 2000

Product Form	Retail Price (Baht/can) (155 g. net contents)	Retail Price (Baht/can) (185 g. net contents)
Sardines in tomato sauce	10	n/a
Tuna in mayonnaise	n/a	25
Tuna in curry sauce	n/a	25
Tuna in oil, solid pack		30
Tuna in oil, chunks	n/a	25

Source: field surveys carried by counterparts.

Seafood reaches consumers in Bangkok through a multi-level system, which may involve at least three to four transactions before a fish or fishery product is purchased by consumers in a public fish market or supermarket, or eaten at a restaurant/food stall. The channels of distribution incorporate locally caught and processed seafood, as well as live and chilled cultured species.

Bangkok's Retail Fish Market

The Bangkok urban area is home to a variety of retail establishments offering live, fresh, frozen, cured and canned seafood to consumers. The range of shopping options includes public retail markets, supermarkets and street hawkers that offer a wide selection of fish and fishery products. Public markets and street vending currently hold a significant share of the retail market of chilled and live fish, fresh, fermented and cured fishery products. Large supermarket chains and medium-sized independent supermarkets offer mainly chilled, frozen, cured, fermented, processed (surimi-based fishery products, dried seafood snacks, and roasted squid/cuttlefish) and canned seafood. Supermarkets currently hold a fairly low portion of the retail market share of chilled fish and fishery products, but sales of surimi-based products, snacks and canned seafood are significant. Most supermarkets have well-defined seafood product sales strategies, including adequate product mix and variety of frozen and fermented fish products, fish sauce, surimi-based products, roasted squid/cuttlefish, dried snacks and canned seafood products.

Table 37 shows the estimated distribution of retail outlets in Bangkok, according to data provided by the Bangkok Metropolitan Administration (BMA).

Table 37: Estimated Number of Retail Outlets in Bangkok

Type of Retail Outlet	Number
Wet (public/municipal) markets	154
Supermarkets	107
Minimarkets	700
Minimarkets (within petrol stations)	300
General grocery stores	17,000
Total	18,261

Source: BMA, March 2000.

The most popular product form is whole fresh fish; the species most in demand are: catfish, snakehead, gourami, Spanish mackerel, Indian mackerel, tuna, squid, cuttlefish, red snapper, groupers, cockles, arc shells, topshells, mussels, shrimps and giant freshwater prawn.

Live giant freshwater prawn is a well-established product in the domestic market and retail selling of the species in aerated tanks/aquariums is a traditional and attractive marketing approach. Sales through the catering sector are also an important outlet for giant freshwater prawn. Some of the restaurateurs interviewed indicated strong consumer preference for prawn served grilled/roasted, or fried with vegetables (with curry and/or coconut milk). Squid and cuttlefish are usually offered in public and street markets as whole and skinless tubes/fillets; some retailers indicated that skinless tubes/fillets have a good demand among working housewives and young couples. In restaurants, squid/cuttlefish dishes are either grilled/roasted, fried with vegetables (with spicy sauces) or served as spicy salad.

Table 38: Comparative Retail Prices of Fresh Fish at Selected Street Fish Markets and Public Markets in Bangkok

Period: March 2000

Species	Street Seafood Market Price (Baht/kg)	Public Market Price (Baht/kg)
Live Seafood		
Snakehead	75 - 85	
Average: 80	80 - 85	
Average: 82		
Catfish (*Clarias* spp)	38 - 44	
Average: 40	38 - 48	
Average: 44		
Swamp Eel	110 - 120	
Average: 115	110 - 120	
Average 115		
Giant freshwater prawn	n/a	Small: 170
Medium: 250-360		
Climbing perch	100 - 110	
Average: 105	100 - 120	
Average: 115		
Fresh/chilled Seafood		
Seabass	140 - 145	140 - 145
Black Pomfret	70 - 80	78 - 80
White Pomfret	n/a	295 - 300
Black tiger shrim	n/a	
Small: 175 - 200	Large: n/a	
Medium: 290 - 325		
Giant Freshwater Prawn	Small: 110 - 120	Small: 110 - 120
	Medium: n/a	Medium: 190 - 260
Squid:		
Whole	95 - 100	100
Skinless	170 - 180	180
Cuttlefish	100	100 - 110
H&G Snakehead	n/a	100
Snakehead (with roe)	n/a	150 - 170

Source: field market surveys carried out by the author and counterparts in March 2000.

Table 38 shows the comparative retail prices for fresh fish at selected street fish markets and public markets in Bangkok. In general, retail prices at street fish markets were slightly lower than public markets with a price difference range of 2.5 to 9.5 percent; however some products like eels, giant freshwater prawn and seabass were at the same price level. Taking into consideration that most supermarkets have similar or slightly higher prices than public markets, we can conclude from this relatively limited data that street seafood markets are currently offering the lowest retail prices for fresh fish in Bangkok.

Table 39 shows a comparison of average wholesale and retail prices for selected fish species in Bangkok. From the data, the estimated marketing margins for chilled fish ranged from 8.3 to 66.6 percent, with an average margin of 37.9 percent. Although based on the relatively limited data obtained from the field surveys carried out for this study, in general the results obtained were in line with the marketing margins from retailers in public markets. In most public markets, there are full-service seafood stalls which prepare orders from consumers. This may include weighing a specific quantity of fish or shellfish, gutting, cleaning or cutting a whole fish to the desired size or product form. Orders are then wrapped in plastic bags.

Table 40 shows a comparison between average retail prices of fresh meat, poultry and fish offered in Bangkok's retail food market. When compared with popular small pelagic species, beef was the most expensive animal protein source, with an average retail price of US$ 4.35/kg for beef tender chuck, followed by chicken breast and lean pork with average retail prices of US$ 3.04 and US$ 3.13/kg respectively. Dressed chicken with an average retail price of US$ 1.76/kg, and small pelagics such as Indian mackerel and hardtail scad, with an average retail price of US$ 0.79/kg and US$ 0.66/kg respectively, were the cheapest protein source. However, when compared with available fresh meat, poultry and seafood in general, the most expensive animal protein sources were black tiger shrimp and white pomfret with average retail prices of US$ 8.31 and US$ 7.28/kg respectively. It is important to note that the popular freshwater fish species such as catfish, snakehead and eel, are direct competitors in price with respect to chicken products (the main substitute for fish in Bangkok market), with average retail prices of US$1.08, US$ 2.13/kg and US$ 3.03 respectively. The highest retail prices for red meats and poultry were seen in supermarkets and the lowest in public/private markets and street vendors.

Table 39: Average Gross Marketing Margins for Selected Chilled and Live Fish Species in Bangkok Period: January - March 2000

Species	Average Wholesale Price (Baht/kg)	Average Retail Price (Baht/kg)	Marketing Margin (%)
Chilled Seafood			
Indian Mackerel (*Rastrelliger kanagurta*)	18	30	66.66
Spanish Mackerel (*Scomberomorus* spp.)	29	50	72.40
Threadfin (*Nemipterus* spp.)	90	130	44.44
Seabass (*Lates calcarifer*)	105	142.5	35.71
Black Pomfret (*Formio niger*)	65	77	18.46
White Pomfret (*Pampus argenteus*)	255	297.5	16.66
Squid (*Loligo* spp.)	65	98.3	51.20
Black Tiger Shrimp (*Penaeus monodon*)	Small: 180 Medium: 300 Large: 425	Small: 200 Medium: 325 Large: n/a	Small: 11.50 Medium: 8.30 Large: n/a
Live Seafood			
Giant Freshwater Prawn (*Macrobrachium rosenbergii*)	Small: 110 Medium: 240 Large: 520	Small: 170 Medium: 358 Large: n/a	Small: 63.60 Medium: 49.20 Large: n/a
Catfish (*Clarias* spp.)	35	42	20.00
Snakehead (*Ophicephalus striatus*)	60	81	35.00
			Average margin: 37.90%

Source: FMO and market surveys carried out by the author and counterparts.

Table 40: Comparative Average Retail Prices of Meat, Poultry and Fish in Bangkok

Period: March - May 2,000

Product	Average Retail Price (Baht/kg)
Red Meats:	
Lean pork	80 - 138 (118)
Pork loin	79 - 80 (79)
Beef loin	90 - 120 (100)
Beef tender chuck	120 - 190 (165)
Poultry:	
Dressed chicken (chilled)	45 - 79 (67)
Chicken breast/chilled)	68 - 139 (115)
Chicken, drumstick (chilled)	50 - 82 (71)
Small Pelagics (whole)	
Indian mackerel	30
Round scad	25
Other Fish Species (whole)	
Spanish mackerel	70
Catfish (*Clarias* spp) (live)	42
Eel (live)	115
Snakehead (live)	81
White pomfret	276
Black tiger shrimp (medium size)	315

Source: market surveys carried out by the author and counterparts.

The retail market for surimi-based products includes fish balls, squid/cuttlefish balls, fish noodles, fish burgers, fish sausages, fish satay and surimi analogues. In addition, minced dried fish/shrimp crackers and seasoned dried fish mince (locally processed) are also offered in the market. Public retail markets and supermarkets currently offer a variety of traditional minced products and surimi-based products. Traditional fish and squid balls, fish cakes, and fish satay are consumed mainly deep fried, grilled/roasted, in soups or sautéed with mixed vegetables. Surimi-based dried snack foods with different seasonings, either shredded or as small portions (rectangular sheets) are increasingly gaining popularity among consumers, competing with roasted dried squid/cuttlefish products.

The shelf space devoted to chilled/frozen surimi products in two medium-sized Bangkok's super-markets was considered adequate in comparison to the main seafood counter at the same supermarkets. The surimi-based product shelves area were located in the same section as fresh and frozen processed seafood items. Surimi-based snacks and traditional roasted dried squid/cuttlefish were located in the food snacks section.

Besides the above-mentioned minced fish products, value-added items such as fish portions, fish fingers, nuggets, tempura fillets, squid rings, cuttlefish/squid/fish/shrimp patties and value-added shrimp products were locally processed and marketed in several supermarket chains.

Live Fish Marketing and Basic Equipment

It is a well-known fact that live fish and shellfish commands a premium price because of its guaranteed quality, freshness and intrinsic flesh characteristics (better texture and delicate flavour) in comparison with fresh/chilled seafood. The tastes, traditions and cooking styles of the population determine Bangkok's live fish and shellfish market requirements. In general, the live fish sold in Bangkok are mainly freshwater species such as catfish (*Pangasius spp; Clarias spp.*) carp (*Puntius gonionotus; Cyprinus carpio; Probarbus jullieni; Hypophthalmichthys molitrix*), gourami (*Trichogaster pectoralis*), snakehead (*Ophicephalus striatus*), swamp eel (*Fluta alba*) and giant freshwater prawn (*Macrobrachium rosenbergii*). Live high value marine finfish is a niche market for affluent tourists, the upper class population and businessmen. On the other hand, giant freshwater prawn has a wider market than high value finfish and is offered in most public markets. Live low-priced freshwater fish and giant freshwater prawn are well-established products in the catering business.

There is a significant live grouper export trade, with production coming both from capture fisheries and cage culture. About 85 percent of the total production of cage cultured grouper is exported, with the marketing channels involving brokers/collectors and exporters. Live groupers for the domestic and export markets are transported in plastic bags filled with water, ice and oxygen; the bags are packed into polystyrene foam boxes with an average gross weight of about 12 - 15 kg/box. Marketing margins[24] for live grouper represent about 44 - 45 percent of the export price, of which 7.5 percent represents the local wholesaler's/ collector's margin and 37 percent the exporter's margin.

Live aquatic food display systems have traditionally been an effective marketing device in public and street food markets and restaurants. Tourist seafood restaurants as well as traditional Thai and Chinese seafood restaurants offer a selection of live aquatic food, such as giant freshwater prawn, oyster, eel, snakehead, catfish, gourami and seabass.

Live seafood is displayed in tanks, plastic containers and aquariums for customers to appreciate the variety of species available and facilitate the selection. There is a premium on size, with larger fish often commanding higher prices than smaller fish; demand is significant for live fish within the range of 1 - 2 kg in the specialised seafood restaurant market sector.

Vivier Trucks

Currently, vivier trucks transport live freshwater fish from the fishponds. The main features of vivier trucks include portable tanks filled with water, mounted on flatbed trucks; the majority of tanks used in Bangkok are locally made from galvanised iron and externally lined with wooden planks. These portable tanks are of two sizes: the larger ones can hold about 60 kg of live catfish or 40 kg of snakehead; smaller tanks can hold about 40 kg of catfish or 30 kg of snakehead. A typical example of live freshwater transportation system is as follows:

Main equipment:

(a) Truck: 2 tonne payload flatbed truck

(b) Portable tanks (30 units)

(c) Scoop nets (stainless steel frames and nylon netting)

(d) Weighing baskets

(e) Weighing scales.

On arrival at the wholesale market, the live fish is sorted into species and size and distributed to wholesalers, retail markets and restaurants at mutually agreed prices. Fish which are not sold on the day are kept in portable tanks. The fish are normally not fed. During the entire collection, storage and distribution operations, the handling of the live fish is reduced to a minimum to avoid excessive injuries. At the retail or restaurant destination, the fish is transferred to aquariums or portable containers until sold or required for consumption.

Freshwater prawns (*Macrobrachium rosenbergii*) are often held in oxygenated water in portable tanks or in plastic bags and placed within polystyrene boxes. Wholesalers noted that they could obtain increased survival rates when live prawns were packed in oxygenated water, provided that ambient temperatures were not too high during transport. In general, packaging, road transport and distribution operations are relatively short (less than 8 hours) and involve short distances from farms to the market.

Retail Outlets for Live Fish and Shellfish

The main retail outlets for live freshwater fish in Bangkok are public food markets and some street markets. The equipment used for display and retail of these live freshwater fish and shellfish at public and street markets included mainly display tanks/plastic container units. The usual display tank unit (used mainly in public food markets) is equipped as follows:

- Galvanised iron or fibreglass display tanks (rectangular in shape)
- One water pump (for water circulation)
- One mechanical filter.

A typical display tank unit had an estimated capacity of about 140 to 160 kg of giant freshwater prawn or 80 - 100 kg of freshwater fish. The display tanks units are an important promotional tool for the fish section and assure consumers of the good quality of live fish being offered. Simple portable tanks/containers filled with water are also used for displaying live catfish, snakehead and gourami in some street food markets.

Most retailers in public markets display portable galvanised iron or FRP tanks equipped with air pumps to maintain adequate oxygen levels.

During retail operations, the main quality control measures for live giant freshwater prawns are to keep them below water level, regular addition of small quantities of crushed ice to lower the water temperature and the prevention of injuries caused by rough handling. On arrival at the public markets, freshwater fish and prawn are carefully examined; the weak or dead specimens are removed from the tanks and sold as chilled seafood.

Catfish and snakehead can survive for prolonged periods out of water, provided they are kept moist and relatively cool, as well as handled carefully. Wholesalers and retailers take advantage of the high survival rates of these fish.

Daily supplies of live freshwater fish are delivered to public markets to replenish stocks. On average, each retailer holds stocks of live seafood for at least two working days.

Street Food Hawkers in Bangkok

Street food hawkers in Bangkok, in particular those selling fresh fish and ready-to-eat seafood, are considered to be catering to the middle and low-income consumers. Current data on the total number of street food hawkers indicates about 26,000 operating in authorised areas. According to Bangkok Metropolitan Administration (BMA) officials, there are three different types of street food vending operations in the 50 Bangkok districts, namely:

(a) Those in authorised areas (287 sites of street vending were identified)

(b) Those in private areas (21 sites of street vending were identified)

(c) Those in non-authorised areas (407 sites of street vending was identified).

The total number of street hawkers includes those vending ready-to-eat foods and beverages, raw food (fruits, vegetables, seafood, poultry), local sweets and delicacies, dry and processed food, manufactured goods (including clothes, toys, footwear, cosmetics) and providing services such as small repairs. Street seafood hawkers currently play a significant role as fresh/chilled seafood suppliers in Bangkok. However, there is no updated detailed data on the number of street fish hawkers operating in the city, besides the 1993 figure of 6,040 street hawkers selling raw foodstuff (vegetables, fruits, meat and seafood), which represented about 30 percent of total street hawkers at that time. The main characteristics of fresh/chilled fish street hawkers include the following:

- Setting up temporary stalls in busy streets around public markets during certain times of the day. These vendors usually operate at fixed and regular locations, mainly using portable equipment, umbrellas and tent-type stalls. It is the simplest type of market available, making use of existing infrastructure and with a low level of investment. In general, facilities/equipment can be relocated easily to another site. When operating in areas surrounding public markets, they compete with the permanent fish retailers
- Carrying fresh fish in HDPE fish boxes, plastic tubs or insulated boxes from the wholesale markets to the street marketing areas using either motorcycles, taxis, public transportation, private cars and vans
- Limited availability of potable water supplies and wastewater disposal systems at the stalls; however, all street fish markets visited had an acceptable common solid waste disposal system and a regular cleaning schedule
- In addition to the regular selling by weight, it was usual to offer a kind of "pantry" service, selling fish and fishery products in extremely small quantities, e.g. sales in small dish lots
- In general, street fish hawkers, when compared with public markets or supermarket chains, offered less variety of fishery products, but with the advantage of being comparatively cheaper. In most street markets visited, besides fish and fishery products, vegetables, fruits and other items such as noodles, rice and fresh chicken were also offered.

Retail sales of raw food, in particular fresh fruits, vegetables and fresh fish at busy streets or around public markets by informal vendors in Bangkok are an integral part of the local market place. The "floating market" is a traditional way of street food vending using small boats (blunt-nosed sampans) gathering at various locations along the Chao Phraya River canals (*klongs*). These retailers sell mainly fresh fruits and vegetables.

Currently Bangkok is confronted with the problem of street hawkers and the need to control street litter, effluent disposal, pollution and obstruction of pedestrian traffic. The municipal authorities authorise and regulate street vending through the city police and district Public Health Sections.

Significant improvements in the ready-to-eat food and beverages street vending operations have been achieved through a 1994 FAO-supported pilot project aimed at improving the quality and safety of street vended food in Bangkok. In addition, sanitary requirements for street food stalls were formulated and implemented by local authorities. Another FAO- supported project aimed at improving the quality and safety of street vending in Bangkok was implemented in October 1997.

The Public Health Act (B.E.2535) issued on 5th April 1992 regulates street food vending operations. Chapter 8 (*Marketplace, Place where Meals are Sold and Place where Foodstuff is Stored*) sections 34 to 37, indicated the need for an official license to establish a marketplace and to be subject to supervision by local government authorities. Chapter 8, sections 38 to 40, indicated the need to notify local authorities and obtain a certificate of notification in order to set up a place where meals are sold or where foodstuff is stored, if the said place has an area not exceeding 200 m2. This Act also describes the powers and duties of local officials and public health officials; the issue of licenses; fees and fines; procedures of appeal and penalties for violations of the Act. In addition, local officials have the authority to establish the basic requirements for street food vending practices, suitable locations of stalls and non-selling zones in the city.

With the implementation of this Act and FAO-assisted pilot projects, the National Department of Health (DOH) and Bangkok Metropolitan Administration (BMA) launched specific activities to provide technical advice on improved street food vending infrastructure and handling practices, and to update general information about street food vendors, in particular socio-economic information and current food handling practices.

The main factors for the growth of street food vending in Bangkok can be explained as follows:

(i) Local eating habits, cultural significance of street food hawkers, socio-economic conditions, high unemployment rates, rapid urbanisation and urban population growth

(ii) Loyal patronage of a growing clientele; street food vending has emerged in response to a socio-cultural need for inexpensive nutritious foods and the convenience that street ready-to-eat foods offer. In addition, it is recognised that a large number of tourists are also regular consumers of ready-to eat foods offered by street vendors. In the particular case of fresh raw seafood, informal street markets operating in strategic locations (mostly around public food markets) at busy hours of the day serve customers, thereby saving them time and/or money in search of other markets or supermarkets

(iii) The effects of the Asian financial crisis, which dragged Thailand's economic growth down, had severely hit the urban poor population. Consequently, street food vending activities flourished.

In general, it was observed during field surveys that fish and fishery products offered by street hawkers were of acceptable to good quality. Consumers appreciated the convenience of obtaining readily available seafood at street fish markets, which also provided personalised services with adequate seafood expertise. Some street fish retailers indicated that low-income families purchase their food (including fish) on a daily basis, since they don't have enough money to purchase large amounts of food. Therefore, they usually purchase fish by the small dish in street markets, as it is more convenient for them. Apparently, the sale of fish by the small dish is a traditional service only offered by street seafood vendors. Our limited retailer's survey also indicated that street vended fish is purchased by people from mostly all income levels and not exclusively by low-income families. Based upon a relatively limited knowledge, it cannot be assumed that customer satisfaction is necessary for loyalty and that loyalty is necessary for repeat purchases of street vended fish. This hierarchical assumption can be inaccurate because repeat purchasing is not necessarily contingent upon customer satisfaction and loyalty. Convenience, strategic location and affordable prices can also directly influence repeat purchase of street vended fish.

At most of the informal street seafood markets visited, adequate to fair conditions were observed regarding fish handling practices. Generally, seafood was displayed without ice; however shrimp and squid were usually displayed and kept in plastic tubs or trays in a slush of ice and water. However, most street fish vendors had at least one insulated box to keep chilled fish with crushed ice and one (1) 15 - 20 litres capacity plastic bucket for storage of potable water for fish cleaning. Some large stalls had at least one HDPE- lined insulated container to keep fish with ice. Regarding the variety of fish and fishery products at street markets, most stalls offering fish had less than ten (10) fresh/chilled fish species or 5 to 6 fishery products (mainly minced, cured and fermented) on display. Most fish hawkers indicated that they were handling inventories of fresh fish from one to two working days. All street fish hawkers were somehow specialised, selling either fish/ chilled fish, live fish or cured fish; however live fish hawkers were also offering dead specimens in fresh/chilled form. On average, street seafood vendors operate about 6 - 8 hours daily; most indicated that the average number of working days is about 7 days per week. The average daily sales per stall are about 45 - 50 kg of fresh fish and shellfish, 6 - 8 kg of dried/cured fish and 6 - 9 kg of fermented fish/shrimp paste.

The use of simple dial metallic thermometers is suggested to regularly measure temperature of seafood on display at street fish markets. These thermometers can easily be calibrated to a known temperature by adjusting a hex nut located under the dial. They were locally available at some supermarkets and specialised shops. This basic tool could be included as part of the training kit for street fish vendors. In addition, adequate supplies of potable water (tap water), as well as adequate wastewater drainage systems should be made available to each street fish stall. Our limited street seafood/freshwater fish wholesalers and retailers survey indicated that women are actively involved in the operations of street seafood stalls in Bangkok. Their involvement in the street seafood wholesale and retail trade reflects the need of most poor women to balance the earning of income with household responsibilities. A limited gender analysis showed that women and men run street seafood vending as a family business. Few women indicated the difficulty in balancing the demands of business and family. Most said that street fish vending gave them greater time flexibility than other types of jobs/businesses, with the advantage that it does not need as much capital or as many skills.

To be effective, statutory requirements for street food vending (including licensing), should be properly linked to training, monitoring, supervision and equipment/infrastructure development programmes. In particular, street fish vending should have adequate provision of basic facilities for handling, chilled storage, preparation and wastewater disposal, which can be provided by targeting busy street areas where seafood vendors regularly operate.

Regular training courses on fresh/chilled seafood handling and hygiene should be part of any development programme for street seafood vendors organised by the Bangkok Metropolitan Administration (BMA) in co-ordination with the relevant specialised government agencies. This training should be aimed at providing adequate guidance and technical assistance to seafood hawkers on proper seafood handling and personal hygiene practices. All stall holders and their assistants who are involved in the preparation and sale of seafood should be required to attend and pass this training course.

Basic technical fields, which may be relevant for training courses intended for street fresh seafood vendors, are as follows:

(i) Introduction to the concepts of freshness, quality, wholesomeness and nutritive value

(ii) The care of live and fresh fish, handling methods, use of ice, receiving deliveries, quality inspection, storage of live and chilled fish, hygiene and sanitation for fish retailers, selection and application of detergents and disinfectants

(iii) Quality and quality aspects at retail level, display of fish, and promotion of fish sales techniques. Avoiding bad marketing practices

(iv) National and municipal regulations and codes of practice for seafood vending

(v) Introduction to business planning; simple economics for fish retailing

(vi) Equipment and facilities development programmes for street seafood vending.

Examples of Street Food Market Outlets in Bangkok

Phrannok Street Seafood Market

Phrannok street seafood market operates in one of the streets beside the Phrannok private food market located within the Bangkok Noi district area. The latter sells meat, poultry, seafood, fruits and vegetables, as well as dry groceries and cured and fermented products. During the survey period, a total of 300 fixed stalls were operating inside this retail market, of which about 10 stalls offered live and fresh/chilled seafood. The seafood section consists of typical concrete fish stalls, equipped with washing basins, potable water supplies, concrete display platforms for chilled fish, insulated boxes, concrete cutting area lined with tiles, display lighting adequately mounted on the wall and galvanised iron holding tanks or portable containers for live fish storage.

In this street seafood market outlet the following food items were offered:

(i) Fresh seafood

(ii) Cured fish (traditional dried fish and smoked fish)

(iii) Fermented fish sauce and shrimp paste

(iv) Squid/fish balls

(v) Fresh fruits and vegetables.

Bangkok's typical street seafood outlets are usually located near public and private markets. They operate during the same working hours of the markets, including special days such as religious holidays and other days when the markets are closed. According to vendors interviewed in Phrannok street market, all stall displays are ready in the designated locations between 07:00 hours to 09:00 hours. At the end of the working day (14:00 hours to 15:00 hours) street vendors should remove all their equipment away from the streets. The solid and liquid wastes are collected by the market cleaning staff and placed in offal bins for further disposal. Daily stall rental fees are 16 Baht/day for fixed stalls located inside the covered market and street seafood vendors are charged 10 Baht/day.

The basic equipment of street seafood vendors consisted of folding umbrellas, cutting boards, HDPE round containers, trash bins, water containers for washing fish and maintaining the cleanliness of the stall area, insulated boxes, weighing scales, small stainless steel display dishes and round display trays (made of stainless steel, aluminium or plastic). Some large stalls were equipped with stainless steel slabs for fish display. The typical sales or table area per seafood retailer would be in the range of 1.5 to 3 m^2. In addition, they use up some space to keep some insulated boxes that cannot fit below the round display trays and the chopping board. A typical area for a seafood stall would be in the range of 3 to 6 m^2. The most commonly available live and fresh fish species/presentations were as follows:

- Live fish: catfish, snakehead and eel
- Fresh/chilled whole marine fish: groupers, snappers, mackerels, squids, cuttlefish, banana shrimp, black tiger shrimp and giant freshwater prawn. Molluscs: mussels, arc shell, top shell, clam

- Steaks: tuna and Spanish mackerel
- Fillets: skinless squid and cuttlefish tubes.

The most common materials used for manufacturing the round display trays are aluminium and plastic. In most locations visited, retailers displayed their fish in standard aluminium round display trays; in some stalls, whole shrimp was displayed in small stainless steel dishes (on top of a round display tray) and sold by volume. The round display trays were placed on top of a framework made of galvanised steel pipe (threaded) of about 63.5 mm in diameter. After market hours, all equipment was washed with clean water; wastes were collected in plastic bags and placed in offal bins and the stall area was rinsed with clean water. The services of cleaning personnel are included in the daily stall rental fees.

According to the street seafood retailers interviewed, about 90 percent of the freshwater fish in the consignments arriving at the market are still alive and these fetch the highest prices, according to the size and condition upon arrival. The retailers do not usually buy the fish that have died, but often when supplies are limited they are forced to; these fish fetch about 50 - 60 percent of the price of live specimens. Based on their experience, street fish retailers were aware that storage in clean freshwater allows catfish and snakehead to survive from 3 to 4 days and eels from 4 to 5 days. Most street freshwater fish retailers said that the traditional galvanised iron containers (50 - kg capacity of live fish) used for transportation of live freshwater fish is also used for stowage of live fish at the stalls. Survival rates of giant freshwater prawns at retail level vary according to the available facilities. For example, retailers with fixed stalls in public/private covered food markets, equipped with galvanised iron tanks (1 m x 1.2m x 0.5 m) or large size aquariums, air pumps and air distribution piping at the bottom of the tanks, indicated that the average survival rate for healthy specimens of giant freshwater prawns held in tanks was about 7 -15 days, with regular feeding.

Lowering the water temperature in the tanks to about 24 - 28°C with small amounts of crushed ice, is usually practised by these retailers, in order to make handling easier and less stressful for the prawns. However, they know by experience, that if the giant freshwater prawns are chilled too much, they will not survive. Adult freshwater prawns are tolerant to a wide temperature range from 18 to 34°C.

Table 41 shows the details of the estimated investment costs of basic equipment used by a typical street fish retail vendor in Bangkok.

Table 41: Estimated Investment Costs of Basic Equipment used by a Typical Street Fish Retail Vendor in Bangkok

Description of Item	Quantity	Cost per Unit (Baht)
Umbrella	2	1,325
Round display trays (aluminium)	10	100
Small display dishes	15	40
Plastic container (trash bin)	1	60
Plastic containers	10	60
Insulated box	1	2,200
Container for live fish (50 kg capacity of live fish)	1	600
Water bucket	1	50
Plastic bags	100 pieces	0.45
Weighing scale (20 kg capacity)	1	480
Chopping board	2	300
Filleting knives	2	40
Total Cost:		18,965

Source: field surveys conducted by the author and counterparts.

Street Wholesale Market for Live Freshwater Fish

An interesting variant of the street seafood market is the wholesale market for live freshwater fish, located in one of streets behind the wet vegetables and meat, poultry and seafood retail hall within the premises of the Fresh Food Market complex (also known as the "Thai Market"). This privately-owned wholesale outlet is specialised in sales of a variety of foodstuff, including agricultural and fishery produce at reasonable prices.

The main characteristics of this street wholesale market for live freshwater fish are as follows:

(i) This marketing scheme usually operates seven days a week, from 13:00 hours to 22:00 hours. Wholesalers/retailers are charged a daily fee by the Fresh Food Market management for stall space allocation. Most wholesalers are trading live freshwater fish, but there are also some small-scale wholesalers/retailers who sell fresh/chilled whole freshwater fish and minced fish. The wholesalers transport the live freshwater fish from fish farms or rural areas to the market area, using pick-up vans/lorries for temporary live fish storage at the market place

(ii) The Fresh Food Market complex provides the following services:
- Rental of stall space allocation according to the needs of each wholesaler
- Market price information
- Adequate security and logistic services to attract institutional buyers, retailers and consumers
- Supervisory services to manage wholesalers' requirements and ensure adequate levels of cleanliness
- Parking provision for pick-up vans and lorries carrying live fish

(iii) All the live freshwater fish wholesalers operate from vans and small trucks; live fish is displayed in metal tanks with an umbrella to provide protection from the rain and sun. Whole chilled freshwater fish is usually kept with crushed ice in insulated boxes. The typical wholesale street stall for live fish consists of about 3 - 5 galvanised iron display tanks filled with water in which fish is kept, two umbrellas, weighing scales and scoop nets. This type of stall has the advantage that it can be easily assembled at site and after market hours can be loaded on the vans and moved to another market location. The typical sales or tank area per wholesaler would be in the range of 2 to 3.5 m^2

(iv) Live freshwater fish supplies were mostly from fish farms while fresh/chilled freshwater fish supplies were collected from small-scale fishermen. Most of the street fish vendors were wholesalers, but who also retailed to consumers. They indicated that the frequency of purchases of fresh seafood was 6 - 7 days/week. Average daily sales were about 400 - 600 kg of live fish. The unit of sales of live and fresh fish at the wholesale level was the plastic bag (±10 kg. net weight); at the retail level, the fish were sold by weight. Some retailers selling live fish at public markets usually purchase their supplies by the container (50 - 60 kg) based on the total weight of the lot

(v) The most common live and fresh/chilled freshwater species identified at this street wholesale market were as follows:

- Catfishes (*Clarias spp. and Pangasius spp.*), snakeheads (*Ophicephalus striatus and Channa spp.*), snakeskin gourami, climbing perch, spotted spiny eel, whisker sheatfish, great white sheatfish, swamp eel, tilapia, grey featherback, Jullien's golden-price carp, silver common carp and common carp
- Pond snail (*Sinotaia ingallsiana*) was offered as whole and shucked meat; frogs (*Rana spp.*) were mostly offered alive. Most giant freshwater prawns were offered alive or in whole fresh/chilled form at fixed stalls inside the fresh food market section
- During the market surveys there were some wholesalers/ retailers offering minced fish (made from spotted featherback, Jullien's golden-price carp and catfish), chilled eel steaks, H&G climbing perch and gourami.

Table 42 shows the average wholesale prices of selected freshwater fish traded at the street wholesale market located in the premises of the Fresh Food Market complex in Bangkok.

Table 42: Average Wholesale Prices of Selected Freshwater Fish at the Street Wholesale Market, Fresh Food Market in Bangkok

Period: March 2000

Species/Product Form	Wholesale Price (Baht/kg)
Live	
Catfish (*Clarias* spp.)	28
Swamp eel	60
Climbing perch	50 - 55
Pond snail	10
Snakehead	45
Giant freshwater prawn	
Small size	170
Medium size	250
Fresh/chilled	

Catfish (*Pangasius* spp.)	15 - 23
Spotted featherback	40 - 45
Tilapia	
Small size	12 - 13
Medium size	15 - 20
Large size	30 - 35
Silver common carp	20
Yellow *Mystus*	60
Great white sheatfish	70
Jullien's golden-price carp	20 - 23
Giant freshwater prawn	
Small size	100 - 110
Medium size	130
Shucked pond snail	30 - 35
Minced Jullien's golden-price carp	35 - 38
Minced spotted featherback	120
H&G gourami	35
H&G climbing perch	35 - 36

Source: field surveys conducted by the author and counterparts.

Table 43 shows the estimated costs of basic equipment used by a street wholesaler of freshwater fish (mainly catfish) operating in the "Thai Market". This wholesaler makes daily trips to farms (about 50 km. from Bangkok) collecting about 600 kg of live catfish. The catfish are graded according to sizes, placed in galvanised iron containers filled with fresh water and transported. At the street wholesale fish market, the wholesaler parks his pick-up van parallel to the sidewalk of the main street and assembles the display facilities on the street. Average daily sales are about 500 to 600 kg of catfish. Some large wholesalers are equipped with one lorry and two pick-up vans and reported daily sales of five tonnes of live fish. Some of the large wholesalers run their operations as a family business, with the father and elder sons working as drivers and the mother and daughters conducting the daily sales at the street market. One large wholesaler indicated that he paid daily rental fees for five stall space allocations (each stall space allocation is about $2m^2$).

Table 43: Estimated Costs of Basic Equipment used by a Street Wholesale Vendor of Freshwater Fish in Bangkok

Description of Item	Quantity	Unit Cost (Baht)
Pick-up van (1 tonne) with wooden body (second-hand)	1	300,000
Galvanised iron container for live fish transport (galvanised iron inner walls and external wooden planks frame; 50 - 60 kg capacity)	10	600
Stainless steel live fish display tanks (0.9m x 0.57m x 0.2 m)	2	2,500
Weighing basket (iron frame with nylon netting)	2	500
Scoop net (steel frame and wooden handle)	1	250
Umbrella	1	1,300
Plastic bucket	1	60
Plastic tray (for removal of live fish from the display tanks)	1	90
Price board	1	300
Plastic bin (offal collection)	1	90
Weighing scale (20 kg capacity); platform type	1	500
Portable calculator	1	200
Total Cost of Basic Equipment		**314,790**

CONCLUSIONS AND RECOMMENDATIONS

This study aims to draw a profile of low-cost retailing equipment and facilities for fish marketing in the large urban areas of Southeast Asia, as it examines the status, problems and needs of those in the fish retail trade, in particular the street fish vending sector.

The study made use of secondary data from four major sources, the national agencies in charge of fisheries affairs, national fish marketing agencies, local governments and the FAO statistics database. For the study to accurately reflect low-cost fish retailing equipment and facilities in large urban areas of Southeast Asia, surveys were conducted as a source of primary data. The data was related to the available equipment/facilities being used, technical characteristics, investment and operational costs, as well as street fish vending operations and critical issues; improved technologies for urban street fish retailing; training programmes for street fish vendors; national legislation; and improvement programmes related to urban street fish vending. Direct observation during field visits provided qualitative and quantitative data on matters such as: current situation of street fish vendors; the selling prices of fish at both wholesale and retail levels; physical and operational conditions prevailing in street fish markets; local costs of equipment; live and chilled fish handling and display practices, as well as sanitary conditions and design deficiencies at marketplaces.

Currently, some of the street fish vending operations in Manila, Bangkok and Kuala Lumpur exhibit specific characteristics according to the pattern of operation, the location of the stalls, the type of fish and fishery products offered, the equipment used and the working hours. In Singapore, all street fish vendors have been resettled into public markets and food centres since 1986. In general, two main patterns of operation were identified:

- Street seafood/freshwater fish vendors selling from mobile facilities. These are typical motorised retail outlets specialised in the trade of fish and fishery products. In this category we can include marketing schemes such as "Fish on Wheels" and *Pasar Tani* as well as the street wholesale and retail live freshwater fish outlets. There were also ready-to-eat fish/squid balls and traditional sausage vendors peddling from place to place using wheeled pushcarts
- Street fish vendors with equipment that enables them to operate a temporary street retail outlet (unmotorised facility). In this category we can include the typical informal street seafood markets. However, traditional itinerant street seafood vendors peddling from place to place and carrying two baskets on shoulder poles were not very common in urban areas

Most street seafood/freshwater fish vending operations were characterised by the use of low-cost equipment and facilities. In some large urban areas, the available low-cost fish retailing equipment and facilities showed some deficiencies, particularly regarding design, limited potable water supplies and wastewater disposal systems. Water is used extensively in fish markets, not only for fish cleaning, but also to flush offal and blood from equipment and floors, and to flume wastewater to floor drains and collection sumps. The first step for the implementation of adequate potable water supplies to individual stalls at street fish markets should be to analyse water use patterns, install water meters and regularly record water consumption. The next step should be to undertake a survey of all market area and ancillary operations to identify wasteful practices and undertake corrective actions. Street fish vendors should pay according to their water consumption and proportionally for the provision of wastewater drainage systems. In two of the three large urban areas where street fish vendors operated regularly, solid wastes collection and disposal, as well as daily cleaning schedules were provided by the municipal authorities or private management and service charges were paid by the street fish vendors on an individual basis.

Live fish trade was the usual practice in all the large urban centres investigated. Most street live fish retail vending operations can be characterised by the use of low-cost equipment, with the exception of Singapore. Live fish was usually sold at higher prices than dead fish; most consumers were prepared to pay premium prices for live fish, which is considered the best guarantee of freshness, quality, and intrinsic characteristics of its flesh (better texture and delicate flavour) in comparison with fresh/chilled seafood. Primarily, the tastes, traditions and cooking styles of the local population determine the live seafood market requirements.

The consumption of high-value live seafood is a niche market for affluent tourists, the higher income group, and businessmen, and for special celebrations/festivities and wedding parties. Gradual economic recovery in most of the large urban areas investigated is slowly bringing consumers back, which is helping the markets for high-priced produce like shrimp, prawn and crab. Shrimp and crab are well-established products in the catering business and regulars in supermarkets, either live or chilled. On the other hand, the consumption of low-priced live fish is a well-developed market for consumers from all socio-economic levels as well as through the catering sector. Domestic markets absorb most of the low-priced aquaculture products like milkfish, tilapia, carp, catfish, eel, snakeheads, oysters, mussels and edible seaweeds.

In some cases, street markets, despite their limitations, are among the most dynamic channels for seafood/freshwater fish marketing. The need for street fish market outlets has arisen as a result of the inability of the existing market infrastructure to keep pace with the rapid population growth, relatively high urban unemployment rates and the negative impacts of the economic crisis on real incomes. Based on limited data and direct observation, we recognise that convenience, strategic location and affordable prices directly influence repeat purchase of street vended fish, rather than customer satisfaction and loyalty.

The study identified some of the problems faced by street fish vendors. These were as follows: the effect of the financial crisis on business and the ability to survive, the lack of access to specialised training on fish retailing, credit, and improved infrastructure and technologies. Hoewer, most street vendors interviewed indicated that street fish vending, in comparison with other types of jobs/businesses, had several advantages, such as that it does not need as much capital or as high a skills requirement. Generally, street vendors used ice to transport and keep fish either in fish boxes, metal tubs or insulated containers. However, in most cases, only high-value fish and shrimp were displayed, well- iced to maintain adequate quality levels. It was noticed that in most street fish markets, there was a lack of adequate chilled storage facilities for common usage by vendors.

The other fish retailing system, which is identified as the modern marketing sector, comprises self-service stores and large supermarket chains. In most cases, these shops cater to the middle and higher-income population groups, which generally have a family car and the capacity to purchase and store relatively large quantities of food. This high volume of sales allows these large market outlets to compete with regard to prices and terms of sale. However, with the exception of Singapore, where there was no street fish vending in all other large urban centres investigated, street fish vending was competing well with the modern marketing sector.

In all large urban centres investigated, there was available legislation regulating the operation of street food vending in general, including fish and fishery products. In most cases, the regulatory framework included the compulsory registration and licensing of street vendors. In the case of Singapore, the main legislation dealing with hawkers was the Environmental Public Health Act, No.32. This was also the case in Bangkok, where the regulations dealing with street food vendors were under the Public Health Act, BE 2535. In Manila and Kuala Lumpur, regulations related to street food vending have been enacted in terms of a law established by a local government authority. Regulations through codes of practice are used in most cities for street ready-to-eat food vending operations. Specific codes of practice for street vending of raw fish and fishery products are still lacking. Although the role of the informal sector, in particular street fish vending, in providing employment opportunities is recognised, in some cases, its importance in terms of supplying essential services to urban dwellers as well as generating income to the urban poor, is overlooked. Challenging much conventional wisdom about the informal sector, this study documents street fish and fishery products vending as an economic activity that produces an income ranging from minimum wage to higher than average income as compared to public or private clerks. Most successful street fish vendors work in the trade for a lifetime, but there are also a few casual street vendors selling as a supplement to other activities.

The findings support the efficacy of local governments in assisting informal micro- entrepreneurs improve their facilities, food handling practices and sanitation. In addition, adequate official attitudes and policies toward the street ready-to-eat food trade, and efforts within and outside the government to train street ready-to-eat food vendors in food handling and sanitation are positive steps in the right direction. However, similar efforts are needed in relation to street fish vendors, particularly regarding assistance to improve their facilities, fish handling practices and provision of credit.

Based on the findings of the study, recommendations and suggestions to promote the activities of street fish vending and improve fish retail marketing include the following strategies aimed at improving the technology and infrastructure:

- Provide more focused research on the design of improved low-cost fish retailing equipment and facilities aimed at obtaining the most profitable output, through a better selection of alternative materials suitable for fish vending operations. Therefore, it is important to develop adequate low-cost designs, which should include improved technological features in relation to clean water supply, and collection and disposal of solid and liquid wastes
- Formulate and implement adequate training programmes for street fish and fishery product vendors regarding improved facilities and equipment as well as fish handling practices. It is of utmost importance that local governments organise suitable information campaigns concerning the improved facilities and

equipment and stimulate the effective participation of the private sector in the provision of low-cost prototypes to the street fish vendors

- Promote agreements between street fish vendors' organisations, local governments, fisheries and health government agencies, NGOs and international technical co-operation organisations for the technical evaluation and dissemination of information regarding improved low-cost prototypes. The main objectives should be focused on the demonstration of the technological advantages as well as the improved sanitary operations of the low-cost prototypes both for the vendor and the consumer
- As the legal status of some street fish vendors remains informal, registration and licensing procedures should be simple and straightforward. In return for the license and fees paid, each street fish vendor should be entitled to access to water taps, regular wastes collection and disposal as well as cleaning services. Stall space should be allocated based on agreements with street vendors' organisations, which should be responsible for the equal distribution of stall space among associates and for monitoring the vending operations
- Formulate adequate small-scale credit programmes for street fish vendors aimed at the introduction of improved low-cost facilities and equipment. These programmes should be designed with the necessary promotion, evaluation, follow up and credit recovery components. In addition, suitable training programmes for personnel from lending institutions should be implemented in order to ensure an adequate administrative and operational framework to carry out credit operations for street fish vendors
- Organising street fish vendors will strengthen their group activities, allow better communication and strengthen their bargaining position with the government. Groups of street fish vendors could facilitate the provision of small-scale credit through lending institutions for improved facilities and equipment. The cost of purchasing fish supplies and ice could also be reduced through group activities
- Encourage national fisheries agencies to develop profiles of successful street fish vendors, including reference to low-cost fish retailing equipment and facilities, to serve as role models

- Strengthen street fish vendors' organisations/groups to help catalyse the dissemination of information on a regular basis in the following areas:
  - Government rules, regulations, taxation
  - Models of improved low-cost fish retailing equipment and facilities, including results of demonstrations, cost estimates and sources of financing
  - Specialised fisheries/fish marketing training programmes offered in the city
  - Updates of fisheries business trends including fish market information services
  - Specialised fisheries/fish marketing fairs, exhibits and others
- Taking into consideration women's active role in street fish marketing, particularly in Metro Manila and Bangkok, it will be desirable to promote women's participation in training activities in the fields of small business management, fish handling and marketing
- It is evident from this study that the amount of research information about low-cost fish retailing equipment and facilities in large urban areas of Southeast Asia, does not yet match the level of interest and need. Therefore, more information is needed about street fish vending operations and their businesses, their number and level of economic contribution, growth trends, the issues and challenges they are facing, and access to improved infrastructure and technologies. Deficiencies in information constitute a major impediment in the planning of improvement programmes for street fish vending. Efforts to reduce these information gaps will be useful in stimulating governments to move toward more effective management of street fish vending, both by indicating the significance of the benefits and the ways in which the benefits can be achieved. Such data should come both from official government surveys, and from non-governmental organisations such as associations and universities. International agencies could remedy these deficiencies by supporting and possibly conducting research, provide expertise for the design and implementation of training programmes, as well as asist in specific technical areas.

3

Current Status and Information Needs

INTRODUCTION

The inland capture fishery statistics for many countries are commonly regarded as being poorly reported and/or inaccurate. Those who are familiar with officially reported figures, and how they are derived, frequently mock them as meaningless. Whilst some exceptions exist, this perception is probably valid. But such statistics are important as they still tend to form the basis of opinion, policy, planning and management decisions, even amongst those who recognise the weaknesses of the statistics. Unfortunately, those who are unfamiliar with the shortcomings of this information often take it at face value. Therefore, official inland fishery statistics, whether good or bad, do significantly influence perceptions. Not surprisingly, this has tended to promote significant under-valuing of inland capture fisheries.

Recognising the need for improvement, a mission was initiated by FAO Regional Office for Asia and the Pacific, to review the current status of inland capture fisheries in Southeast Asia. Short field missions were made to four countries (Indonesia, Malaysia, Myanmar and Thailand) and further information was based upon recent professional experience in three other countries (Cambodia, Lao PDR and VietNam). The objectives of this review were to:

1. Assess the quality and relevance of existing statistics on inland capture fisheries
2. Assess the extent that the statistics meet management objectives
3. Suggest cost effective ways in which the existing statistics might be improved

4. Explore the information needs for inland capture fisheries
5. Recommend strategies for obtaining the required information.

This review takes a broader perspective of the problem and goes beyond simplistic reviews of shortcomings in statistical approaches. The opportunity has been taken to highlight the flaws in the current information system and point to the significant opportunities that exist to re-evaluate the information requirements and look at novel approaches to how to meet them. Some country-specific observations and recommendations are reported in Part II. Even for these, time has not permitted a thorough analysis of each situation, nor in-depth recommendations. Each country needs to follow-up on this report in much more detail locally. What has been learnt, however, is that the countries do have common problems for which there are common solutions. This is the focus of the first part of this report.

Throughout this review conclusions have been made based upon two important factors, these are:

- That solutions to meet information needs should be cost-effective (most countries have limited financial resources and will be reluctant or unable to suddenly make substantial investments into improving their inland capture fishery statistics).
- That there is considerable scope for information sharing between countries (in many respects this is essential because for many countries the only way to verify the current figures, or obtain indicative ones from scratch, is to use information from elsewhere).

A desk-top review of inland fishery statistics was undertaken by FAO (2000b) which included several generic recommendations, most of which are endorsed here. The current report extends that review by exploring the problems and opportunities in more detail based upon the mission to selected countries. It presents a more detailed analysis of the data currently being produced, its actual origins, potential accuracy and relevance. Particular attention has been given to information needs for inland fisheries and the practicalities of addressing those needs in the countries in question.

STATISTICS VERSUS INFORMATION

"Statistics" generally refers to the recurrent (repeated) collection of data for specific information purposes. This is normally done through specialised agencies, *e.g.* departments of statistics, which may or may not operate through, or delegate collection duties to, sub-divisions of relevant line agencies (*e.g.* departments of fisheries). These agencies report the summarised information to national authorities and to FAO usually on an annual basis.

According to the *Oxford English Dictionary* statistics means:

" 1) the science of collecting and analysing numerical data, especially in or for large quantities, and usually inferring proportions in a whole from proportions in a representative sample; 2) any systematic collection or presentation of such facts"

The same dictionary defines data as:

"known facts or things used as a basis for inference or reckoning"

FAO (1999a) defines the term data in relation to capture fisheries as:

"facts that result from measurements or observations"

The first conclusion of this review is that, in general, the published figures for inland capture fisheries in Southeast Asia do not qualify as "statistics" because most are not based upon data. Even for the exceptions, qualification of the information as "statistics" is debatable as none of the information is based upon measurement or observation. This in itself is not necessarily a problem, but the difficulty lies with the fact that the information is reported as real data, which are subsequently treated as such.

This review considers the subject in question more broadly, preferring the term "information", which includes but is not limited to "statistics" or "data". According to the dictionary: information means *"knowledge"*. This implies that the subject matter has a certain degree of utility. This is not necessarily so for statistics or data, which can take on almost abstract features and their collection become an end in itself; as witnessed admirably by inland capture fishery statistics.

In view of this background, two recent initiatives have significant relevance to the current review:

(i) FAO (1999a) provide guidelines for the routine collection of capture fishery data. At first sight this publication would appear to have significant relevance to the subject of this review. But since few of the statistics for inland capture fisheries reported for Southeast Asia are based upon actual data, the publication is of limited use. It does, however, remain the definitive work for guidance for those who are thinking about obtaining some data in the near future. All of those interested in the specifics of data collection, sampling strategies and protocols, statistical approaches etc. are referred to this work.

(ii) The "STREAM" initiative (STREAM, 2001) provides support to regional aquatic resources management in the Asia-Pacific region. The objective is to promote participation, communication, and policies that support the livelihoods of poor aquatic resource users in the Asia-Pacific. A cornerstone of the initiative is improved information generation, communication and sharing between countries. The subject of this review is, of course, highly relevant to STREAM. Although STREAM focuses on sharing information relevant to improved management, and not directly to that relating to fishery valuation/ assessment/monitoring, these two aspects of information are, of course, closely related. For STREAM to function effectively, it is, for example, essential to have knowledge of the realities of the relative importance of various sub-sectors in the aquatic resources arena (*e.g.* capture *versus* culture). STREAM, for example, is itself influenced by an over-reliance in its formulation upon existing national statistics for inland capture fisheries, which might potentially lead to a bias towards aquaculture. But more importantly, improved information on the aquatic resources sector is essential if governments and other stake-holders are to support STREAM to the extent warranted by the actual importance of the sector, as opposed to that indicated by the current statistics.

THE NATURE AND PERCEIVED STATUS OF INLAND CAPTURE FISHERIES

Inland capture fisheries are characterised by an extremely diverse range of gears, environments in which they are used and socially and culturally complex societies within which they operate. They include all features of marine fisheries and many that the latter sub-sector does not possess which makes them much more complex. Some generalised differences between inland capture fisheries and marine fisheries, in relation to statistics, are summarised below:

Inland Fisheries	*Marine Fisheries*
• Bulk of the catch taken by dispersed small-scale gears	• Bulk of the catch taken by large commercial/industrial gears
• Fishing activities largely dispersed and less visible because of (i) informal nature, and (ii) operating in remote rural areas masked by geography/vegetation	• Activities more visible in open waters/sea
• Bulk of landings dispersed and informal	• Bulk of landings centralised and visible
• Part-time fishing the norm, especially mixed farming/fishing lifestyles on river floodplains	• Professional fishing dominates the sector
• Most produce consumed domestically and much of it within the communities where fishing occurs	• Most is exported

These differences have a major influence upon the nature of statistics and the problems of obtaining them. In general, they favour the marine sector, both in ease of collecting information and motivations for doing so (taxation, export generation etc.). Comparisons with aquaculture also suggest that statistics for the latter are easier to collect.

Aquaculture is invariably household based, or site specific. Activities are more visible and participants tend to have better monitoring of outputs because they must gauge this against inputs (labour, feed etc.) in order to track profitability. Information may be more difficult to obtain for some small-scale and more extensive aquaculture activities (typically small-scale aquaculture represents the weakest of the aquaculture statistics). Although statistics for marine fisheries and aquaculture are not perfect, they are likely to be more representative than those for inland capture fisheries.

The habitats in which fishing occurs can be numerous and have very different characteristics. In most, if not all, countries in Southeast Asia, almost all areas of inland waters, which are not polluted beyond the ability to sustain fish, have vibrant and active capture fisheries associated with them. They can be very roughly divided into categories, each of which has particular relevance to the subject of statistics:

Reservoirs and Lakes

These can be of significant importance nationally. Fisheries on larger reservoirs and lakes are relatively visible, often with well-organised landing sites. Access is from the shore. The use of boats (motorised or not) is common. Problems facing data collection are similar to smaller-scale marine fisheries. The fish stocks, in terms of natural variations, tend to be more stable both within and between years. Problems with reservoir fisheries management, in general, centre on managing over-exploitation. Management actions tend to generally include stocking. Small reservoirs and water bodies can be a significant resource and cumulatively more important than larger reservoirs. Deeper lakes with higher gradient banks present similar features to reservoirs. Lakes that are part of river floodplains (*e.g.* the Great Lake in Cambodia) tend to take on features of river floodplains (see below).

Rivers

Rivers (*i.e.* flowing freshwaters, including streams) form networks covering nearly all inland areas, except extreme deserts. Traditionally, human settlements are located near rivers. Rivers, consequently, are traditionally heavily fished. Access tends to be from the shore. Use of boats is more limited on smaller tributaries and hill streams. On rivers with extensive floodplains, resource availability in river channels is highly seasonal as fish migrate through channels in response to flood conditions on the plains. There can also be large variations in resources between years due to between year variations in flood extent (rainfall). Rivers are generally suffering from severe environmental degradation arising from other sectors. Riverine fisheries are very diverse, generally informal and dispersed. They have been traditionally extremely difficult to get representative statistics for.

Floodplains

River and lake floodplains are very productive and their fisheries highly seasonal. Peak catches are taken as flood waters recede and migrating fishes are caught in appropriate gears (especially barrage fences with traps). Most people tend to be already living on floodplains themselves and do not "access" the fishery (*i.e.* travel to it) because it comes to them. The seasonal cycles, and fish migrations they stimulate, can produce significant opportunities for migratory fishers. In Southeast Asia, a mix of farming/fishing lifestyles predominates on river floodplains. Floodplains are very productive for agriculture too and represent the best land. They support some of Southeast Asia's highest concentrations of human populations. Floodplains and adjacent river fisheries are intimately linked. Key fishing grounds or opportunities tend to be leased, either officially or through community-based management systems. Floodplain fisheries are very diverse covering the full spectrum of gears. They are very resilient to over-exploitation. Main threats are habitat loss and environmental degradation (particularly loss of floodplain area through flood control and water extraction from rivers). Floodplain fisheries are very difficult to get statistics for: the larger gears produce valuable catches, information for which is jealously guarded, corruption over licensing is common; smaller-scale operators, particularly part-time, are difficult to see and monitor. Catches from all gears are highly seasonal. The bulk of catches can often be taken within very limited periods. Such variation is difficult to monitor.

Estuaries and Deltas

These areas can be extensive and their fisheries often have a mixture of river and floodplain characteristics, depending upon the hydrological conditions. In addition to freshwater riverine species, large migrations of brackishwater/estuarine species can occur, including for marine prawns. Environments vary from freshwater to full seawater according to flood and tidal conditions. Estuaries receive large nutrient inputs from floodwaters. Their fisheries are naturally highly productive. Estuarine fisheries can be hugely important. One problem with statistics is that many coastal/marine fishers are based in estuaries and deltas and land their catch there. Separating coastal/marine production from inland catches can be problematic. Some countries report their catches based upon classifications of salinity (freshwater vs. marine), some based upon geography (inland v. coastal). Much of the catch from inland areas near the coast (estuaries/deltas) is reported as coastal or marine fisheries production. Again, this significantly under-values inland fisheries. Estuaries in Southeast Asia tend to have severe environmental problems due to pollution and water management activities arising both upstream and locally, particularly through deforestation and the conversion of wetlands.

Rice-fields

Rice is the main staple crop throughout most of Southeast Asia. Traditionally "wet" rice is grown, particularly in lowlands through paddy farming. The local aquatic fauna naturally tends to treat rice fields as floodplain and colonise fields during the aquatic phase of rice farming. This can result in significant quantities of aquatic animals (not only fish, but also a wide variety of crustaceans, molluscs, reptile, amphibians and insects) being taken regularly from rice-fields throughout the growing season or when they are drained. Most rice farmers have traditional systems for enhancing aquatic animal production mainly centring on enhancing recruitment and controlling predation. Traditionally, external feeds are not used. Intensification of systems has included stocking with fish and supplemental feeding. Separating production between capture and culture can be very problematic. Rice intensification has led to sub-optimal water management regimes and increased pesticide use, which has resulted in significant losses of this secondary crop of aquatic animals. Capture fisheries production from rice fields can be very significant but is rarely accurately reported, if at all.

Categories of Fishing Activities

(1) *Commercial/industrial fisheries* - where activities produce significant commercial quantities of fish at localised sites, usually involving high capital input gears and often using significant inputs of professional labour. Some impressive commercial/industrial river fisheries occur in Southeast Asia. Examples of gears used

include river bagnets and large barrage fences. Such fisheries are usually found where resource availability and access to markets justify significant capital investment (financial, manpower and/or in the construction of gears) and where access can be controlled. Key fishing sites or opportunities are often allocated through well developed licensing and auction systems. Many of these systems were in place in historical times.

(2) *Middle-scale fisheries* - here catches per operating unit are smaller and gears are normally operated at the individual or family level. Examples are: trawlers, beach seines, long-lines.

(3) *Small-scale fisheries* - a very diverse and diffuse sub-sector whereby individual catches generally are not high and activities tend to be rather informal. Part-time fishing dominates. Participation in this sector can be very high. Catches per unit can be small but cumulative catches are significant and can surpass those from commercial and middle-scale fisheries combined.

Activities associated with inland capture fisheries such as: processing, marketing and transportation can be significant. In particular, the seasonal nature of floodplain fisheries can result in huge local surpluses, which enter significant processing routes particularly in Southeast Asia for fish paste and fish sauce. This produce helps spread the benefits of the fishery throughout the year and is very important for local and regional food security.

There are three main motivations, or objectives, for fishery-related activities:

(1) *Commercial/profit.* This is a primary motivation for many fishers, including at the small-scale level. This group is not limited to the commercial/industrial sector since the scale of profits generated is not relevant.

(2) *Food and subsistence.* Where the produce is consumed directly by the fisher or the immediate family or household.

(3) *Sport and recreation.* Where the fishers do not depend directly on the fishery for employment (although others may be employed servicing sport fishers), and fishing is undertaken for leisure purposes. The fish may be returned to the fishery, used as a trophy or eaten or sold but neither of the latter are the main motivation for capture.

Throughout this review, the term "*subsistence fisheries*" (where the catch supports the family diet directly) will be avoided for several reasons. This is because true subsistence fishers are in fact quite rare, fishers in poorer communities will still tend to sell their catch if they have access to suitable markets. The definition "subsistence fisher" is more often concerned with lack of opportunity to derive income rather than a deliberate livelihood strategy; this term also under-values the importance of fishing activities. Even where fish is not sold but consumed locally, it has an economic/commercial value because it contributes to family, local or regional welfare and food-security, thereby enabling other more obvious financially oriented activities (such as commercial fishing, aquaculture) to take place. "Subsistence" fisheries are included here under small-scale fisheries.

A detailed study of sport/recreational fisheries is beyond the scope of this review. They are, however, important for several reasons. They can have an extremely high economic value, which is not always obviously related to total catches and landings. The requirements for information and statistics are considerably different, not least because total landings are irrelevant, since much of the catch is returned live to the fishery after being caught. Sport/recreational fisheries tend to develop as countries become more affluent, a process which provides both financial resources to invest beyond basic needs and a higher priority on leisure time. Sport/recreational fishers can be extremely influential as they may represent more affluent sections of society who have leisure time and the sector tends to become very well organised and politically and economically powerful.

This presents both management opportunities and challenges. Inland sport fisheries are not limited to the rich industrialised countries of the west. Southeast Asia already has well-developed inland sport fisheries and the sub-sector is developing rapidly, particularly in Malaysia and Thailand (amongst the countries covered by this review). The sub-sector is also very relevant because elsewhere, where they have developed further, they present some of the best examples of effective co-management approaches in fisheries. The fishers are usually well organised. They also, in general have little motivation to withhold information about catches (possibly being the only group to tend to actually exaggerate catches!). Sport fishers also can be one of the most active and influential groups promoting improved environmental management, restoration and rehabilitation. In the mission's experience, several countries in Southeast Asia are under-estimating the value and potential of their inland sport fisheries.

This is largely because they have no statistics on them. There is a need for separate and more detailed advice to relevant FAO member countries regarding information and statistics issues relevant to sport/ recreational fisheries. For the present purposes it is sufficient to note: (i) that information systems can, and should, be funded through revenue generated from the fisheries themselves (user pays); countries with developing sport fisheries need not re-direct funds away from pro-poor fisheries management and development; and, (ii) co-management approaches to information generation and management are not only logical, as elsewhere, but are likely to be much more easily implemented (sport fishers are better educated, better resourced, and better organised).

REVIEW OF CURRENT INLAND CAPTURE FISHERY STATISTICS IN SOUTHEAST ASIA

The countries for which inland capture fishery statistics are reviewed have a wide range of population characteristics, economies and natural resources. Not surprisingly, their inland fisheries differ according to level of economic development and freshwater resource availability. They all have significant inland capture fisheries, particularly in areas where poor rural communities live in proximity to significant freshwater resources.

Methods of Statistics Collection and Reporting

The methods that the reviewed countries use to collect or compile their national statistics for inland capture fisheries are summarised in Table 2. A wide variety of methods are used to estimate inland capture fisheries production ranging from estimates made in offices (verging on guesses), through basic or elaborate sampling based surveys to attempts to obtain full cover of the entire fishery based upon (officially) compulsory licensing of all gears.

There is also either suspected, officially admitted or known (confirmed) differences between the official systems in place and the actual practices. Of the countries covered in this report, there are only two for which there is a degree of certainty (*i.e.* recognized by government) regarding the level of accuracy of the system that is actually used in practice: Lao PDR, where there is no sampling system and reports are entirely based upon estimates derived in the office, and Cambodia, where discrepancies between figures generated through the official system, and more accurate figures that have been established through significant independent research spanning the last six years.

Table 1 Some population, land, economic and resource data for the countries reviewed.

Country	Population (year)	Land area (km^2) & population density (no./km^2)	GDP per caput US$ (year)	Major freshwater resources*
Cambodia	10 000 000 (1995)	181 035 55.25	309 (1995)	Mekong River Floodplains, Tonle Sap and the Great Lake
Indonesia	206 338 000 (1998)	1 900 000 108.6	1 018 (1997)	Reservoirs. Large river systems particularly on the islands of Kalimantan (Kapuas and Mahakam Rivers), Sumatra, Sulawesi and Irian Jaya. Widespread estuaries, deltas and mangrove systems.

Lao PDR	5 032 000 (1995)	236 725 21.25	362 (1995)	Large rivers. Mekong mainstream and large tributaries.
Malaysia	21 830 000 (1999)	329 758 66.2	4 523 (1998)	More limited on peninsular Malaysia. Substantial rivers in Sabah and Sarawak provinces (Borneo). Inland fisheries differ significantly between these two areas.
Myanmar	50 000 000 (2000)	676 577 73.90	220 (1994)	Very large river and floodplain systems, particularly the Ayeyarwaddy (Irrawaddy) River and a number of others. Resource area rivals that of the entire lower Mekong Basin.
Philippines	73 130 000 (1998)	304 212 240	890 (1998)	Limited to several lakes, most rivers severely polluted, major islands Luzon and Mindanao, large number of reservoirs

Lao PDR	5 032 000 (1995)	236 725 21.25	362 (1995)	Large rivers. Mekong mainstream and large tributaries.
Malaysia	21 830 000 (1999)	329 758 66.2	4 523 (1998)	More limited on peninsular Malaysia. Substantial rivers in Sabah and Sarawak provinces (Borneo). Inland fisheries differ significantly between these two areas.
Myanmar	50 000 000 (2000)	676 577 73.90	220 (1994)	Very large river and floodplain systems, particularly the Ayeyarwaddy (Irrawaddy) River and a number of others. Resource area rivals that of the entire lower Mekong Basin.
Philippines	73 130 000 (1998)	304 212 240	890 (1998)	Limited to several lakes, most rivers severely polluted, major islands Luzon and Mindanao, large number of reservoirs

None of the countries estimate the statistics based upon direct observations, report verification, catch or landings sampling or any other form of independent monitoring. This includes Cambodia where recently the statistics have been revised (*i.e.* corrected) based upon new information produced by research, not through an improved statistical system. The degree of estimation inherent in most of these systems ranges from responsible attempts to estimate actual catches through to arbitrary guesses. Most are genuine attempts by over-worked and under-resourced staff to actually reflect the situation with the fisheries. However, it must be said that underlying some of the estimates at field level is a general disinterest in accuracy and, on occasion and as openly reported by the relevant authorities themselves, mis-reporting.

The Statistics Produced

In view of the analysis of the methods used by each country to produce these statistics, the information should in general be regarded very sceptically. The statistics do not necessarily represent reality. Nevertheless, they do show some interesting features. First, there is no apparent trend of declining production for any country (except possibly for the Philippines, less so for VietNam). This is somewhat at odds with the widely held view that inland capture fisheries are declining and illustrates that perceptions of the fisheries are held independently of the statistical information. There are two explanations of this: (i) perceptions are wrong and the fisheries in general are not in decline, or (ii) perceptions are not based upon statistics, which begs an obvious question as to their function. The most relevant point for the present purposes is that for most countries the statistics produced do not enable any confidence in the analysis of trends.

The increase in reported production for Cambodia in 1999 is due to re-estimations based upon scientific surveys. However, two countries report significant increases in actual production. That for Thailand is stated to be due to the impacts of stocking in reservoirs; and the Thai statistics apply mainly to reservoirs. Myanmar reports significant increases in production from river and floodplain fisheries over the past 4-5 years. It was achieved without any significant physical inputs (*e.g.* fish feed) and is based purely upon improved aquatic resources management (environmental restoration and rehabilitation, restocking floodplains and improved governance). Of all of the countries reviewed, Myanmar has the most extensive and comprehensive inland capture fishery statistical system and there is more confidence than in most countries that the reports may be representative (but likely still underestimates). This is a most interesting case, which demonstrates the great benefits on offer through applying management effort to riverine fisheries. The reported increased catches are 45 percent and 65 percent per annum from leased (large fenced areas of floodplain) and open fisheries respectively; and this is from a fishery of already significant proportions. This example eclipses any known benefits arising from investments in aquaculture (when starting from similar production levels) and emasculates the widely held view that river fisheries cannot be improved and therefore do not warrant investment.

However, the general degree of confidence in these statistics, based upon methodologies applied to generate them, varies considerably. Assessing their accuracy is of course difficult, because better statistics are normally not available for comparison. But a number of approaches can be taken to try to verify the figures. The mission stresses that such verification should be done in more detail, and by the competent authorities in question. Statistics should not be revised externally. The current analysis is used to provide a general overview of the possible extent of mis - and under-reporting.Riverine fisheries in the tropics, for example, are known to be highly seasonal. Statistics for inland capture fisheries for areas dominated by rivers should, if representative, reflect such seasonality. The mission has been able to obtain catch statistics dis-aggregated by month or by quarter in only a few cases. Unfortunately, monthly (or quarterly) reports for areas dominated by riverine fisheries in Indonesia and Malaysia show no such seasonality and question, if not discount, the validity of the underlying data.

It is known that in many countries the statistical methods exclude or seriously under-estimate some parts of the fishery. Estimates for such sub-sectors can be applied based upon experiences from scientifically based surveys from elsewhere (preferably within the same country, or for equivalent types of fishery in broadly equivalent areas). It is also known that statistics based upon reporting can be unreliable and potential corrections can be applied using known variations between actual and reported catches. This applies particularly to the more prominent licensed and leased fisheries where large taxes are levied or revenues extracted.

For all of the countries reviewed, the analysis shows that production from inland capture fisheries is clearly seriously under-reported. In many cases, reported production has been checked by making comparisons with independent survey data available for the same countries. For those countries, or areas, where survey data are not available there is no reason to assume that the statistics reported are any more accurate. The discrepancy between officially reported catches (where available) and estimates based upon independent scientifically based surveys (*i.e.* collecting actual data for the same areas) varies by a factor of between 4.2 and 21.4. Overall, for all the countries combined, total reported catches from inland waters appears to be under-estimated by a factor of at least between 2.5 and 3.6. Based upon actual survey data the latter figure could still be an underestimate of the discrepancy. This margin of error agrees with the minimum thought to be applicable to reported catches from inland waters worldwide (FAO, 2000a).

Total reported freshwater aquaculture production in the same Southeast Asian countries for 1999 was 1 268 968 MT. This figure is already surpassed by only the reported freshwater capture fisheries production (1 303 247 MT). Actual production from inland capture fisheries, amongst the countries in question, likely exceeds reported aquaculture production by a factor of between 2.5 and 3.6. This is also after the supposed "decline" and "degradation" of inland capture fisheries. If the decline is real, one is left wondering what production was like before. The most interesting question that these figures raise is why most countries (Myanmar and Cambodia to a lesser extent) continue to disinvest in inland capture fisheries, some favouring aquaculture almost exclusively. A common answer, apart from the perceived decline, is that it is assumed that production from inland capture fisheries cannot be increased. This is not the case, as clearly demonstrated by Myanmar in this review. And even if true, is not a fishery of these proportions worth effort in sustaining it?

Naturally, many will find the figures in Table 3 difficult to accept. They are, however, based upon available information; amongst which the mission has only been selective by favouring facts over fiction. All the calculations need to be repeated properly and methodically and not be done externally to appropriate government authorities. At the very least, Table 3 suggests that this is worth doing.

Sources of Error in the Official Statistics

Potential sources of sampling error when routinely collecting data for capture fisheries are covered in detail in FAO (1999a). This includes much more attention to statistical errors and adequate sampling approaches. The following summary refers to general problems with inland capture fishery statistics in the countries in question.

Although problems and their significance vary between countries, the following general errors are inherent in the current inland capture fishery statistics.

Errors in Catch Reporting

Obviously, catches reported by fishers depend on two major factors:

(a) The ability to recall what actual catches were. Most methods of collecting statistics require at the best monthly recall of catches, many require yearly recall. Scientific surveys have shown that the ability to accurately recall (remember) what catches were drops off significantly beyond only 48 hours. Most inland fishers do not record their catches, but many do and this group falls generally under the problem area below. Recall is particularly a problem where household heads are asked about total household catches. They tend to report only their own catches and are unaware of catches made by other household members, particularly women and children.

(b) The willingness to report. In most countries, fishers are subject to licensing and other regulations enforced by the same personnel that collect catch information. Quite logically, they see links between catch reports and taxation or other costs to them. Not surprisingly this does not encourage accurate reporting. [Although this is a potential problem with marine fisheries also, in that sub-sector reports can be reconciled against landings, processing/marketing, export records and expectations based upon catch/effort, *e.g.* vessel size].

These problems can be significant. For example, even with the relatively well monitored commercial, industrial and middle-scale sections of inland capture fisheries in Cambodia, by the Fisheries Department's own estimates, catches are under-reported by a factor of at least 3.0.

Under-estimates of the Importance of Small-scale Fishing Activities

This is particularly a problem in inland fisheries. The high levels of participation in small-scale activities may produce small catches per caput but cumulative catches can, and usually do, exceed those from the more professional, full-time, fishers. This is a serious problem because most, if not all, countries that produce statistics based upon some consideration of fishing effort and reported catches derive these on the basis of records of professional fishers. The few examples which reportedly include small-scale activities, seriously under-estimate their extent.

Mis-reporting by Government Officials

There are examples of mis-reporting by local government officials for inland capture fisheries in Southeast Asia. Some fisheries produce very lucrative licensing or other forms of revenue; the most valuable ones generally associated with auction or tender systems. Corruption encourages officials to down-grade the catch reports they submit, to be more in-line with reported revenue, which is less than that paid by fishers.

This is recorded in the literature for fishing lots in Cambodia and probably occurs elsewhere. This has a knock-on effect on national statistics, because many countries will also estimate small-scale production as a proportion of reported production from licensed gears.

Estimates made without collecting data

Obviously, estimates made without collecting data or information are subject to significant potential sources of error. Some countries openly report that their estimates are made in this fashion. But for others, at field level, such estimates often substitute for those that are officially supposed to be based upon sampling.

Some people are actually quite good at producing reasonable estimates but they require much local knowledge, experience and motivation. Invariably, they favour the more visible and "commercial"/ professional parts of the fishery.

But more often than not, such estimates are produced in an arbitrary way by people whose main interest lies elsewhere; often with aquaculture. Such methods are also more vulnerable to subjective assessments of trends. Nevertheless, there is considerable scope for improving this method through better quantified approaches, appropriate training and increasing transparency. The method does offer some significant advantages, low-cost being one.

OTHER CONSTRAINTS WITH THE EXISTING STATISTICS

Recording Participation in Capture Fisheries

Very few of the countries record participation in the capture fisheries sector to any significant degree in their statistics. Most do not record it at all. Some only report licensed fishers. None record participation in fishery-related activities of processing, marketing, transportation and gear construction etc.

In addition to some indicative figures for participation of households in fish capture the following information illustrates the extent to which participation is an important element:

- Indonesia reports approximately 500 000 fishers operating in inland waters and part-time fishers outnumber full-time fishers by a factor of about two to one; but this is still considered an under-estimate and likely excludes small-scale (un-licensed) fishers and activities in rice-fields. This compares with about three times as many fishers reported for marine fisheries where the split between part- and full-time is about equal. Correcting inland figures to include small-scale fishers and rice fields would certainly exceed the number for marine fisheries.
- Myanmar has a more extensive licensing system and reports 1 398 410 fishers operating in inland waters in 2000-2001. This is higher than for the marine sector (1 278 000 fishers) and is approximately 3.5 times the number of fish farmers. Even so, the figure for inland waters is based on license records, in practice many small gears are not included and rice-field and reservoir fishing is excluded.
- In Luang Prabang province in Lao PDR (a more remote, mountainous region with a relatively low-key fishery by Mekong standards), 83 percent of households are involved in fisheries and on average 41 percent of those household members actively fish, 20 percent of which are children. If this pattern is typical, this gives an estimate of about 1.7 million fishers nationally (in a country of only about 5 million people).
- In a single province in the Mekong delta in VietNam, survey data suggest that about 1.35 million people rely to various extents on capture fisheries, out of a total of 2 016 949; 45 percent of people actually actively fish (900 000 fishers), 9

percent of these are children and 30 percent women; 5.7 percent of households are involved in fish processing and/or trading, with 32 500 traders in the province, 60 percent of which are self-employed; 66 percent of households are involved in capture fisheries compared to only 14 percent in aquaculture. Yet the popular perception of the inland aquatic resources sector in VietNam is one dominated by aquaculture, where even the existence of capture fisheries in rivers/floodplains is widely denied in some circles.

- A conservative estimate is 1.7 million fishers in the VietNamese part of the Mekong delta alone.

According to FAO (1999b), globally there are 28.5 million people fishing or involved in aquaculture. Of these 15 million are marine fishers, 9 million are fish farmers (freshwater and marine combined) and only 4.5 million are inland fishers. The latter number, however, is exceeded amongst the countries reviewed in this report. The figures above also suggest that at least for Southeast Asia the numbers of inland fishers may at least equal or exceed the number of marine fishers and certainly surpasses involvement in aquaculture by a significant margin. It is unlikely that the countries reviewed are unique in these respects, although the prominence of rice farming in Asia, which includes rice-field fisheries, significantly increases involvement in fishing. The FAO (1999b) report also suggests that globally 41 percent of fishers are full-time (*i.e.* those receiving at least 90 percent of their livelihood from fishing), 35 percent are part-time (deriving between 30-89 percent of their income from fishing) and only 6.5 million people (23 percent) are occasional fishers who derive only less than 30 percent of income from fishing. The latter figure is ludicrous in the extreme.

The problem with these FAO figures on fishers, of course, is that they are based upon a survey of reports from countries. The majority of these do not have figures for numbers of fishers, those that do usually cover full-time professional fishers (usually only for marine) and fish farmers. It is hardly surprising, therefore, that the reports bias perspectives. This is yet another illustration of the danger of summarising the fisheries sector based upon incomplete, inaccurate and in many cases prejudiced reporting.

There will be controversy over the inclusion of occasional and part-time fishers in such statistics. A common argument is that most inland occasional fishers are not "real" fishers. This is an inappropriate view for two good reasons: First even if "occasional" fishers were a lower status category, the definitions used by the FAO report require that proper numbers should still be included (the figures reported ostensibly include any kind of fishing). Second, and more importantly, the relevance of fishing to a person's livelihood is not directly or simply related to the total amount caught or whether fishing is the main "occupation". Does the average catch of 280 MT per person per annum make professional fishers in Iceland a higher status category than the 50 kg per annum caught by a poor rural fisher in Southeast Asia, who may not have an income upon which to calculate the contribution of fish to, but without which the family would literally starve?

The importance of fisheries cannot be determined externally and certainly not by applying western formal economic criteria. The valuation of a fisheries and its importance should be defined by the stakeholders themselves and it is crucial that they be given the opportunity to do so. As a basic indication within the complex livelihoods of rural people, nothing is done without reason and we can assume that the level of participation in fishing is a clear indication of its importance.

FAO reports are influential (FAO, 1999b) and may have significant influence on policies. It is suggested that FAO seriously reconsider the potential impact of the inland fishery statistics it reproduces if the figures are known to be inaccurate. An effective first step in this process would be an explanation as to the possible sources of error in relation to inland capture fisheries, coupled to some indication of likely veracity.

Species Composition of Catches

Most countries report only very basic information on the species composition of catches from inland waters; some countries have slightly better information on species composition at field levels. Where species composition is recorded it tends to include only those considered to be economically important, even then, many taxa tend to get grouped into species groups. Even the most comprehensive systems are generating only basic information and the quality of such information is widely regarded as suspect by most agencies. Some countries do not even have catch composition data enabling them to properly evaluate their own stocking programmes.

Without exception, none of the countries are compiling statistics that are in any way useful for obtaining information on trends in biodiversity; although some obtain such information independently of their statistical systems, usually via research. Monitoring vulnerable species for example is almost impossible using the current statistical system because such species are not common enough in catches to warrant inclusion as a distinct category (although in theory such could be done).

The Philippines was visited at the end of this mission and unfortunately could not be reviewed in as much detail as would have been liked. The country, however, reports some curious things. An example is the reported catch from inland waters (about 145 000 MT per annum recently), of which about 65 percent is accounted for by molluscs (which is not from culture). This includes a mix of brackishwater (inland) but also freshwater species. There is no reason to assume the country has the only mollusc fishery in Southeast Asia. What is intriguing is how, or if, this catch is reported elsewhere. It is common for fishery statistics to be biased towards fin-fish and it is possible that in many cases these mollusc fisheries are ignored. This is also a problem with rice-field fisheries where a significant proportion of the catch is non-fish, but often only fish are reported, if at all. The prominence of molluscs in the Philippine catches suggests that this subject deserves closer attention.

Monitoring Fishing Effort

Catch per unit of effort (CPUE) data are useful for monitoring trends in the fishery, particularly for monitoring the state of stocks. A number of countries also base their statistical system on the foundation of calculating catches using CPUE. calculations (based on total numbers of gears and total numbers of fishing trips). However, with inland capture fisheries defining and monitoring fishing effort is extremely difficult. Certainly, effort cannot be defined simply in terms of the existence of gears in an area (which is what most countries currently record). The real effort applicable to any particular gear depends largely upon where, when and how it is used, which is not necessarily best enumerated by number of trips. These problems are no different to other fisheries but become more important in inland fisheries because of the predominance of smaller gears, which take the majority of the catch. Also, passive gears are common in inland fisheries and are particularly difficult to assess effort for. Gear use is also influenced largely by social factors external to the fishery. Changes in participation in the fishery can be significant and rapid. For many gears, effort also varies in response to environmental conditions (and the latter are not recorded). For example, effort for some of the larger industrial sized gears such as barrage fences and river bagnets depends on river flow rates (how rapidly floodwaters recede), which can vary significantly within and between years.

These difficulties result in two problems: First, attempts to calculate total catches for the whole fishery based upon CPUE data for gears is very problematic and likely requires a depth of knowledge of effort currently unavailable, and likely unattainable, for most fisheries as a whole. For small-scale activities a better unit of effort is the household (by ignoring for present purposes how fish are actually caught). But most countries do not record catches by household and those that do often fall into the trap of applying CPUE approaches for gears to household activities. Second, without adequate data on CPUE, statistics for total catches, even if accurate, are of limited use for tracking trends in the fishery stocks in any detail. This does not mean that CPUE data for individual gears are not valuable. They are, and should be collected where feasible and cost-effective. But such cannot be obtained for the whole fishery, not even for the bulk of it.

Aquarium Fish

A number of countries have capture fisheries based upon the collection of ornamental species for sale in the aquarium trade. It is important in Indonesia and should not be under-estimated in Thailand (possibly Malaysia and Myanmar also). Few of the countries collect statistics on the activities. It is therefore difficult to establish the relative importance of this fishery, but the ornamental fish industry in Southeast Asia is huge. Capture of ornamental fishes can be locally quite significant and many activities tend to be concentrated in more remote areas where other sources of income are more limited. The fishery is also unusual in that as species become rarer they become much more valuable which can contribute to over-exploitation. This is a specialised area which might perhaps be subject to a regional review, including information and statistics requirements.

Uncritical Acceptance

A serious underlying constraint with the current statistical systems in Southeast Asia is the uncritical acceptance of the information that is produced. There are numerous reasons why this happens including:

(i) Complacency; some authorities are little motivated to try to improve the interpretations of their statistics

(ii) In some cases there are vested interests at stake in keeping the production figures low (especially where large revenues are involved with licensing, but also sometimes to justify investments in alternative sectors)

(iii) Reluctance to admit previous figures are wrong (this is especially a problem for districts and provinces reporting to higher authorities)

(iv) Incompatibility between statistical systems and data or information arising externally to them (government statistics are compiled in certain ways and it is often difficult to incorporate better information into them from other sources)

(v) There is a tendency to treat the information that is collected an actual statistics that are based upon data. When working with data there is less scope for interpretation than when acknowledging that a figure is an estimates or even a guess ('ballpark figures'). The official statistics that are produced are often regarded rigidly; although for any data, the methods used to obtain them, including sampling aspects, leave more flexibility than is currently used for inland fishery statistics. Most, if not all, statistics on inland capture fisheries in Southeast Asia are not founded upon data, thus presenting them as data limits options for interpretations. Formal acknowledgement of the limitations of information collection would allow greater flexibility and ultimately more meaningful information. Hopefully, this report will be comforting to many countries as they lcarn that they are not alone in having unreliable statistics or problems with the methods of collecting them. Perhaps the greatest progress can be made by simply admitting this.

Relationships between the Methods used and the Accuracy of the Statistics

A major objective of the current review is to advise countries how they might improve upon their information and statistics for inland capture fisheries. With such a wide range of countries, methods used to compile the statistics and the growing knowledge on the accuracy of the information, it should be possible to draw some conclusions by comparing experiences between them.

The first conclusion is that countries cannot be ranked in order of those having the "best" statistics. The current statistics must be viewed not only in terms of potential accuracy but in terms of effort expended (cost) in obtaining them. For example, Lao PDR has statistics that differ from survey based estimates by a significant margin but spends practically no money generating them. Its system also has the considerable advantage that, in theory, figures can be modified relatively easily in the light of improved information availability from non-statistical sources. But most importantly, its figures are not that much less accurate than some countries that spend significant effort compiling them. Some countries with elaborate, formal and rigid statistical systems are in fact arguably worse off. Costs are high and they tend not to work. But because these systems are in place it can be difficult to produce better information in different ways, and more cheaply.

Perhaps the most relevant example is for Cambodia. Two "data" points are provided in Fig.1-04, the first for statistics up to 1999, the second for 1999. The mean factor of uncertainty in the latter estimate is about 1.55 compared to 5.2 prior to 1999 (that is, the 1999 estimate has improved in accuracy by 335 percent). However, both estimates for production are based upon the same statistics collection system. Infrastructures and data collection methods were not significantly changed. The 1999 figures essentially represent earlier figures re-estimated in response to considerable research. Therefore, Cambodia has shown that statistics can be improved without changing statistical effort. The same statistics could indeed quite likely be obtained with significantly less effort; in fact, probably without any statistical data collection effort at all (by estimating from research data). However, what is most informative about the Cambodia experience is that despite a considerable (donor funded) investment in research and survey work spanning six years, and focussing heavily (but not exclusively) on improving fishery statistics, the current estimates of actual production made by the Department of Fisheries itself shows a range of 290 000 to 430 000 MT which is still 1.25 to 1.86 times the official statistics. It would appear, therefore, that there is a limit to narrowing the inaccuracy of such statistics (within reasonable limits of investment and effort). Two further conclusions can therefore be drawn:

(i) There is a level of accuracy with inland fishery statistics beyond which it is unreasonable, if not impossible, to go beyond. In other words, statistics should purposefully provide indicative figures, not necessarily highly accurate ones, and

(ii) In addition to this "optimal range of accuracy", due to statistical methodologies, there are known significant but unpredictable natural variations in the fisheries between years. Therefore, statistics of the nature currently collected will be near useless for tracking all but the most drastic of trends, even if their accuracy is improved. And they certainly will not be able to explain why the trends are occurring. This is the likely explanation as to why most statistics indeed do not currently reveal any trends, not that they are not there. In other words, information on trends must be obtained in other ways.

The purpose of inland capture fishery statistics in Southeast Asia

One of the most interesting and relevant areas investigated by the mission was that of the objectives of compiling inland capture fishery statistics and the use to which the information is put. The following is a general synthesis of opinions of senior managers and a summary of actual practice:

(i) There is a definite feeling, in many countries, that "statistics" are compiled because central governments request them. But the use to which the statistics are put is often uncertain.

- *Whilst many specialists appreciate the shortcomings of the information compiled, forwarding incomplete or unrepresentative information to central government agencies is extremely dangerous.*
- *Those that know the data might moderate policy considerations accordingly, but those that do not, might take the statistics at face value. Hence, there are examples of planners in central governments who are unaware that significant inland capture fisheries exist in their countries. Getting appropriate information to these people is important.*

(ii) National fishery statistics are frequently compiled primarily as a perceived obligation to FAO.

(iii) The information requested by FAO has a major influence on that which is collected or compiled.

(iv) Countries are reluctant to admit to FAO (and often to their own agencies) the true nature of the information compiled.

Consequently, the "statistics" are often taken as factual.

- *For example, of the 8 countries reviewed, only the statistics for VietNam are listed in FAO documentation as estimates. Those for Lao PDR are listed as estimates to 1992 but thereafter presented as actual statistics (which is not the case; the Lao figures have never been based upon data collection). Of the other five countries, in reality most also estimate their catches.*

(v) Most countries report that the statistics are used for "fisheries management purposes"

- *but few countries are actually managing their inland capture fisheries, at least at the national level (except for reservoirs, usually through stocking)*
- *even if they were managing the fisheries the information produced through their statistics is not adequate for most management purposes*
- *in the few cases where fisheries management occurs, the national statistics are of limited use in assessing the impacts of management; or meaningful statistics are only gathered where management is in place (e.g. for reservoirs)*

The most important conclusions, however, are that without exception, the countries:

(i) Regard the main value of their inland capture fisheries as relating to sustaining the livelihoods of poor rural communities and associated aspects of food security (not withstanding that many countries still have significant commercial/industrial inland fisheries). By contrast, in general, marine fisheries are regarded as being important for revenue generation, export earnings and formal economic benefits, and in many cases so is aquaculture.

(ii) Agree that the current information collected (even if it were accurate) does not provide information of the kind necessary for addressing, monitoring or managing rural livelihoods issues

(iii) Have a clear realisation of the need to obtain such information but considerable uncertainty regarding how it can be done and who should do it

(iv) Agree that the main threats to inland fisheries, particularly for rivers and associated wetlands, less so for reservoirs, is habitat loss and environmental degradation, the information currently collected does not assist in monitoring such trends, nor with moderating the degradation itself

(v) Recognise the importance of issues relating to sustaining biodiversity in inland waters, but that the current statistics are widely regarded (correctly) as irrelevant to this subject

(vi) Recognise that improved and effective governance of the fisheries must be founded upon co-management approaches.

During this review, the mission could not avoid the overall impression that the countries in Southeast Asia, in general, struggle with limited resources to compile information that, in many cases, they do not themselves trust, need or use. Meanwhile, most appreciate what information would be more logical to collect but lack the methods and support to obtain it.

HISTORICAL INFLUENCES UPON THE CURRENT STATISTICAL SYSTEMS

The history of fisheries research and management has had a significant impact upon statistical collection. The subject of research was reviewed by SIFR (1992). Development projects in the 1950s and 1960s promoted improved gear and vessel technology, almost to the exclusion of other, non-technical considerations. The quest was for increases in gross production to maximise profit and to feed rapidly growing populations, no matter what the other implications were. This was based originally partly upon the concept of inexhaustible stocks or exploiting new ones as existing ones showed signs of fatigue. In some areas there were deliberate policies of maximising "profit" by using more and more effective gears, which required, often deliberately, the reduction of participation in exploitation, especially marginalisation of the poor.

But in the 1970s it became apparent that the marine fisheries were in trouble and that limits to production were being reached. Some stocks were even collapsing, a trend which escalated thereafter. Fisheries began to run out of stocks. Aquaculture became the argued panacea for the problems and was to save the world from starvation, despite much of the initial effort being devoted to high value luxury species that are net consumers of fish. Aquaculture did indeed progress well and even later included more attention to the production of fish for less affluent consumers. It was particularly successful in Asia, but aquaculture production was frequently promoted solely on the concept of maximising production and profit. Equity, participation, livelihoods, food security were not issues that had been considered until recently. Neither were the environmental impacts of aquaculture or underlying constraints to its development immediately acknowledged. This situation has been slowly changing as we begin to better understand the potential role of aquaculture and also its limitations.

The emphasis of attention through this period was on declining marine catch, and subsequently aquaculture development. Inland fisheries were largely ignored and they were not covered in detail by the SIFR report itself. Research and development in the fisheries sector was dominated by marine scientists, a trend which continues. Additionally, the dispersed nature and relative inaccessibility of many inland fisheries resources made it difficult to maximise profits by placing exploitation in the hands of a few. The fact that the major inland fisheries were not easily (or rather comfortably) accessible to most western scientists contributed to their neglect. Most inland fisheries were also, and still are, so well developed in terms of traditional exploitation that the opportunities for improved gears and technology were limited, leaving technocrats in a quandary about what to do in freshwaters. To this day, the level of participation in inland fisheries, the near impossibility of compartmentalising the resources into the hands of the few and the extent of use of appropriate technologies remain their greatest assets. In the light of recently changing policies towards more livelihoods centred approaches, these attributes may yet be properly acknowledged and some overdue attention paid to the valuable role played by inland fisheries.

This brief history of fisheries was accompanied by three other relevant developments:

(i) Capture fisheries research was driven mainly, if not exclusively, by the presumed need to understand biological and ecological aspects of fish stocks and their responses to increased exploitation. The objective was to establish maximum sustainable yields (which, with hind-sight does not appear to have prevented the decline of many stocks). Technology centred on how to catch the most fish and what to do with it once it was caught. Aquaculture research also focussed on biological and ecological aspects, the objective being to maximise production with minimal inputs of feed. The concept of aquaculture was narrow, focussing only within easily managed boundaries (*e.g.* ponds, cages, raceways) that could be easily defined. Simplification of production was the goal, to be achieved through complete control the production cycle and, as far as possible, by deliberately minimising participation. More people meant more overheads and less profit. (Extensive aquaculture is a relatively recent area of interest, at least for western scientists). Economics figured largely in both sectors but only in the narrow sense of maximising profits. The more qualitative social, environment, equity and alternative management aspects were largely neglected.

(ii) Alongside this, a fisheries training and education infrastructure developed to support these perceived and narrow needs (e.g. large numbers of people were taught how to calculate mortality rates for fish and why it was essential to know this, yet few were taught about practical issues such as what poor people needed in order to survive, and how their options were narrowed by the degradation of their local environment).

(iii) The current statistical systems in place, by-and-large, grew up in parallel with this process. We can only speculate if the statistics reflected the above developments or were responsible for them. The reinforcement of one by the other resulted in serious lack of attention to inland fisheries.

One result of this process has been that the research and management needs of inland fisheries have generally been addressed by trying to impose upon them approaches and methods developed for marine fisheries. The most relevant illustration of this is the inland capture fishery statistical systems in place in Southeast Asia. They are all based upon concepts, methodologies and objectives developed for marine fisheries. Some have even recently been modified as a result of experiences from aquaculture. Of course, it is prudent to learn and improve by experience, but are inland fisheries just small, poor relations of marine fisheries and aquaculture? This review has attempted to show that in fact inland capture fisheries are neither small nor "poor" and that the time has arrived to accord them their deserved status. These fisheries are important enough to develop statistics/information systems and also management approaches that are specific to their unique characteristics.

The above description has been included because this history continues to dog attempts to better the situation of inland fisheries. In

Southeast Asia, inland capture fisheries at least equal aquaculture in terms of production based only upon official statistics, and actually is likely to be at least double. Participation is probably in the order of at least three times higher than aquaculture and is dominated by the rural poor. Despite this, there is not a single regional institution or agency providing significant long-term support to inland capture fisheries (management, research or training) in Southeast Asia; and probably very few at national level. Projects supporting the sub-sector are also rare. The situation is no better worldwide; institutions covering marine fisheries or aquaculture are almost so numerous as to be vulnerable to claims of duplication of effort. What has been the role of statistics in this historical neglect?

Shifts in Policy Emphasis by Countries, Donors and International Agencies

Recently, there have been three significant and inter-related shifts in policy emphasis. Firstly, towards policies in which poverty issues are becoming more prominent, if not central (social exclusion from fisheries, poverty reduction and alleviation, equity, gender, food-security etc.). Secondly, greater emphasis on the environment, the biodiversity it supports and how these are linked to sustainable development. Both of these are part of *"livelihoods centred approaches"*. Thirdly, the promotion of co-management systems for fisheries, based largely on the concept of participation of stakeholders in the governance process. It has already been noted that the existing statistical systems fall well short of addressing the first two needs, to which now can be added the observation that they are also, being based essentially on extractive methods, not particularly compatible with the third.

Opportunities for Shifts in Information Support at FAO

FAO has historically been one of the few international agencies with competence and interest in inland fisheries and has had its achievements in this field. Nevertheless, FAO has been an active participant in the aforementioned history of fisheries research and development and its implications for current perceptions of inland fisheries. FAO has had a high profile role in some of the priorities and policies that have been developed over the years, particularly so in developing countries. FAO is also the leading international organisation in terms of statistics for food and agriculture. In this respect it continues to have a pivotal role. Many countries have based their statistics either upon advice from FAO or upon the information that FAO requests. Many will continue to do so.

The *Strategic Framework for FAO 2000-2015* prominently includes an institutional strategy focused on poverty eradication and food security. Among its main components that Member Nations decided to indicate as fundamental are:

(i) Improving the opportunities available to the rural poor to strengthen, diversify and sustain their livelihoods by taking advantage of the potential synergies between farming, fishing, forestry and animal husbandry, including through pre- and post-production income-generating enterprises;

(ii) Supporting efforts to strengthen local institutions and to enact policies and legislation that will provide for more equitable access by both women and men to natural resources (particularly land, water, fisheries and forests) and related economic and social resources;

(iii) Improving the efficiency and effectiveness of public and private sector response to the multiple and differing needs of disadvantaged rural populations, notably of women and youth;

(iv) Promoting gender-sensitive, participatory and sustainable strategies and approaches, based on self-help, capacity-building and empowerment, to improve the skills of the rural poor and local, civil society and rural people's organizations;

(v) Assisting in the targeting of investment in the agricultural, fisheries and forestry sectors - from public and private, domestic and international sources - that contributes to food security and poverty eradication.

The framework includes sustainable livelihoods as one of its goals, therefore, it is mandatory. Sustainable livelihoods principles (rather than a particular framework) are to be more widely and systematically incorporated into FAO's normative and field programme. The strategy includes a number of proposed initiatives to internalise and consolidate sustainable livelihoods approaches. Oddly, this does not appear, based upon a superficial review by the mission, to have explicitly included amending statistics to incorporate more meaningful cover of livelihoods relevant information (although such would be implied from the strategic framework).

A visit to the FAO website (www.fao.org) reveals that the Fishery Information, Data and Statistics Unit (FIDI) describes its function as:

"FAO is the only source of comprehensive global fishery statistics and most reviews of the state of world fisheries, past trends and future prospects rely on FAO statistics. FAO analyses these statistics in order to monitor many aspects of world fisheries such as fishery production from capture fisheries and aquaculture, production and trade of fishery commodities, fish consumption, fishery fleets, and employment in fisheries. On the basis of these analyses, FAO prepares advice on fisheries policy to member countries."

FIDI maintains various databases relevant to these fields, based largely upon information inputs from member countries, and they are indeed widely used. The information currently collected is important. However, as already intimated, statistics for "production", "trade in commodities" (by which is largely meant international trade), "fleets" and "employment", whilst relevant, are not those areas of most direct relevance to sustainable livelihoods issues (especially for inland fisheries). "Food security" is more directly relevant but the current FAO statistics favour simplistic analysis at the national level based upon information on domestic supply (production, minus exports, plus imports).

The information strategy of FIDI "—— *aims to remove constraints relating to effective and efficient utilization of data and information for the sustainable contribution of aquaculture and fisheries to the food security and improved nutrition for all, thus helping the Member countries to address new and emerging challenges in the management and development of aquaculture and fisheries sectors."* Subsequent descriptions of activities, however, are not particularly focussed on sustainable livelihoods. Again from the stated strategy: *"The whole purpose of compilation and analysis of data and information is to put usable information in the hands of target users, thus facilitating problem solving and informed decisions and actions."*

It is not obvious that "sustainable livelihoods" related information is a priority requirement currently at FIDI. If it is, none of the fisheries departments in the countries covered in this review appear to be are aware of it.

A significant challenge for FAO and an important step in the new millennium, is whether it is able to respond rapidly to shifts in policy and emphasis by adjusting its information generation and dissemination activities to cater for these new needs. It will be constrained in doing so because many member countries themselves will have difficulties in shifting emphasis to more pro-poor, livelihoods oriented, information generation. But there is the opportunity for FAO to be pro-active and to start to request such information, and to member countries on how it can best be generated. Presently, alerting countries to this need is more important than obtaining the information itself.

"Sustainable Livelihoods" Approaches

All people interviewed in the countries visited are aware of the subject of "sustainable livelihoods" and why it is important in relation to inland capture fisheries. There is however considerable confusion over terminology. There is also widespread uncertainty as to how to incorporate such approaches into information and management systems, but full acknowledgement of the need to do so. Unsurprisingly, local communities, who have the relevant livelihoods most at risk, understand the concepts better than scientists or managers do. Sustainable livelihoods and co-management approaches therefore go well together, if not being the same thing. There are a number of frameworks or descriptions of livelihoods principles one of which is illustrated below (DFID-FAO, 2000).

SUSTAINABLE LIVELIHOODS FRAMEWORK

For anybody experienced in inland fisheries, such livelihood framework concepts are not new. We have, in fact, been arguing for such approaches, in differing ways, for a long-time. The frameworks do no more than formalise the setting of inland fisheries within rural livelihoods. And inland capture fisheries fit very nicely indeed into such a framework. The "livelihood outcomes", of management/development actions (see above) are exactly those most relevant to inland fisheries.

The promotion of sustainable livelihoods focused information does, however, present a number of challenges. Livelihood "capital" (human, natural, financial, social and physical; see above) can obviously vary according to circumstances. Some communities might, for example, have substantial financial capital (money), others less so but have more natural capital (natural resource assets, *e.g.* wetlands). It is obviously the combination of these assets that underpins livelihoods. However, it is quite legitimate to exchange different kinds of capital assets, provided the overall outcome is improved livelihoods.

For example, reduced reliance on natural assets is achievable if compensated by increased sustainable financial assets. This in effect is the argument put forward by many planners for decades regarding river fisheries; that is, that the natural assets of rivers should be stripped or re-allocated for the benefit of macro-economic growth (improved financial capital); degradation of the environment, and the fisheries along with it, was justified; damages were argued to be compensated for through reservoir fisheries and aquaculture. There is a certain simplistic superficial credibility to such a policy, but applying the above sustainable livelihoods framework would force those promoting it to justify their claims and to show that those incurring the impacts of river degradation were net beneficiaries of the developments causing it.

This trading of benefits of various forms of assets forces the inland capture fisheries sub-sector to adopt a more holistic position. For example, sometimes it is indeed logical to sacrifice fisheries for other benefits, provided it is planned and the livelihood outcome objectives are reached. But this has significant implications in terms of information requirements. That is, information on livelihoods and fisheries is only relevant in relation to information for other livelihoods assets. Therefore, fisheries information must not be generated independently. This requires all the various sectors to work together much better. Fortunately, the challenge is not as daunting as might be thought: First, most government agencies are, or should be, moving in the same directions regarding information. Second, co-management requires participation of the stakeholders in the processes; and the rural agrarian poor, generally, and particularly on floodplains, tend not to compartmentalise their livelihoods into sectors in the first place.

The biggest challenge, however, is to develop the tools with which to cost-effectively generate information (statistics) relevant to livelihood considerations. Some background to the kinds of information relevant to such policies is provided, for example, by DFID (1999 - and related information). For those without adequate access to such information an overview of information requirements is included in Annex I. Unsurprisingly, the information required to cover the full spectrum of livelihoods relevant considerations is substantial. However, those interested in improving livelihoods and poverty aspects of inland capture fisheries information should note the following:

(i) Nobody expects authorities to make sudden and drastic leaps towards these goals, it is more important in the short-term to recognise the needs than to meet them.

(ii) A gradual shift towards relevant information is logical, by identifying where opportunities exist and, where necessary, within existing information systems.

(iii) Fisheries related agencies would not be expected to produce the full spectrum of information; they would be working alongside others with similar goals, including other agencies, NGO's and local communities.

(iv) Fisheries related agencies may, in fact, not be required to produce the information at all. Requirements might be met by such agencies promoting others to generate the information. An appropriate role of fisheries agencies, in the long-term, could well be overseeing the information generation and compiling that part of it relevant to government statistics.

(v) It is not necessarily the case that existing information generating activities be abandoned (although priorities, methodologies and approaches should be reviewed - but that is necessary in any case).

But reviewing current literature and information will not help most agencies interested in such approaches to decide what to do in practice nor how to do it. Therefore, this review recommends that a priority is to produce guidelines (or provide direct technical assistance) to assist countries how to move their information generation activities, for inland fisheries or more broadly, towards livelihoods centred approaches.

Co-management and Information Generation

The move towards co-management approaches for fisheries offers significant opportunities to improve information generation. Information systems based upon catch reporting by fishers will always be unreliable as long as fishers and government officials are at odds with each other. In fact, it is largely because current information systems are extractive by nature that they are inherently unreliable. Effective co-management should improve confidence between fishers and government staff and along with it the willingness to divulge more accurate information. Not only does this obviously offer potential improvements in accuracy but it could well significantly reduce information generation costs (enabling government staff to focus on other aspects of information generation).

The current inland fishery statistics in Southeast Asia, in general, are notable for the apparent absence of links between the information and management. This does not encourage either government officials or fishers to take their generation seriously. What is required is for stake-holders to be able to recognise that the information that they provide results in benefits accruing to them, or to the broader community in which they live. Co-management and revenue generation are not incompatible and it is incorrect to assume that stakeholders are always unwilling to pay fees or taxes. They do however, expect to see benefits from it in return and making appropriate, and visible, links between revenue and benefits is not easy. Myanmar (see Part II) has shown that it can be done, even with complex river fisheries, by re-investing a substantial part of its revenue from lucrative lease fisheries back into visible improvements in the fishery. Others in Southeast Asia can learn from that example. But perceived links between revenue and information on catches may continue to be a problem for report-based statistics. Agencies should remove these links wherever possible.

Recommended Strategies

Strategies that might be adopted by particular countries will depend upon the extent of their current inland statistical systems and the degree to which they have specific requirements. Some countries, for example, have extensive licensing systems for their fisheries, which are coupled to information generation. For others, licensing requirements (if any) are separate. Each country will need to establish at what point it enters the level of considerations below and the need for restructuring.

Some of the following recommendations are low-cost activities that can be implemented immediately. Some may even reduce actual costs of information generation. But some will take much longer to implement (although do not necessarily involve significant costs).

(1) All countries should review their existing statistics based upon impartial desk-top appraisals using existing information.

This is the immediate priority and is by far the most important short-term task countries can undertake. It should be done more thoroughly and in a more systematic fashion by the appropriate agencies themselves. The re-assessment of information would also serve as a better basis for frame surveys for future data collection, or at least contribute to it. Consideration should be given to coupling this activity with a review and description of their inland capture fisheries sector. This would serve to inform relevant authorities (other agencies, donors etc.) of the features of inland fisheries, their extent and importance.

Very reasonable estimates of the importance of the sub-sector can be obtained using existing local information, comparative data from elsewhere and fishery independent information. In many cases, this can be done without the need for additional surveys. Inland fisheries can be described and estimated by a number of simple variables: the location, nature and area of the resources, population distributions (access to resources) and socio-economic variables.

Resource Areas

This information can be obtained from locally available maps. Some countries already have basic information on this, but it tends to be outdated and only general. Much more detailed, and recent information, can be obtained using remote sensing imagery which is already available in most countries (although not necessarily in Departments of Fisheries). Areas of wetlands, including reservoirs, lakes, river/stream systems, floodplains/swamps, rice-fields and coastal marshes and mangroves should be clearly located. It is particularly important to obtain accurate information on the location, extent and duration of flooding in river basins. The information should be kept in digital, geo-referenced format, so that it can be used in a GIS (Geographic Information System).

Population Distributions

Population census data should be compared with resource availability. Human populations, located nearby inland aquatic resources, translate into inland fisheries. The nature of the fishery will depend largely upon these two factors. If countries are lucky, their population census data will already be digitised and enable go-referencing. Once it is in that format it can be analysed in a GIS - enabling computer aided analysis of relationships between populations and resources. If the census data is not digitised or geo-referenced, it is a relatively simple task to put into this format. Disaggregated data on populations must be obtained. Summaries by district or province are usually not discrete enough but can be used as a last resort.

Socio-economic Considerations

These can usually be quite basic and are very much country specific. Some relevant factors are:

(i) *The level of economic development in areas.* Areas with better economic development tend to be less dependent upon inland capture fisheries. But care should be taken to use disaggregated data (average income, for example, is not necessarily the best indicator of the absence of poverty, or poorer communities).

(ii) *The level and kind of agricultural development.* Rice-farming for example usually has considerable fisheries activities associated with it, oil-palm less so.

(iii) *Access to markets.* This is important because fishery resources will be exploited only to the level of demand. Demand is not unlimited. Access to markets can usually be evaluated, for example, in relation to closeness and accessibility to urban areas.

(iv) *Ethnic, cultural or religious considerations.* Some ethnic groups (or religions) may be more or less dependent upon inland capture fisheries than others. In Southeast Asia, this consideration is usually only important in local areas.

Pollution and Habitat Degradation

Pollution as such is usually less of a problem than thought, except near urban or industrial areas. Heavy use of pesticides in farming should be accounted for (particularly in rice-fields) but it does not normally totally reduce fish production. An idea of the general level of habitat degradation should be obtained (but will usually already be known). The relationship between water quality and fish production can, however, be difficult to assess. It has to be severe to totally halt fish production. Actual habitat loss is often more important and information relating to this should be accounted as described in '*Resources areas*' above.

Once this information is compiled, it is relatively easy to apply certain relevant and reliable assumptions about the fisheries based upon local information and information from other similar areas. When doing this it is essential to favour information based upon impartial research and survey work where actual data are available. Making comparisons to other areas where information is based upon dubious or uncritical statistics is pointless (because most countries under-estimate or under-report).

Estimates for inland fisheries should not be limited to gross production. Particular attention should be given to obtaining indicative figures for livelihoods aspects of fisheries. It is usually possible, for example, to make rough estimates of the involvement of people in fishing (as well as processing, transportation, trade and gear construction etc.). Indicative figures for household dependencies on fishing are valuable.

This approach is guaranteed to provide a more reliable and representative estimate of inland capture fisheries than most of the statistical systems currently in place in Southeast Asia. The information will not necessary be of any use for monitoring trends, unless of course the approach is repeated at intervals and the information up-dated; but neither are most current statistics. Obtaining a reasonable idea of the base-line situation is the priority. The activity will also clarify, or form, the frame upon which other surveys are, or can be, based.

(2) Countries should incorporate improved and more accurate information into their current national statistics.

Obviously, improved assessments of the inland capture fisheries (as above and elsewhere) should be reflected in national statistics. Although the current statistics are often mistrusted, even sometimes ridiculed, they are important. They have a major impact on government policies and on donor perceptions. National statistics reported to FAO have the same impact on the international/global scale. It is important to correct them.

(3) Where necessary, countries should make significant efforts to explain the inadequacies of their current statistics to relevant parties

It is important that those that use inaccurate, unrepresentative or unsubstantiated statistics are made aware of the pitfalls of the information.

(4) Where appropriate, countries should endeavour to incorporate inland capture fisheries information (questions/surveys) into surveys done by other agencies.

Often fisheries departments have more limited resources for survey work than others (*e.g.* agriculture departments, statistics agencies). A great deal of very valuable information can be obtained by incorporating information requests into these other surveys.

Opportunities for questions can be limited in surveys designed for other purposes and time should be spent considering the most appropriate information. A priority is to get information on dependency upon fisheries. For example:

(i) In Lao PDR, a very reliable estimate of inland capture fisheries production was obtained by asking a very limited number of simple questions in a national income and expenditure survey.

(ii) In Myanmar, the mission advised the Department of Fisheries to incorporate some simple questions about rice-field fisheries into a proposed agriculture census (because the department's statistics did not cover rice-fields).

(5) Countries should promote more research on the production of, participation in and dependency upon inland capture fisheries.

Much progress can be made by using existing information from within Southeast Asia, but for full accuracy there is usually no substitute for specific data obtained for local situations. Research should be promoted amongst all relevant agencies (line-agencies, universities, aid projects, NGO's etc.). Researchers, and particularly social scientists, often need to be encouraged to produce quantitative data which enables extrapolations to be made to none surveyed areas. Research should focus upon quantifying dependency of households on inland capture fisheries and on the relationships between such dependency and the environment. Studies can be broadened to include "aquaculture" to investigate dependency on "aquatic resources" more generally. The latter is more appropriate but often better information on aquaculture is already available. Care has to be taken to avoid an aquaculture bias in such research and surveys (history has shown that aquaculture specialists can be remarkably uncritical in such surveys). Countries should focus the research on priority areas, which compliment existing national or regional information.

(6) Countries in Southeast Asia should share their information on inland fisheries and statistical/information systems

In all countries, human and financial resources are limited. Their inland fisheries also do not compete. There is little point in countries trying to re-invent the wheel in terms of research work. And there is much valuable information to share. For example, Lao PDR has some good experience and information now with fisheries in mountainous areas and using national surveys to obtain basic information on fisheries where there is limited information to start with. Cambodia has much experience in assessing the true nature and production of commercial/ industrial fisheries on floodplains (and small-scale fisheries), of considerable relevance to Myanmar in particular, but also Indonesia, Malaysia and VietNam. In Myanmar, there is much knowledge to share on enhancing lease fisheries (lots/Inns) relevant in particular to Cambodia but also others. All countries now have considerable cumulative information on rice-field fisheries and reservoirs. Most countries have undertaken extremely valuable local studies of river and swamp/floodplain fisheries. Sharing this information base is a fundamental part of improving overall assessments of inland fisheries (as recommended above). They also all have different systems for collecting the information and can share experiences on what works and what does not.

(7) Those countries with existing extensive inland capture fishery statistical systems should consider how best to improve them, without necessarily incurring significant additional costs.

This should include:

(i) Investigating the reduction of costs where feasible. Some countries arguably try to collect too much information

(ii) Re-allocation of survey effort. More emphasis should be placed on quality of information, not quantity. The existing human resources, for example, could perhaps be divided, each unit to focus better on smaller sections of the fishery. Some people could concentrate on rice-fields, some on reservoirs, some of floodplains, some on commercial gears etc. Trying to get the same people to collect all information (including in most cases for marine fisheries and aquaculture) will not encourage accuracy of the information.

(iii) A good baseline understanding (frame survey) of the fisheries is required as a starting point (see recommendation # 1). Sampling strategies (where they occur) should be re-assessed in the light of recommendation # 1 above.

(iv) Extensive reporting systems based upon the same individual personnel trying to cover everything will often result in selective reporting. Where too much is expected reports will tend to focus on the more visible activities (reservoirs, aquaculture or only the professional/commercial activities).

(8) Those countries currently with more limited statistics collection activities should be very careful about investing in improved systems based upon the models currently in place in other countries.

(i) There is no evidence that the current systems will necessarily yield accurate information, even if significantly up-graded (within reason)

(ii) Short-term donor funded investments in strengthening domestic capacities (manpower) are unlikely to be sustained (but technical assistance including training and improving communications and co-ordination may be appropriate)

(iii) Countries should be innovative and take the opportunity to adopt new and more appropriate approaches (some of these are outline here, more can be developed)

(9) Countries should recognise that as policies and priorities change; that the information requirements also change

(i) In particular, recent attention to pro-poor, livelihoods centred, policies and sustainable development and biodiversity issues require different information approaches

(ii) This represents an opportunity for countries to re-vitalise their statistical systems in response to these opportunities

(iii) There is in any case no evidence that, in general, the current type of information collected through statistics actually influences policies. In fact, the opposite appears to be the case. Therefore, the correct information is not being collected.

(10) Countries should focus on livelihoods related information in their statistics and information generation activities

(i) Information on gross production is still relevant and should be produced, as should ancillary existing information on licensing etc. where necessary and appropriate.

(ii) The true value of inland fisheries lies in their relevance to rural livelihoods. Information generation should reflect that.

(iii) Livelihoods based information is quite likely the only kind of information that will influence policies, particularly those relating to natural resources allocation and use (*e.g.* water resources management planning). It is certainly well proven that information based upon gross production and participation in licensed fisheries does not generally influence policies for the benefit of fisheries; at worst it may well reinforce inappropriate policies.

(11) Countries should amalgamate co-management approaches and the generation of fisheries information

(i) The accuracy and relevance of information can only be improved and sustained if stake holders are fully involved in the information process

(ii) Generally, and in the longer-term, fishery dependent communities or groups should be the main focus of information generation. They should be motivated and empowered to produce the necessary information. This will also reduce the costs of information generation (to fisheries departments).

(12) Countries should be more flexible in the way they treat and report their statistics

(i) Information systems are not currently based upon data. The information should therefore not be treated as data (*i.e.* taken at face value).

(ii) Where known errors or misrepresentations occur, these should be rectified at the reporting stage. This is more important, and much cheaper, than trying to improve the statistical basis of the reports themselves.

(13) Statistical and information systems should be reviewed, revised or developed with the full involvement of appropriate stakeholders at governmental level (i.e. appropriate statistical agencies)

(i) This is somewhat obvious. But there are examples where information relevant to statistics has been generated externally. It is subsequently often difficult to incorporate into existing statistical systems, even where motivation to do so exists.

(14) Existing statistical systems should be revised to make it easier to incorporate ancillary information into estimations and subsequent reports

(i) Currently, statistics are often produced with rigid methodologies (*e.g.* regular surveys undertaken by specific agencies). Subsequently it can be difficult to incorporate ancillary information that can improve the accuracy and relevance of the information, even when it is accepted as valid by the appropriate agencies.

(15) It should be widely and openly acknowledged that most existing statistics are not useful for monitoring trends in the fisheries

(i) They are currently not accurate enough to pick up anything but drastic changes.

(ii) Even if significantly improved (within reason) they will still likely not yield information of the quality required for trend analysis.

(iii) In any event, trends in production may not be the primary information required. Trends in livelihoods are more relevant (and current systems do not track this).

(iv) A significant issue related to this recommendation is that countries need to re-assess whether they need to collect the current kind of information every year. Why do it regularly if it is not accurate enough for time-series considerations? This question should be assessed on a case-by-case basis. But it is essential to ask it.

(16) Countries need to explore options for obtaining better information enabling trends to be tracked - using low-cost and sustainable methods

(i) The fisheries should be assessed to see which parts of it can be accurately, cost-effectively and sustainably monitored.

(ii) Countries should avoid trying to obtain accurate information (enabling trend monitoring on a year-by-year basis) for the entire fishery. It will not work and scarce resources would be better used in ensuring quality rather than quantity of data.

(iii) There is no substitute for long-term catch-effort data for assessing the state of fish stocks. But in multi-species, multi-gear inland fisheries, care must be taken in selecting which gears are monitored. It is important to record effort properly and the effort for many gears inland is influenced by environmental variables. For example, fishing "lots" ("Inns") and river bagnets offer easily accessible and relatively obvious gears to monitor, but their efficiency is influenced by environmental variables (extent of flooding, river flow rates) which must also be monitored. It is also not necessarily easy to get truthful catch reports. Care must be taken to avoid assuming that trends with any gears represent trends in the overall fishery; and covering all gears is near impossible. An option is to monitor selected gears on an annual (including daily, monthly, as appropriate) basis, together with less frequent, but broader reaching surveys that cover a wider range of fishers and gears.

(iv) Countries should not assume that monitoring fish stocks is the priority. It is important, but so are trends in livelihoods and the environment. Some would argue the latter to be more important. But where livelihoods information is linked to fish species groups and the environment (which it should be) then monitoring livelihoods trends should provide information on trends in stocks.

(17) Countries should devote more effort to monitoring trends in environment relevant to inland capture fisheries.

(i) Most commentators agree that the greatest threat to inland fisheries, especially riverine fisheries, is habitat loss and degradation. Most "trends" in these fisheries, and in biodiversity, are argued to be due to environmental influences. Therefore, it is essential to monitor these trends in the environment if trends in the fisheries are to be understood.

(ii) This is arguably more important than trying to monitor the fisheries themselves. A strong case can be put for river fisheries that as long as the environment stays intact, the fisheries might be sustained. Most river fisheries have been lost not because we did not monitor them properly, but because the environment that supports them was undermined and at least in part because it was not monitored.

(iii) Whilst this may not appear immediately to be the role of fisheries agencies, and in some countries may not be, those agencies must become more pro-active in promoting appropriate environmental monitoring.

(iv) Where necessary, environmental agencies need to be made more aware of which environmental changes are relevant to inland fisheries. In particular, aquatic specialists may tend to focus on water quality issues, whilst the major issues (particularly for larger rivers) can be habitat loss and degradation.

(v) Inland fisheries specialists must adopt the philosophy that environmental management is an important part of fisheries management.

(18) Countries need to adopt better strategies for monitoring trends in biodiversity

(i) Biodiversity is a fisheries issue (Coates, 2001). Countries need to explore how biodiversity in their inland fisheries can be better monitored. Naturally this should be done in conjunction with other initiatives in this area. Monitoring biodiversity should incorporate the same concepts as for other information (statistics) collection systems. Ecosystem diversity should be monitored as noted under recommendation 17. Cultural and social diversity should be monitored through livelihoods monitoring. The role of fisheries agencies should include advising other agencies on aspects of biodiversity relevant to fisheries. An obvious problem in practice with genetic diversity is that concerns tend to become greater as species (or varieties etc.) become rarer. One option is for countries to short-list their most vulnerable genetic resources and implement monitoring programmes for them - using fisheries based information collection systems where appropriate (*e.g.* catch-effort data for selected species).

(19) The current statistics for inland capture fisheries produced by FAO should include better indications as to their basis and meaning

(i) Inland capture fishery statistics are likely to be more unreliable than any other statistics that FAO reports.

(ii) The general tendency is for under-reporting.

(iii) Statistics should not be published in the absence of details as to how they were collected. This should include explanation as to likely sources of error and possible extent of under-reporting. It is not unreasonable, for example, to suggest that FAO include such a by-country explanation in its yearbooks of inland fisheries.

(iv) Statistics that have been based upon estimates should be clearly indicated in both yearbooks and FAO reports. This would also include an indication as to the basis of the estimations. This requires both that countries report such information to FAO and that FAO requests it.

(20) The information and statistics activities at FAO should reflect the requirements for improved livelihoods related information more obviously and explicitly

(i) This can be achieved by FAO requesting better livelihoods focussed information on fisheries.

(ii) Alerting countries to this need is an urgent priority.

(21) FAO should provide improved advice to member nations on what kinds of livelihoods relevant information should be collected and how it can be cost-effectively obtained

(i) For inland capture fisheries there is a need to back-up the broad recommendations made in this report (with emphasis on the deriving information on the role of fisheries and livelihoods) with specific and practical advice on how to implement.

(ii) Logically, this might be better implemented as a compliment to a broader based strategy regarding livelihoods information.

4

Inland Capture Fishery Statistics in Asia

In most countries where information is actually collected, the process originates at district/sub-district level. Often, the only way to fully investigate the statistical validity of such an information system is to review activities at that level. The travel schedule of the mission did not allow this. This report is therefore based upon information obtained primarily in head offices and analyses of the officially reported statistics. This is sufficient for the purposes of this general review, which concentrates on information gaps and needs at the planning and management levels. It should be followed by more in-depth reviews of the national statistical and information systems by the appropriate authorities in the proposed follow-on activities (including a proposed regional TCP on Addressing the Quality of Information on Inland Fisheries, AQUIIF).

The mission visited four countries as part of the current assignment (Indonesia, Malaysia, Myanmar, and Thailand). A fifth (the Philippines) was visited as part of the AQUIIF formulation mission and more brief details of the inland capture fishery statistics have been incorporated into this report as an addendum from that mission. In addition, the mission has recent experience with inland fisheries data in three others (Cambodia, Lao PDR and VietNam).

COUNTRIES VISITED AS PART OF THE MISSION

INDONESIA

Indonesia is a very diverse country. The nation includes several islands with significant land mass, high rainfall and, consequently, has significant freshwater resources, especially rivers. Particular mention can be made of Sumatra (which has several good sized rivers), Kalimantan ("Borneo"; which includes the Kapuas and Mahakam Rivers both of which are large by world standards, plus several others), Sulawesi and Irian Jaya. The latter is the eastern half of the world's largest tropical island, New Guinea, which has the large Idenburg/Mamberamo system in the north, equivalent to either the Fly or Sepik Rivers in Papua New Guinea, and several other decent sized systems to the south. Although inland waters in parts of Indonesia are reported to be suffering from severe environmental stress, good inland fisheries are known to still occur, particularly on Kalimantan and the mid to southern region of eastern Sumatra. The least environmental degradation likely occurs in Irian Jaya, partly due to lower population pressures there.

A notable feature of Indonesia is that the islands cover two of the word's most prominent zoogeographic zones separated at "Wallace's Line" running roughly north-east to south-west between Sulawesi and Kalimantan. East of this line (notably New Guinea), primary freshwater fishes, for example carps (cyprinids), do not naturally occur and the depauperate nature of the fish fauna limits biological production (Coates, 1985; 1993); although a large number of species have now been introduced into that area. Inland fisheries in Irian Jaya are significantly different from the rest of Indonesia (especially Sumatra and Kalimantan) but fortunately, for current purposes, valid comparisons can be made with fisheries in the eastern half of the island (Papua New Guinea).

The licensing requirements for inland fisheries vary widely between provinces and districts. In general licenses are officially required for the more commercial gears but compliance (and surveillance) may be reduced beyond Java. Access to prime fishing opportunities (either by sites for major gears or by demarcated areas) is often allocated by auction systems. This is especially so for the major opportunities (or areas) on river floodplains. The system is similar to the "lot" system of Cambodia and the "Inn" system of Myanmar. Auction income can provide an important source of revenue for government agencies (up to 75 percent of income in some areas, for example, southern Sumatra). Auction systems are widespread on Kalimantan but tend to be more village based. They are traditionally absent on Irian Jaya because of the resource base limits the partitioning of exploitation in this fashion.

Fisheries associations are common in inland areas, especially for reservoirs. Fishing competitions are popular (using hook and line). This fledgling recreational/sport fisheries sub-sector appears to be growing rapidly.

Most commentators agree that a major requirement for inland waters is improved environmental management but that a major constraint to achieving this is limited co-ordination between the various agencies involved.

Indonesia has no significant national management policies or strategies for its inland capture fisheries excepting a general policy of sustaining the resources. There are many localised activities, such as stocking, which can be widespread and significant, especially in reservoirs. A substantial degree of survey work and/or research has been done in localised areas (southern Sumatra, Kalimantan). The country includes some of the best studied freshwater fisheries in Asia although, as usual, the mission found it difficult to obtain published information on fisheries production based on empirical survey data.

The Directorate General of Capture Fisheries has a stated policy to emphasise co-management approaches within a national policy promoting the increasing role of local communities in managing areas.

The Statistical Collection System

Previously, "freshwater" and "brackishwater" fisheries were jointly covered under an inland fisheries section. Now there are separate divisions for marine, freshwater and brackishwater fisheries. Production from inland brackishwaters is still included under inland production statistics. The definition of "inland" is problematic locally but this is thought not a serious problem with the statistics. The definition of aquaculture is more of a problem (ref. how to treat production from extensive stocking). In Indonesia, the term "inland fisheries" includes both aquaculture and capture fisheries activities (the latter sub-sector is referred to locally as "inland open water fisheries").

Indonesia has a very elaborate fishery statistical collection system involving a large amount of manpower and information collection based upon a structured sampling approach applied nationally but implemented at provincial and district levels. Sampling approaches are based on earlier designs with significant inputs from FAO (as is the national statistical systems for agriculture/forestry/fisheries at large). Recently, modified sampling strategies and forms for inland areas have been introduced based upon experiences from a JICA aquaculture project. Statistics are compiled at district level with actual information collection being accomplished through staff at sub-district level. District officers report the information to provincial offices, which compile it and forward it to the Sub-Directorate for Data and Statistics within the Directorate General of Capture Fisheries (DGCF) in Jakarta. From there it is forwarded to the National BPS Statistics Indonesia and to FAO. DGCF Jakarta is largely responsible for determining the content of the statistics themselves.

Three types of forms are used. Those prefixed "S" for actual field surveys, "E" for estimations based upon the surveys (*i.e.* from "S" forms), and "L" for reporting the figures (derived from estimates, "E" forms) to the central office.

Sample villages are determined by staff at district level as are the households sampled within sample villages. Ostensibly, selection of sample villages is based upon a previous frame survey with households being selected at random. The *SP1* form covering inland open water fisheries provides a list of every household in sample villages and details of all vessel types held by the households, including no-vessel households, and the total number of fishing units by gear type. The list of gear types naturally favours the more commercial gears and/or those requiring licenses. Information on *SP1* forms is recorded by quarter (3 months) but the actual survey is reportedly undertaken only once a year. Between 3 and 5 households in each village sampled are then surveyed using *SP2* forms. *SP2* attempts to obtain production by household based on numbers of trips and average catches per gear type per trip (*i.e.* catch-effort sampling based on reported catches by gear type). Information is collected for each month but surveys are reportedly done every three months.

Species composition and estimated values of the catches are also recorded. Information is also collected by habitat type where the fishing occurred: "river, lake, reservoir or swamp". This requires a separate *SP2* to be completed in each household for each habitat type where fishing occurs by that household (although it is reported that sample villages are often selected based upon habitat criteria, the basis of which is unclear). Information from *SP2* forms is then entered directly onto E forms from which point estimates begin to be derived based upon information from *SP2's* in relation to sample sizes etc. derived mainly from *SP1s.* Various known raising factors are applied to the original information to obtain estimates. *EP1* estimates from *SP1* the number of households, boats and fishing gears etc. *EP2* estimates total production by vessel, gear type, species and by habitat type (from *SP2* forms). *EP3* estimates the value of catch by habitat type (from *SP2*). An *EP4* form is specifically designed to estimate the nature of disposal of the reported catch and information is collected by species (Part 1 covering weight of fresh fish, Part 2 - weight of preserved products). *SP1* and *SP2* do not contain information on disposal. *EP4* information is based upon a separate estimation process, which in theory involves discussion with the sample groups. At all levels, the information recorded is officially based upon reports by households and/or fishers (presumably biased towards the latter). At no time does the survey method measure any production (etc.) directly.

The current system is labour-intensive also at the level of information compilation, analysis and reporting. DGCF Jakarta intend to computerise the system to streamline the operations including using appropriate statistical software.

A comprehensive annual fishery statistics bulletin is produced. At the time of drafting this report the latest available was for 1998. Figures for 1999 have now been produced.

There are a number of constraints with this system:

(1) *The sampling frame.* The original frame survey upon which the current sampling strategy is based originates from an agricultural frame survey done in 1973, which apart from now being 28 years out of date, likely did not cover inland fisheries considerations anyway. Although household based sampling surveys are generally a good approach for inland fisheries, it is unclear for example, how the system covers those gears which are not owned by the household (*e.g.* some very productive gears can be leased or owned communally). The mission did not have time to investigate the sampling strategy in detail (the strategy is implemented at district/sub district level) and cannot currently make valid detailed comments on how the strategy might be improved. To do so would require a much more substantial study. It can be concluded, however, that there are serious doubts about the statistical validity of the official sampling programme in relation to inland fisheries (a point well acknowledged by DGCF themselves).

(2) It was reported that the information required is comprehensive but complex and time consuming. The most serious problem reported by DGCF Jakarta was insufficient manpower (budget) to undertake surveys properly. Each district has only one staff assigned to statistics. Each sub-district (where information is actually collected) usually has only one person assigned to statistics collection part-time (their duties also include *e.g.* extension work, licensing/surveillance duties etc.). Where appropriate, these staff are expected to collect statistics for marine, open water inland fisheries and aquaculture. Not surprisingly, it was reported that sub-districts will often (usually?) complete the *L* forms (reporting forms) without undertaking surveys (using *S* forms). District offices may also do this on behalf of sub-districts.

(3) The survey design is based upon the application of a system and strategy developed for marine fisheries, which is applied to inland areas. The emphasis in the forms to recording vessel types and gears represents these origins in design (although in theory the surveys include households without vessels). There are serious doubts about whether surveys of this nature based upon trying to record catches through estimating effort and catch per unit of effort are, in general, suitable for inland fisheries. Although it may be valid for certain prominent gears, the approach is problematic for more informal and dispersed fishing activities. It is also unclear how the survey technique was "improved" through experiences with aquaculture. Whilst considerable overlap between culture and capture tends to occur, in most river basins there tends to be an important geographic separation between the two. For example, aquaculture tends to be more important in areas where inland fisheries are less so; for example, away from floodplains (primarily because aquaculture, in general, cannot compete with productive inland fisheries).

(4) In common with all systems based upon reporting, the information provided by respondents will depend upon (a) the willingness to be truthful, and where there is an actual or perceived link between information and licensing/regulation it is realistic to expect under-reporting; and (b) even if motivated to be truthful, the ability of the respondent to accurately estimate

actual production; the sampling strategy requires a three-month recall by respondents, more importantly, for household based surveys for inland fisheries, key respondents (*e.g.* household heads or main fishers) have been shown to seriously underestimate household production as they tend to report only their own catch and can be unaware of other catches in the household (Sjørslev, 2000; 2001).

The Information Produced

There is an apparent peak in the years 1994-6. However, given the known natural variations between years in inland capture fisheries, based on this information there is no evidence that production has declined over the 10 year period in question. A relatively high gross production (for Southeast Asia) is reported but this is consistent with the high population and extensive freshwater resources. There is no apparent trend in species composition of catches except that "others" (= mainly freshwater fishes not elsewhere included in FAO Statistics) apparently account for most of the aforementioned increase in reported gross production over the period 1994-6. The large proportion of the catch being recorded as miscellaneous is a common constraint in inland capture fishery statistics. Amongst other problems, the information is effectively useless for analysing trends in vulnerable/rare species.

Again, obvious trends are absent. Not much can be made of this information except that most production arising from "other" gear types is likely typical of inland fisheries where normally a huge variety of gears are in operation. It is odd that set gill nets and hook and line, each account for a higher proportion of catches than guiding barriers (barrage fences). On river floodplains, the latter gears are normally very efficient and produce high catches. However, the most productive of such gears are usually associated with stringent licensing and revenue collection systems where under-reporting of production is likely common (if not universal). There may also be a bias in the information towards reports from reservoirs and lakes (which would also account for the dominance of production from gillnets).

The high catches from guiding barriers are also evident from Table 1 but the reported catch per gear is still only about 4 or 8 times that from gillnets and hook and line respectively. The mission would expect catches per gear to be relatively much higher for guiding barriers. Hoggarth *et al* (1999) report that such barriers account for 49 percent of the catch from an Indonesian river. Also, the mission considers that the mean catches reported per gear are high for many of the other gears. If the reports represent actual catches, this is quite possibly because there is a reporting bias towards commercial/professional fishers.

For example, an average annual catch per gillnet of about 450 kg for a professional fisherman is reasonable but as a mean catch per gear perhaps less so (since there are likely a large number of gillnets in only part-time use).

However, the best illustration of peculiarities in the reports is the extremely high catch per gear under "other gears" which is the fifth highest ranked gear by production per unit and rivals that of gillnets; it is also higher than the mean catch per gear for all gears combined (meaning the majority of gears have a mean catch lower than that for "others"). The majority of gears under the category "others" for tropical inland fisheries should include a myriad of small gears in intermittent, low-profile use (for example, millions of small basket traps in rice fields catching only a few kilograms per year). Even if some individual gears do produce large catches, the mean catch per gear unit should be relatively low.

Table 1 Indonesian inland open water fisheries - mean catches per gear (1998)

	Number of gears	Total catch (kg)	mean catch per gear (kg/yr)
TOTAL	678 826	288 666 000	425.2
Drift gill nets	36 014	16 229 000	450.6
Set gill nets	85 350	59 046 000	691.8
portable lift net	29 642	9 414 000	317.6
scoop nets	41 304	11 292 000	273.4
long lines	35 211	11 979 000	340.2
hand lines	161 783	311 96 000	192.8
guiding barrier	20 395	333 26 000	1 634.0
stow nets	9 304	91 22 000	980.4
portable traps	102 314	40 037 000	391.3
others	157 509	67 024 000	425.5

One possible explanation for high unit catches for "other" gears is that production comes from a productive (per unit) gear type(s) but the gear type(s) is not listed elsewhere (if so, it should obviously be listed separately). Even so, this explanation would require that the large number of small, less productive, gears is not recorded under "other". Again, the reports, if meaningful, could be biased towards commercial/ professional catches. Such problems may be significant because the gear category "others" accounts for roughly 25 percent of the reported total catch. Much would depend upon the methods applied in the field and an analysis of disaggregated catches within the category "other" gears. For example, there would be a serious error if the data for availability of "other gears" (or by disaggregated category if applicable) were not collected on SP1 forms (*i.e.* it is necessary to know within the population sampled what is the overall ownership of "other gears").

It is unlikely the category "others" is uniform throughout the country. These examples illustrate the difficulties, and some possible pit-falls, of attempting to estimate inland capture fisheries production based solely on catch-effort data, particularly in the absence of a good frame survey.

Reports for production are available by province. These also show no consistent trend over the last ten years. However, analysis of reported production over a one year cycle provides information. Inland capture fisheries in rivers in the tropics should show gross seasonal changes in production related to river flood cycles (see notes for Cambodia and Myanmar). Whilst there is much variation in reported production within years in some provinces, there is little consistency between them.

For purposes of illustration, the annual cycles of reported fish production for all provinces where river and swamp fisheries account for more than 75 percent of total production (the remainder coming from lakes/reservoirs) that is for those provinces expected to have the most seasonally variable fisheries. Three of the seven provinces show flat lines. In the others, variations occur but they are not consistent between provinces (they should be because all provinces have approximately the same seasons) and do not relate to monsoon river hydrological cycles. The absence of consistent natural cycles in these reports raises serious doubts as to the validity of the underlying information. Reports on numbers of fishermen per fishing household make very interesting reading. It is not certain whether reports are gender biased or whether the term "fishermen" includes women and children fishing. There is some logic in the figures in that provinces with probably more important inland capture fisheries have a higher mean number of fishermen per household. What is surprising is that a large number of provinces have a mean of less than one fisherman per fishing household (which is impossible; unless fishing households include households with no fishers). For other provinces the mean number of fishermen per household seems rather large, even for inland capture fisheries. Whilst it is not uncommon for all members of households to be involved in fishing, the mean number of fishermen in households in Sumatra Selatan, for example, is 6.5 compared with a mean provincial household size of 4.6 (BPS, 2000). For Kalimantan Barat and Kalimantan Timur, mean number of fishermen approximately equals mean household size (which has a national mean of 3.9 with a range from 3.4 to 5.0 by province, BPS, 2000).

As might be expected in inland capture fisheries, households with non-powered boats greatly outnumber those with motorised vessels. Reports suggest that part-time fishers outnumber full-time fishers by a factor of about 2, which is logical for inland capture fisheries, although possibly still an underestimate of part-time fishers. It is unlikely that fishing in rice-fields or small water-bodies/canals/streams etc. on an infrequent basis is included in these reports. If it were, we would expect the number of part-time fishers to vastly outnumber full-time fishers.

First, there should be a trend in all these reports showing an increase in households involved in fishing, total numbers of vessels and gears in operation and total numbers of fishers due to population growth over the 10 year period (about 15 percent, BPS 2000). Second, there should be a clear increase in all these reports as a result of the "Asian Economic Crisis" (early 1997) which was accompanied by a significant return to fishing as a low capital activity, accompanied with emigration from urban areas. Several reliable commentators in Indonesia confirmed that in inland areas participation in fishing increased by an estimated 30-40 percent as a result of the economic down-turn. But this is nowhere to be seen in the reports. However, both the long-term trend in participation in marine fisheries due to population growth, and the more rapid increase expected in 1997/8 are clearly evident for reports for marine capture fisheries. Not only does this analysis reinforce the view that the reports for inland capture fisheries are unreliable, the latter observation suggests that the reports are much more meaningful for marine fisheries.

Table 2 Total fish consumption (from fish consumption surveys, BPS 1999) compared with reported catches from inland capture fisheries for selected provinces in Indonesia

	Total population	Reported production from inland capture fisheries MT (1998)	Total fish consumption (kg/caput/yr) Urban areas	Total fish consumption (kg/caput/yr) Rural areas	Estimate total fish consumed (MT)	% of consumption arising from reported inland catches
Sumatera Utara	11 476 000	6 979	19.9	18.7	229 520	3.05
Sumatera Barat	4 228 000	6 651	10.6	10.4	44 394	15.0
Riau	4 734 000	12 488	18.9	19.2	89 946	13.9
Jambi	2 401 000	5 287	12.0	11.5	28 091	18.8
Sumatera Selatan	7 756 000	45 523	10.3	11.5	77 560	58.7
Bengkulu	1 405 000	3 359	10.9	11.0	15 314	21.9
Lampung	6 654 000	6 078	8.4	8.1	54 562	11.1
Kalimantan Barat	3 740 000	10 969	21.0	14.6	63 580	17.3
Kalimantan Tengah	1 801 000	34 524	18.7	20.2	36 020	95.8
Kalimantan Selatan	2 970 000	56 494	20.0	18.6	59 400	95.1
Kalimantan Timur	2 436 000	16 240	18.6	16.4	48 720	33.3
Sulawesi Utara	2 821 000	528	25.8	23.6	67 704	0.8
Sulawesi Tengah	2 066 000	366	22.1	16.0	39 354	0.9
Sulawesi Selatan	7 787 000	25 570	20.3	24.7	171 314	14.9
Sulawesi Tenggara	1 772 000	7 974	30.7	25.6	49 616	16.1
Irian Jaya	2 113 000	2 582	26.6	12.8	31 695	8.1

Data from fish consumption surveys are available (BPS, 1999). Total fish consumption estimates for various provinces are shown in Table 2 together with reported landings from inland capture fisheries. These comparisons are useful as a rough and independent test of the reported catch figures. Fish consumed, of course, can include that from any source (imported, marine, inland capture or aquaculture). But in freshwater resource rich areas with large rural populations, contributions from inland capture fisheries should make the major contribution to fish consumed locally. This is partly reflected in the information for Kalimantan Tengah and Kalimantan Selatan where reported inland catch accounts for more than 95 percent of fish consumed locally.

However, it is unclear why the contribution of inland catches to consumption should be drastically lower in Kalimantan Timur and especially Kalimantan Barat (Kapuas River system). Similarly, for the Sumatera region, Sumatera Selatan has a reasonable contribution from inland capture of 58.7 percent of fish consumed but it is unclear why Riau and Jambi, for example, have significantly lower contributions at 13.9 and 18.8 percent respectively. Production figures for inland capture for Sulawesi would appear to be particularly low in relation to fish consumed. Unfortunately, for these figures, it is not known which reported catches (at provincial level) are the most representative, if any. It is also likely that the fish consumption estimates (BPS, 1999) are also underestimates since the FAO figure for per caput fish supply for Indonesia (based on production statistics and export/import figures) is about 16.3 kg/caput/year, and this is without allowing for under-reporting of inland catches, compared to the national average fish consumption per caput of 10.5 kg/caput/yr from the BPS reported survey.

Table 3 Indonesian a rea and potential fish yield of open waters (from Sarnita and Djajadiredja, 1968)

Island	Area (ha)	Potential yield (MT per annum)
Java	96 400	30 000 - 35 000
Sumatra	4 053 850	300 000 - 330 000
Bali and Nusa Tenggara	17500	7 000 - 10 000
Kalimantan	9 029 000	400 000 - 450 000
Sulawesi	492 200	50 000 - 55 000
Maluku and Irian Jaya	63 300	13 000 - 20 000
Total	13 752 250	800 000 - 900 000

It is likely that the inland capture figures are affected by overall under-reporting. But the extent of this is difficult to assess. The figures for Irian Jaya are certainly an under-estimate. This province has similar characteristics to Papua New Guinea where inland capture production is estimated (based upon extrapolations from sampling survey data) to be 14 500 MT per annum. Correcting for differences in populations, this would give an estimate of about 6 000 MT per annum (2.3 times the official figure). It is highly likely that the existing reports refer mainly to less remote areas and in particular to Lake Sentani near Jayapura.

Table 3 provides some estimates of the potential production from inland waters in Indonesia. The estimated potential averages about 65 kg/ha/yr which is likely on the low side, especially for heavily fished floodplains.

Even so, the estimates support the view that production from inland capture fisheries is likely, and is feasibly, much higher than official reports suggest. A proper analysis along these lines would need to factor in the effects of environmental degradation on inland waters.

Perceptions of Inland Fisheries and Objectives of the Statistics

It is no secret in Indonesia that there is limited confidence in the statistics for inland open water (capture) fisheries. The mission was impressed by both the frankness of authorities concerning this issue and the genuine desire to try to improve the situation. The issues are complex because quite probably the reports are meaningful (possibly even representative) in some areas but meaningless in others. But this is unhelpful unless we know for certain which is which.

In common with other countries, Indonesian authorities clearly see inland open water fisheries as being important for food security, nutrition, poverty alleviation in rural areas (etc.); although some impressive commercial/industrial inland capture fisheries occur. They also regard environmental degradation etc., together with sustaining biodiversity in freshwaters, to be major issues but possibly ones for which solutions are largely beyond their control. Aquaculture development is regarded as having a major negative impact on inland capture fisheries. The need for improved co-management approaches for fisheries and environmental management is well recognised.

According to DGCF (2000), the purpose of the fishery statistics for Indonesia is *"primarily to provide fishery statistics for the planning of fishery development programmes, evaluation of the progress of fishery development, and stock assessment of fishery resources. However, this book should be of great value also to readers who wish to obtain a picture of the present status of Indonesia fisheries by means of statistics"*. But it is difficult to see how the current statistics for inland open water fisheries help achieve these objectives. In fact, by being unable to reflect trends, and thereby intimating there is none, they may be counter-productive in terms of these aims. Although those familiar with the statistics are unlikely to rely unduly upon them, there are those less familiar who do.

Conclusions and Recommendations

The Indonesia inland capture fishery statistical system essentially suffers from the application of methods promoted for marine fisheries. More recently, perhaps equally inappropriately, the system has been fine-tuned even further by applying techniques from aquaculture statistics. This history begs the question of whether anybody ever attempted to develop a system designed from the outset for inland waters.

Because of its history, the system is focussed on essentially a catch-effort based approached attempting to calculate, via report sampling, landings based upon knowledge of gears in use, the effort for each gear and catches per unit of effort. In itself, this is not illogical, since all fish are caught through fishing effort. The question is not whether the approach is technically valid but whether it is cost-effective and viable. One clear conclusion from Indonesia is that it probably is neither.

The problem with gear based catch-effort approaches in inland waters include: (i) a tendency to under-report for most of the more productive gears (especially where fees are levied, formally or informally), (ii) the complexities and varieties of gear in use and resulting problems in defining effort for most, (iii) usually larger areas need to be surveyed (in comparison with marine fisheries - where fishing grounds may be bigger but activities are more visible and landing sites are more concentrated), (iv) the lower profile of inland fisheries which tends to reduce investment in and motivation for statistics collection (partly because the statistics themselves do not reinforce the need for investment), and (v) the related problem that inland capture fisheries occur in the same regions (inland) where much aquaculture production arises; normally, where government resources are shared with aquaculture, the latter sub-sector tends to get more attention. This does not mean that gear-based catch effort approaches are not valid for some parts of the fishery. There are clear examples of where the approach might be justified.

The DGCF in Indonesia has already identified that investment in computerising the statistical system will yield rewards in terms of increased efficiency of information compilation, analysis and reporting. The mission agrees. There would appear to also be some opportunities for utilising specialist fishery statistics software (an area in which the mission does not claim expertise). But, importantly, improving this aspect of the statistical system will not improve the quality (validity) of the underlying information. For inland open waters, it will be interesting to see what impact computerisation has. If some districts/sub-districts do actually generate information without sampling (as is thought likely), then computerisation may force them to generate the information at a lower level (*i.e.* invent actual sampling data). This could be worse.

There are essentially two broad options for improving the relevance of the information collected via the current system: (i) modify the system with a view to obtaining less information but of a higher quality, in particular by sub-dividing the fishery and applying more focussed sampling to each sub-sector (this requires a decent frame survey); and (ii) make higher investments in the overall system (especially increasing the manpower available, and motivation, at sub-district level etc.). Naturally, the Sub-Directorate for Data and Statistics favours the latter. Although the mission is not against such investments in general, it recommends caution before they are made because: (i) there are doubts if substantial investment in the current system would improve the quality of the information (for technical reasons and others outlined here), and (ii) even if it were achieved it may well generate information that is not entirely in-tine with development and management objectives.

Improving the specific design of the Indonesian survey methodology is beyond the scope of the current report. That will require considerably more inputs and familiarity with the current system. But some general observations/suggestions can be made. One obvious requirement is to improve the frame survey upon which the actual sampling system is based (a point well known to DGCF already). Without that, further investments in the current system may be inappropriate in any case. It is critical that such a survey be designed specifically to cater for the characteristics of the inland fisheries sector. It should provide, for example, comprehensive details of the distribution, seasonality, locations (habitats), methods and timing of deployment, labour requirements etc. for all major fishing gears. The objective should include identifying those gears operating beyond the household level (*e.g.* communally, by industrial operations, operators from beyond the sample area etc.) or those highly productive gears used in low numbers that might bias household surveys conducted at random. Obviously, information on these larger gears might be obtained through statistically valid sampling based upon frame survey guidelines based upon modified catch-effort approaches.

For the multitude of smaller gears the household sampling approach is very appropriate. It is debatable, however, if estimates of household production should rely on gear based catch-effort approaches. In the mission's experience, the most practical approach for small-scale fisheries is to have the household itself as the defined unit of effort. With this approach, it makes no difference how the households catch the fish. Basically, household's catches can be assessed by summating individual household members' catches (including women and children). Meaningful information on this is not easy to collect and care has to be taken in survey design; questionnaires need to prompt household members on various aspects of potential fisheries activities. But it is no less accurate than asking how much was caught by particular gears and the problems analysing the resulting information are considerably reduced. It may still be useful to gather gear-effort information but it is not essential for the estimation of household catches. Information on gears used is also required to determine or interpret a sampling strategy (particularly where random sampling picks up a low-frequency household using a more productive gear). Care has to be taken when sampling households to obtain information representative of the household as a whole. It is important to include the activities of women and children and persons who are not regarded, or do not regard themselves, as "fishers".

The most important need for Indonesia, which is in common with the other Southeast Asian countries, is to re-assess the objectives and requirements for information on inland open water fisheries in relation to the general discussion. There are opportunities for making cost-effective improvements to the current system but it is strongly recommended that this be considered within this much broader framework.

Regarding estimates of the likely production from inland capture fisheries in Indonesia, the most relevant conclusion is that, despite the considerable effort in statistics collection, the answer to that question remains elusive. In addition to doubts about the actual sources of current estimates, the sampling methods will promote under-reporting from the major gears (possibly also for minor ones), almost certainly do not include production from small/informal fishing activities (which cumulatively can be significant) and the sampling frame underlying the whole process likely under-represents inland capture fisheries (probably being more focussed on agriculture and aquaculture considerations). Estimating actual current production is speculative (but so are the current statistics). But based upon the aforementioned considerations and analysis, freshwater resources (although severely degraded in many areas) and inferences from similar fisheries elsewhere (see other sections of this report) it is not unrealistic to suggest that production is at least twice the currently reported level. Guidelines on how to cost-effectively undertake such estimates properly are provided in Part I. But doubling the production estimate does not double the reported value of the fishery. To assess that, better information on the levels of dependency on inland open water fisheries is required.

MALAYSIA

Malaysia is one of the more affluent of the countries in Southeast Asia and therefore, as expected, has a more efficient and effective infrastructure than most. There are, however, major differences between peninsular Malaysia and the distant States of Sarawak and Sabah. The latter account for about half of the total land area of the country but only about 20 percent of the total population. The latter States are the poorest in terms of economic development but both have good freshwater resources including several medium to large sized rivers. Water resources on Peninsular Malaysia are heavily impounded and there are large numbers of ex-mining pools or dams.

Malaysia is notable within the countries surveyed for having the most advanced facilities for remote sensing and GIS. The Malaysian Centre for Remote Sensing (MACRES) is an impressive facility available both nationally and regionally. Currently, fisheries applications at this facility are limited to costal zones, particularly aquaculture mapping and planning.

The Statistical Collection System

Administratively, Malaysia is divided into States (provinces) each divided into clearly demarcated districts, including for inland areas. The State Department of Fisheries has in each district a permanently employed officer who is responsible for compiling statistics (amongst other things). These officers are responsible for compiling statistics for marine capture fisheries, aquaculture and inland capture fisheries. Each district officer reports to the State DOF who then reports to the Federal DOF (Kuala Lumpur) where the statistics are compiled. The Federal DOF has a relatively high degree of control and influence over State DOFs. A good State/district infrastructure exists. Federal DOF has a high degree of confidence in the staff involved and considers them to be comparatively well trained. Training activities continue to upgrade/update skills. Exceptions to this are primarily the large States of Sabah and Sarawak, and likely some minor islands. Here infrastructure is more limited. The problem is compounded by inland capture fisheries and freshwater aquaculture in Sarawak being under the Department of Agriculture. As far as is known, there is basically no effective reporting system for inland capture fisheries for these two States (but time did not allow this to be checked). This is important because these areas have the lowest level of development and the highest availability of inland fishery resources and, hence, are expected to have the biggest inland fisheries.

A special budget appropriation for fishery statistics is made. Annual and comprehensive Fishery statistics are published. District officers "estimate" inland capture fisheries on a monthly basis. The method of estimation involves "visual market surveys, enquiries and observation" but no formal reporting or sampling. In theory, estimates are made by production system: river, ex-mining pools (of which there are numerous), embankments/reservoirs/dams, and others. Estimates are disaggregated (in districts) by species (28 categories included in monthly reports).

Marine capture fishery, and aquaculture, statistics are collected with the same infrastructure and largely by the same personnel. In contrast, to inland capture statistics, those for the marine fisheries and aquaculture are collected through an elaborate and comprehensive system of sampling based upon data collection. These statistics are computerised and considered to be comprehensive. For marine fisheries, information is also collected on numbers of fishers, based upon licensed gears or those working onboard licensed vessels. Aquaculture information includes areas of culture systems, species and marketing data.

The Information Produced

Population data for Malaysia by State are provided in Table 4. Gross production statistics for inland capture fisheries by State are shown in Fig. Estimated gross national production varies around 4000 (+ 500) MT per annum over the six years in question. This estimate applies mainly to peninsular Malaysia. The figures agree with those reported to and by FAO. No estimates are available for Sabah and a fixed 1 700 MT per annum is reported for Sarawak 1995-8 which is reduced to 89.6 and 51.1 MT per annum for 1999 and 2000 respectively (undoubtedly a reporting anomaly). When questioned regarding these apparent trends in the production figures, staff at DOF thought these more likely due to reporting constraints than to actual changes in the fishery. For example, the increased reported production for Selangor State in recent years was explained as likely being due to "increased effort to collect data".

Table 4 Population statistics for Malaysia by State (Department of Statistics, 1999)

State/area	Population (1991) x 1000			Population Density (people/km^2)
	Total	Urban	Rural	
Perlis	190.2	50.8	139.4	239
Kedah	1 364.5	451.3	913.2	145
Pulau Pinang	1 116.8	840.4	276.4	1083
Perak	1 974.9	1072.4	902.5	94
Selangor	2 413.6	1810	603.6	303
Negeri Sembilan	722	306.5	415.5	109
Melaka	529.2	208.7	320.5	321
Johor	2 162.4	1 038.4	1124	114
Pahang	1 081.1	330.4	750.7	30
Terengganu	808.6	360.6	448	62.
Kelantan	1 207.7	406.5	801.2	81
Sarawak	1 718.4	652.6	1 065.8	14
Sabah	1 808.8	600.5	1 208.3	25
Kuala Lumpur	5 048	-	-	-
Labuan	602	-	-	-
Total	**17 098**	**8 129**	**8 969**	

These reports clearly do not reflect the seasonal nature of catches from inland fisheries (especially rivers) that are known to occur in the humid tropics. The estimates may have a bias towards landings reports for reservoirs, which are less seasonal. At the very least the estimates for Sabah, where the resource base is definitely dominated by rivers, are not normal for a tropical inland fishery (landings from rivers, floodplains and swamps should show seasonal increases in catches at the onset of the dry season - see reports for Myanmar and Cambodia). It is possible the reports do not include rivers but it is more likely they do not reflect the true nature of the fishery at all.

Malaysia produces a relatively large number of ornamental fishes for the export trade, mainly through culture especially in Johor, Perak and Selangor States. Department of Fisheries (2001) lists a production in 2000 of 306 million individuals with a reported value of 71.9 million RM (about US$ 18.9 m). However, it is likely that there is also a significant fishery for wild ornamental fishes especially in Sarawak and Sabah but no information on this could be obtained.

Malaysia has a modest open-water stocking programme. Department of Fisheries (2001) lists approximately 4.5 million fish stocked into open water bodies for 2000. The main species are Java Carp, Common Carp, Giant Freshwater Prawn, Red Tilapia, River Catfish and others. This compares with about 17.5 million individuals distributed from government hatcheries to culturists (it is assumed that considerably more are provided by private hatcheries). Fish caught as a result of stocking in open waters are reported as capture fisheries.

Malaysia has significant areas under rice production and the dominant system is wet-rice, mainly irrigated. There appear to be limited attempts to get figures for aquatic animal production from rice fields and it is assumed that this production is not reported. DOF (Kuala Lumpur) consider production of aquatic animals from rice fields to be limited due to the intensified agricultural system and especially the extensive use of pesticides.

Recreational fisheries are undertaking rapid and significant development. A new Act is being developed which covers sport fishing. Whilst marine sport fishing is considered to be a major sector (and possibly is based upon individual license fees) participation in, and gross revenues from, freshwater sport fishing are potentially very significant. Currently, no information is collected or reported on the recreational fishing sub-sector.

Malaysia reports no significant activities or projects in its inland capture fisheries sub-sector except for some local activities relating to attempts at conservation measures for certain threatened freshwater species or stocks. Particular note was made of the problems with the Terubok (*Hilsa macrura*) fishery, which is suffering from a multitude of problems of over-exploitation and environmental impacts.

Most research on freshwater fishery related issues have focussed on the biology/ecology etc. of fishes and the ecology/limnology of freshwaters. No studies on fishery economics or socio-economics, particularly production estimates, for freshwater fisheries, could be located.

It was reported that "most Malaysians prefer marine fish" but this is difficult to reconcile with prices of freshwater fish reportedly often being higher than for comparable marine grades, especially in the interior.

Perceptions of Inland Fisheries and Objectives of the Statistics

Most staff interviewed saw clear distinctions between the inland fisheries situations in peninsular Malaysia *versus* Sarawak and Sabah. In the former region, although locally important inland capture fisheries for food likely occur, the main areas of interest are biodiversity, environment, rehabilitation/restoration and recreational fisheries. In Sabah and Sarawak, authorities are fully aware that issues include poverty, livelihoods and food security values of inland fisheries.

The existing inland capture fishery statistics appear to have limited, if any, use. They do not form the basis of any current management system and appear, generally, not to form the basis of policy generation (accepting in a negative way - to reinforce the view that the sector is not important). The existing statistics are of no use as a basis for biodiversity/environmental management. There are clearly stated needs for information for policy and management in Sabah and Sarawak but useful statistics may be absent there.

The main threats to inland capture fisheries throughout Malaysia, and especially in Sabah and Sarawak, are perceived by most people interviewed to be due to environmental degradation and habitat loss arising through activities in other sectors.

Conclusions and Recommendations

The inland capture fishery statistics in Malaysia are compiled as a secondary activity to the production of information for the marine and aquaculture sectors. Obviously, any system based upon estimates made by district officers in the absence of a statistically based sampling/observation programme, done probably as a secondary activity in most areas, cannot be expected to generate accurately representative information. The skills of staff in estimation would be highly variable. With such systems, at best normally only a cursory estimate of the fishery is made which is normally biased towards the most visible parts of the fishery (both in terms of access by the observer and nature of the activities). In particular, informal fishing activities in rural areas, particularly where fish are not landed at regular sites, and especially for rivers and swamps, are often overlooked. Malaysian authorities are well aware of these constraints.

A general consensus at DOF is that the statistics for peninsular Malaysia under-report actual production by a factor of at least 2 and possibly 3 times. However, even when corrected by an optimistic amount the production remains low relative to the marine and aquaculture sub-sectors. What is intriguing is that despite the entire system being based upon personal estimates, the experienced staff at DOF (whose own personal estimates usually put production much higher) make no attempt to increase the nationally reported estimates to a more realistic level. That is, estimates at district level are treated as though they were actual data, which they are not. The problem here likely stems from having to work within the confines of a national statistical system that, for most information, is based upon statistically valid and assessed data. Appropriately in most cases, this discourages adjustments of figures at higher levels of analysis. But this constrains re-assessments for inland capture fisheries.

For peninsular Malaysia there appears to be limited justification for significant investments in improved statistics aimed at ascertaining gross production through strengthening the existing system. Certainly, this would not be cost-effective in terms of investment returns and it would also yield the wrong information. Where objectives relate to biodiversity/environment issues etc., the information generated should help achieve the relevant objectives. However, gross production figures, even when disaggregated by species and production system, are of limited or no use. Investments would be, and are being, more wisely made in the areas of direct monitoring of biodiversity and the environment.

Malaysian authorities already recognise that Sabah and Sarawak are priority areas for improved information in relation to inland capture fisheries. They voiced the opinion that they would like information for those States to be up to the standard for marine fisheries. They are also keen to develop sound pro-poor development policies and resource management plans in these disadvantaged areas. Investments in improved information there are clearly justifiable. In this report, the two States fall into the category of areas where important inland fisheries for food occur but effectively no data currently exist.

A cursory look at Sabah and Sarawak shows a reasonable availability of freshwater resources. The total population of both States is about 2 274 000 with 65 percent living in rural areas. As a guideline, a reasonable average annual per caput 20-40 kg fish captured from freshwaters in such areas (see comparable data for other regions in this report) gives a first guess production estimate of 50 000 to 100 000 MT per annum for the two States combined. This does not fully reflect the true value of the resource but initially indicates that investment in improved information is warranted.

Malaysia is likely to experience the continued rapid development of its recreational fisheries sector and all of the problems and opportunities that this will entail. Information requirements and data collection opportunities for recreational (sport) fisheries in inland waters differ significantly to those for capture for food. It is recommended that DOF anticipate these opportunities and develop appropriate information and management systems. These should centre on developing co-management systems by promoting the full participation of resource users who, in this sub-sector, are generally are more enthusiastic and able to co-operate effectively with the government.

There is considerable potential in Malaysia in utilising the substantial national capacity in remote sensing and GIS to assist with natural resources and inland fisheries mapping and inventories. This approach is particularly useful for obtaining baseline indicative information in areas where limited empirical data exist.

MYANMAR

Myanmar has impressive freshwater capture fisheries. The inland waters are made up mainly of the interlocking/mingling of riverine and estuarine systems of the Ayeyarwaddy (Irrawaddy, 2150 km long), Chindwin (844 km; a tributary of the main Ayeyarwaddy) and Sittaung Rivers (563 km) plus the large Thanlwin River (2400 km) to the east. The first three have adjacent deltas and are arguably part of a larger joint system. Together these systems extend from the eastern part of the Bay of Bengal to the Gulf of Moattama and along the eastern edge of the Andaman Sea. The Ayeyarwaddy River alone has a mean discharge of 13 500 $m^3.sec^{-1}$ from its catchment of 424 000 km^2 (Welcomme, 1985), notably, practically all within Myanmar. It shares a watershed with the Mekong River which has only a slightly higher discharge (15 000

$m^3.sec^{-1}$) but a greater length (4880 km^2) and larger catchment (795 000 km^2) (MRC, 2001). Aquatic resource area of the river systems within Myanmar encompasses a total of 8.2 million hectares (FAO, 1996); there were 53 123 ha of fishponds in 1999.

The department of fisheries (DOF) in Yangon give a figure of 6 m ha of floodplains, which likely excludes river area and floodplain lakes. This approaches that of the entire Mekong (7 m ha, MRC, 2001). The country also includes a small section of the Mekong River basin but is not a member of the Mekong River Commission. With a total population of about 50 million, Myanmar potentially has an inland fishery greatly exceeding that of any single national part of the Mekong River basin, and quite feasibly rivals that of the lower Mekong Basin in its entirety. Indeed, in 2000-2001, the reported inland catch for Myanmar, at 235 000 MT per annum (excluding rice-fields and reservoirs), is three times that reported for Cambodia in 1998 and exceeds that reported for Cambodia, Laos and the Mekong sections of Thailand and VietNam combined in that year. Cambodia revised its figures upwards in 1999 as a result of research to verify its previous reporting system. Therefore this comparison is not valid for the 1999 onwards reports for Cambodia.

There are also great similarities in the fisheries of the Ayeyarwaddy and Mekong and the country presents a fascinating opportunity to compare statistics and experiences between these regions.

For management (licensing/regulation) purposes Myanmar divides its inland capture fisheries into two main categories:

(i) *Lease fisheries.* These are almost exclusively key fishing grounds on floodplains which are primarily fished through the erection of barrage fences around the lease area with fish collected in various collection pens or traps. The peak season involves capturing fishes migrating off the floodplain at the beginning of river draw-down. Lease holders enjoy exclusive rights to fish the lease area including preventing access by others and a certain degree of environmental management and control. This is referred to locally as the "Inn" fishery. For present purposes it is the same as the floodplain (and Great Lake) barrage fishing components of the "Lot" system in Cambodia. There are currently 3 722 leasable fisheries in Myanmar of which 3 490 are still exploitable. Of these, 1 738 (52.3 percent) are located in Ayeyarwaddy Division (the lower floodplains and delta of the river). Leases have been auctioned ever year but DOF are extending the lease period to up to 9 years to promote improved long-term management. There are no government owned leases. A register of leases is kept and details of lease arrangements held on Land Revenue Forms.

(ii) *Open fisheries.* These are fisheries in all other areas including all types of fishing operation. The right to fish in these areas is licensed out by DOF. All fishing gears require a license. For most this is a set fee. Some of the larger gears, particularly "bagnets" set in rivers (comparable to those used in the lower Mekong), are allocated by a tender system ("tender fisheries"). Fees are variable between regions according to production and capacity. License fees for smaller-gears are low. Although the policy is for complete coverage of licenses for all gears (a monumental task in such a fishery) it was intimated that licenses tend to be neglected for smaller gears and the system concentrates on those people perceived as fishing for "profit".

Officially, it is a requirement for all licenses that holders report their catches. The entire fishery is closed during June, July and August (to allow spawning and recruitment). In practice this is probably enforced only for the Inn fishery, tender fisheries and larger gears. The small-scale fishery occurs year-round and is considered technically "illegal" during these months.

DOF have recently tested an interesting management approach to lease fisheries whereby a modest 1 percent of the revenue is returned to the fishery through a stocking programme. An impressive 30 percent is however returned in the form of grants to lease holders for improved management. These funds are used mainly for undertaking environmental rehabilitation, restoration or enhancement measures. Common activities include, the clearing of floodplain channels to allow improved access of fish to feeding/breeding grounds, and improved capture, the planting of trees and river bank engineering works using local materials. This is important because the impacts of this appear to be reflected in reported catches. Some trials are also being conducted on rearing fish in pens (1-50 ha) within lease areas. Currently this is done on a modest scale and production within pens is included in production reports for leases (if the activity expands then DOF intend reporting productions separately).

Revenue from the fisheries (1999) were as follows: lease fishery - 621.89 million Kyats; tender fishery - 83.519 million Kyats; implements (gears) (= others) - 6.298 million Kyats.

DOF report that reservoirs are now under the control of the Ministry of Agriculture and Irrigation. Fishing there is now officially not allowed, reportedly as a temporary measure to allow stocks to recover, although it is odd that a significant stocking programme for reservoirs has been on-going. For the current purposes it is sufficient to note that reservoir catches are not included in the current or recent reports. DOF gave an estimation of reservoir and lake area of about 1.8 million ha (which is consistent with the difference between the DOF floodplain estimates and the FAO total resource estimate).

A fledgling freshwater aquarium fish industry was reported. Its extent is unknown but it could be quite significant either potentially or in reality.

The Statistical Collection System

Administratively the Union of Myanmar is divided into States (and Divisions) - Districts - Townships - Villages. All fishing license holders are required to report their catches to the local township official. For lease fisheries the lease holders keep records and local officers collect these records. No sampling of catches or landings is undertaken. It is however likely that the reporting requirements are enforced, or monitored, predominantly for the larger gears. Some township officers estimate catches themselves. Township offices obtain reports approximately every two weeks and report monthly to the DOF, Yangon. Local officers are expected to check local reports including visiting fishing locations. Rural areas are covered by the local township office. There are 370 townships in the whole country and 110 fisheries township offices. Some township offices cover more than one township. Usually townships with lease fisheries have a resident officer for statistics, including nearly all those in the delta area and Yangon Division. Officers at township level work only part-time on fishery statistics, their other duties including, for example, aquaculture extension. These staff may call upon other officers to gather more statistics when required. There are approximately 90 staff (DOF) in 15 district offices; a total of 70 in the State and Division offices. DOF Yangon is responsible for the nature of information collected and sends summaries to the National Statistics Organisation.

Planning and Statistics Division (DOF Yangon) has 19 staff in total.

It was reported that the tax register is used as the basis for a frame survey upon which reporting is based. But the system essentially does not officially involve sampling but is based upon attempted complete-reporting. It is assumed that the tax register is used to assess where reports are expected to be submitted. Again, this suggests a possible emphasis on the more commercial sectors of the fishery.

Licenses for gears normally apply to both the gear type and locations where fishing is allowed. Information disaggregated by production system (habitat) is therefore, in theory, available at local level. Lease fisheries divide their catch reports into two categories by value/quality (high and low). Open fishery reporting is not done by any category. There is therefore limited information on species composition. Although some modest surveys have been done, often by university students etc., DOF are not confident about their information on the composition of catches.

Aquaculture statistics are collected through the same system by the same personnel. Rice field fisheries are not licensed and therefore production is not reported. Production arising from stocking in open waters is reported as "capture".

Myanmar Reports Statistics by the Fiscal Year (April to March).

DOF have stated confidence in their data but appreciate the need for checks/verifications. They stated a need to modernise their system for data collection, storage, handling and reporting. Computerisation is a high priority, but funds are limited. There is a need for training to use specialised fishery statistics software. These problems/needs are common to all sub-sectors of their fisheries reporting system and general assistance from FAO in these respects was requested.

The Information Produced

The reports for Myanmar, in general, show some interesting trends and features. They may actually represent what may be happening in the fisheries, which is a useful start. Although not conclusive, there is an apparent trend of increasing production from 1992-3 to 1998-1999, which may well be in-line with population growth. The reports also suggest that most of the increase in total catches during this period arose from the open fishery, which is logical (access to the lease fishery is controlled but open fisheries are more openly accessible and therefore would reflect increased effort due to population changes more). It is, however, problematic that there is so little difference between years due to natural variations in flooding extent (due to long-term global oscillations in weather). But the reports are a refreshing change from the flat-lines common to many other inland fishery statistics.

Most interestingly the reports show a significant increase in production from 1998-9 onwards. DOF attribute this to the results of their management activities: restoration/rehabilitation work and in particular stocking. This is likely correct. Over the period 1997-1998 to 2000-2001 production from lease and open fisheries increased 28 271 and 57 828 MT respectively. From 1994-1995 to 2000-2001 the total number of fingerlings reported to be stocked into lease and open water areas was 335.125 and 363.445 million respectively. This gives an estimated average return per fingerling stocked of 85 g and 159 g for lease and open fisheries respectively. This is not unreasonable, although the environments in question would be expected to harbour a high level of predators. The higher return with open fisheries could be due to differences in fishing methods. Lease fisheries would catch most fish primarily in the same season as stocked. Unfortunately, due to manpower constraints, DOF appear not to have collected adequate information on the composition of catches to be able to confirm links between stocking and production. Obviously, this needs to be done. But the existing reports of stocking and production are not without problems. First, major stocking started in 1994/5 but significantly increased production started only in 1998/9.

This delay in benefits is too long. Second, from 1996/7 onwards stocking levels remain fairly uniform but fish production continues to increase (alternatively, the trend in production increase is more smooth than the trend in stocking). The situation is complicated because other enhancement activities were occurring alongside stocking (e.g. environmental rehabilitation). Production can differ significantly between years through natural cycles and such could either mask or enhance the impacts of management. Also, the recent extension of lease periods has encouraged lease holders to undertake their own enhancement and conservation including promoting re-stocking activities. Production reports when based upon stocking programmes can also include a certain amount of subjectivity (anticipation of a response to management measures). Therefore, analysis of the increased production achieved in recent years is very complex. The mission does conclude that the approaches to river fisheries management adopted in Myanmar should indeed produce benefits of the orders being indicated.

The fishery statistics reports certainly suggest that the recent experiences with management approaches with river fisheries in Myanmar warrant further study. They also illustrate the pitfalls of using traditional fishery statistics to obtain feedback on management activities. Clearly, Myanmar needs to compliment the existing information system with a research programme to look deeper into the impacts of stocking and environmental management. But based upon the reported statistics, they are to be complimented on their approach so far. The reported increase in production over the past three years represents an increase of about 45 percent and 65 percent for lease and open fisheries respectively. This is in a fishery that was already large, with a high level of exploitation. To the mission's knowledge it also eclipses anything ever achieved in aquaculture (when starting from a similar point). Most importantly, this experience annihilates the widely held view that there is no scope to increase production from inland capture fisheries in rivers.

Reported production analysed on a monthly basis showed some encouraging results. Monthly figures over two years for Ayeyarwaddy Division (the heart of the Irrawaddy floodplains/delta). These show the gross seasonal changes that are expected from floodplain fisheries. The peak catches are reported to occur in September which is when floodplain waters begin to recede and thereafter remain higher, declining towards the dry season to the flood season. The more rapid drop-off in catches from lease fisheries compared to open water fisheries is also entirely logical. The former tend to target fish fleeing the floodplain and heading towards more permanent waters fished more by the latter.

It is interesting that the reports show fishing all year-round. It is obvious that the stated "closed" season has little impact on reported production. Also, production from lease fisheries is reported beyond the period of river draw-down which means that the reports cover more than the main lease gear (barrage fences; because these only work for receding floodwaters). Presumably fishing continues in dry season refuges (pools etc.) in lease areas. Also leaseholders may hold fish in pens and sell them later in the year when prices increase. It is also reported that amongst the catch held during the dry season is much smaller fish, which are released again by lease holders at the start of the next flood. This approach is promoted by DOF and is becoming more sustainable in view of the increased duration of leases (giving fishers improved incentives to restock). This illustrates fish stocking undertaken by lease holders and based upon naturally recruited stocking material - a system with much potential for promotion in other countries.

Unfortunately, the reports for aquaculture are incomplete but there is possibly evidence of the expected inverse relationship between production from capture and culture in such an area. Capture fisheries on river floodplains, during peak periods, will easily out-compete aquaculture in their vicinity, as documented for the lower Mekong. The monthly reports for aquaculture also change abruptly which is likely explained by them representing marketing and not production (*e.g.* farmers likely hold back produce until prices recover after the influence of seasonal influences from river fisheries). The sudden drop in freshwater capture production in April 2000 is explained by DOF as being due to a sudden increase in production from the marine fishery at that time which depresses fish prices.

But again these reports are not without problems. Catches outside the period of river draw-down (October - August) appear too consistent (apart from the aforementioned drop in April). Catches would be expected to decline over this period as fish that have retreated into dry season fishing areas are exploited and as they migrate away from the area. (This phenomenon is illustrated for Cambodia later). Significant differences in catches between years, are normal for river fisheries and can reflect natural variations in production. Interpretations here are also complicated by the fact that the reports apply to a fishery where a considerable degree of management effort (stocking/rehabilitation) is being applied.

The average reported production per lease is shown by State/ Division. Some States/Divisions away from floodplains have high reported productions per lease. This is possibly because some leases apply to lake areas, likely, for example, in Shan State and Kachin. The odd thing is the low reported production per lease for Ayeyarwaddy, although having over half the total leases since it represents the best fishing grounds. But lease areas there could be on average smaller. It is also reported by DOF that there are some differences between State/

Divisions in the allocation of catches from "flood fisheries" (a previous category used until 1991) into lease *versus* open fisheries.

Reports of wholesale fish prices (for the 8 highest volume species, excluding prawns) in Yangon markets for 1999-2000 show that the lowest and highest prices for marine fish are only 44 percent and 61 percent, respectively, of those for freshwater fish. These reports confirm experiences in most countries that freshwater fish (by-and-large) are preferred to marine fish; in denial of popular perceptions to the contrary. This is likely due to the majority of people living (or coming from) inland areas (preferring traditionally available fish) but the quality of produce is likely another major factor (inland fish is produced locally and tends to be of better quality).

The reported number of fishers operating in inland waters was 1 398 410; higher than the 1 278 000 in the marine sector, and approximately 3.5 times the number of fish farmers (2000-2001). These figures are entirely logical. Although marine fisheries production is far higher in Myanmar (721 904 MT, 1999), the level of participation in inland fisheries is the key factor.

These reports also should be viewed in the light that it is unlikely they represent all inland fishers. In particular, the multitude of small-scale activities are probably not covered. Rice field fishers are definitely not covered and although catches may be low, rice field fishers could outnumber those in open waters and lease fisheries combined; neither are reservoir fishers included. That this section is not included is also indicated by reports for the narrow coastal Division Tanintharyi where fish farmers are reported but no inland fishers. It is a certainty that even coastal areas have people fishing in freshwaters (reports are missing for Rakhine State).

The mission concludes that there is reason for some confidence in the reports for Myanmar. Despite some difficulties and anomalies, the reports do appear to reflect what is expected to be happening in the fishery and there is reason to believe the reports may be useful for picking-up trends in the fishery (partly because some are already evident). However, giving a picture of the fishery is one thing. Whether they accurately estimate actual production is an entirely different issue. It appears that Myanmar have no actual data based upon sampling the fishery itself (for production, participation or anything else). Obviously, the facts of this matter can only be obtained by having a research programme to investigate and verify the actual figures. But there are good reasons to think that reports are still underestimating the fishery:

- The reporting system probably does not properly cover the small-scale, informal sections of the fishery - although catches per caput can be small, participation can be very high. Such activities can produce significant quantities of fish (for example, three times that reported for commercial/licensed gears in the Mekong Delta, see VietNam this report).
- The system is based upon reporting which, as always, relies on the willingness of the fisher to be truthful and the ability to recall catches (although in Myanmar the system expects a shorter recall period than in most other countries). This is particularly so for fisheries where there are linkages between license fees and catches - especially for commercial gears and lease/tender fisheries.
- Experiences in Cambodia have shown that where large revenues are involved (especially for leased/tender fisheries) not only do lease/tender holders under-report, but government officers deliberately under-report also. The mission has no reason to believe the same problem occurs in Myanmar.
- Cambodia has a fishery very similar to that of Myanmar (at least for the floodplain areas) and a similar reporting system based for the larger gears on catch reporting and license records. Considerable research during the mid 1990's has confirmed that the reporting system grossly under-reported catches. In response to this information, Cambodia elevated its catch reports for 1999 by a factor of about three times. Despite this increase, recent reports are still considered under-estimates (see Cambodia in this report).
- Estimates of catches based upon sampling in the Mekong Delta in VietNam (an area very similar to that in the heart of Ayeyarwaddy Division in Myanmar), showed actual catches to be more than four times higher than estimates made from reports and license information (see VietNam in this report). The latter area in VietNam is a net exporter of fish (as is likely for Ayeyarwaddy) with a per caput catch roughly 100 kg per person (of the total population). If applied to Ayeyarwaddy this

gives a total catch for that Division alone of over 500 000 MT (although a proper comparison needs to take account of a number of variables where information was unavailable to the mission).

- Fish consumption figures for Ayeyarwaddy Division suggest a local product requirement for that area of about 235 760 MT in 1999-2000. But in the same year the Division reported a production of only 90 813 MT (lease and open fishery combined) and 30 317 MT from culture (total 121 130). It is unrealistic to explain the difference through supply from the marine fishery. There is no doubt that such an area would be a net fish exporter (domestically - *i.e.* to other Divisions). Taking into account such domestic export (and much of the culture production is likely also exported) this suggests an under-reporting for inland capture fisheries by a factor of at least 2, possibly 3 times.

It is beyond this report to try to accurately re-calculate catches for Myanmar, an activity that should in any case be done by Myanmar itself. However, it is interesting to note that multiplying the current reports by three (on the basis of experiences in Cambodia) gives a production of about 700 000 MT per annum - excluding reservoirs and rice fields. By taking such approaches, the eventual figure reaches lofty heights, but not unreasonably so. Based on a resource area of about 6 million hectares of floodplain alone, estimated production in Myanmar reaches 900 000 MT per annum based upon figures for capture fisheries for the lower Mekong (150 kg/ha, MRC, 2001). Even very highly degraded floodplains with heavy exploitation may yield in excess of 100 kg per ha (Hoggarth *et al.*, 1999). This brief overview confirms the opening summary of this section, that Myanmar has both the resource area and population to rival the production of the lower Mekong Basin. At the very least, the extent to which this is realised should be investigated through further more detailed analysis and surveys (via methods suggested in Part I of this report).

It is also patently obvious that there is great scope for information exchange between Myanmar and the countries of the lower Mekong Basin (particularly Cambodia, but also VietNam). This is not only for information relevant to interpreting fishery statistics, but also on fisheries management systems, particularly for lease/tender (lot) fisheries.

Perceptions of Inland Fisheries and Objectives of the Statistics

DOF Myanmar is already well aware of the importance of their inland capture fisheries. It is regarded, largely, as a sector which has "looked after itself" for a long time, presenting few management problems. The main threat to the fishery is regarded as environmental degradation. Myanmar is also one of the few countries with comprehensive and active involvement in fisheries improvement for its rivers through stocking and rehabilitation/restoration; apparently, with already significant rewards. Inland fisheries are regarded as primarily "for the local people" whereas marine fisheries, and to a large extent commercial aquaculture (especially prawns), are regarded as export earning sectors.

DOF stated that the fishery statistics are used to draw national plans, determine social factors in communities (*e.g.* consumption/ production), understand the biological dynamics of fisheries for management purposes (stock assessment etc.), to monitor supply and demand, and to identify and monitor strategies for increasing production. The information provided through their reporting system meets some of these needs and certainly more so than in some countries. But it clearly falls short for some other requirements. There was stated concern that the reporting system did not adequately satisfy information needs relating to poverty, livelihoods, food security and other such factors.

Conclusions and Recommendations

It is obvious that Myanmar needs to undertake some studies to verify the accuracy of their reports, or more likely, to evaluate the extent of under-reporting (see Part I for methods). The information currently produced appears to be of sufficient quality to justify this. However, experiences have shown that obtaining accurate information, particularly with licensed fisheries (and especially lease fisheries) can be problematic. It is essential that verification includes impartiality and is perhaps best done through a research process in small representative areas. Even then it is not easy to get accurate data (see Cambodia in this report). But it would appear that there is potential for Myanmar to justifiably use its fishery statistics for basic management and policy considerations, provided they are verified, checked and re-assessed. The important issue is not whether the statistics are accurate but whether they are representative (*i.e.* to what extent they represent a sample of the fishery).

With reasonable information, inaccuracy can be accounted for once the sources of errors are known.

The current reports have limited use for the purposes of assessing management inputs, including assessing the impacts of stocking and other forms of enhancement. For these considerations, precise information on catches, and species composition, is required. Again, this might be obtained through targeted research initiatives and it may not be necessary, or feasible, to modify the entire reporting system to meet these requirements.

One way of investigating the relevance of reports for lease fisheries is to analyse relationships between lease areas (for equivalent habitats), lease fees and reported production. There are logical biological and economic relationships between these factors. Deviations from these are an indication of anomalies in reporting. This should be done and is a relatively low-cost exercise. If research is eventually done to verify production, then these parameters can also be used to extrapolate from researched areas to the fishery as a whole.

The fishery statistical system in Myanmar is based primarily upon a method of revenue generation. The country has already been complimented on its willingness to reinvest some of that revenue back into the fishery. But the issues of statistics and revenue are difficult to divorce. From a purely statistical perspective, a shift from quantity to quality of information would certainly be a benefit. If information is available on the relative abundance of some of the more prominent gears, it is not necessary to have catch reports from them all. But the system in Myanmar still requires near full coverage (at least for the commercial gears) for licensing purposes. The problem then is that it is difficult, without significant increases in investments, to shift the emphasis to a smaller sample in order to get better quality reports. There are also doubts about whether such can be achieved based upon the current reporting approaches. But certainly, for the smaller gears, there is a point at which the costs of collecting licenses outweigh the benefits in terms of revenue (a stage probably already reached, possibly surpassed, in Myanmar). Under such circumstances it is better to have more open policies, which acknowledge the realities of inland fisheries and thereby promote new ways of obtaining fisheries information and less rigid ways of considering existing statistics. A basic problem with the system in Myanmar is not that the reports miss certain parts of the fishery (which almost any system would) but that it portrays itself (officially) as covering it all. And the latter makes it difficult to adjust the figures by acknowledging incomplete coverage.

The strategy of Myanmar should obviously to be to improve its existing reporting system where possible but also to consider inland capture fisheries information more broadly (for example, whether the information collected meets management requirements). The latter is crucial if significant new investments are to be made.

PHILIPPINES

Philippines was visited only briefly and as part of a second mission to formulate a proposed TCP to improve the quality of information for inland fisheries. Brief details of the statistical system in operation, and the information produced, were subsequently included here. The mission was unable to explore the system or data produced in as much detail as for the other countries.

The Philippines is a country composed of many islands, only a few of which are of any size. Not surprisingly its fisheries are certainly dominated by the marine capture sub-sector. Aquaculture is also well developed and has a long tradition in the Philippines which ranks in the top 10 of the world's producers. Even so, the Philippines were ranked fourth in Southeast Asia in 1999 in terms of reported catches from inland waters.

All inland waters are extensively fished. The main producing areas centre on the larger lakes including Laguna de Bay (89 076 ha) and San Pablo Lake in Laguna; Taal Lake (24 356 ha) in Batangas; and Lake Bato (3 792 ha) in Bicol. Most rivers in the Philippines are now highly degraded, as are the lakes. A recent natural volcanic eruption has decimated the inland fisheries in some of these areas.

According to the Philippines Fisheries Code of 1998, inland fisheries occur in freshwater and brackishwater. Resource areas are shown in Table 5. The 1998 Fisheries Code is very comprehensive. Municipal/City Governments have jurisdiction over municipal waters as defined by the code. This includes all inland areas. In addition to problems of pollution and over-exploitation of inland waters there are severe conflicts of interest between capture and culture considerations in inland areas. For example, the extensive development of fish pens in inland waters has limited access to resources by capture fishers.

Table 5 Inland fishery resource areas in the Philippines (ha)

Environment	Ha
1. Swamplands	246 063
Freshwater	106 328
Brackishwater	139 735
2. Existing fishpond	253 854
Freshwater	14 531
Brackishwater	239 323
3. Other Inland Resources	250 000
Lakes	200 000
Rivers	31 000
Reservoirs	19 000

The Philippines has much involvement in "coastal zone management" with many past, current and pipeline projects devoted to this subject. However, there is no parallel for coastal zone management for inland areas, despite the increased environmental and resources management problems there.

The Bureau of Fisheries and Aquatic Resources (BFAR) has undertaken some studies on inland capture fisheries management. One division is engaged in capture fisheries in inland waters but works mainly on fishing technology. Some biological and fisheries assessments studies have recently been undertaken in 7 major lakes. Some livelihoods aspects were covered. The final report on this is pending. There has been a National Stock Assessment Project for Marine Fisheries but not for inland fisheries. In general, for inland fisheries there has been only a limited programme/involvement in biological aspects and very little on socio-economics etc.

The Statistical Collection System

BFAR is the main government agency responsible for fisheries and has the responsibility for management and development. However, responsibility for statistical data collection rests with the Bureau of Agricultural Statistics (BAS). Both BFAR and BAS are under the Department of Agriculture. BFAR has a major role in determining the nature of statistics to be collected but the implementation of surveys, including appropriate methods, is determined mainly by BAS. BFAR is supplied with statistics by BAS. The statistical system used by BAS in general focuses on monitoring landings at a sample of landings sites. However, this information for the inland fishery is supposedly supplemented by a sample survey of households.

The sampling method is simple random sampling of landing centres by province, and simple random sampling of households. The sampling frame for the latter is a listing of municipal fishing households conducted nationwide in 1992. The basis of this frame for the household survey is not clear. Households are stratified by fishing grounds (lake, reservoir, river etc.). According to BAS, for inland fish producing provinces, about 2123 "fishing households" were interviewed in 1997 out of the 34 000 inland fishing households "listed" nationwide. It is unclear how the definition of an "inland fish producing province" is derived or what constitutes a "fishing household". The reported system is confusing because a random sample of all households should be what determines which are involved in fishing and which are not. It is not possible, for example, to have truly random sampling of "fishing households" unless those households fishing, and not fishing, are already known. And that information should be gathered frequently because participation in inland fisheries by households can vary significantly between years in response to a number of factors. It is, however, highly likely that the choice of the sampling pool of households is based upon fishing gear records or records of some other attribute of the fishery recorded in the 1992 survey. The system is, therefore, probably not random but based upon random sampling of a pre-determined section of the fishery (which in any case is now out of date). This can cause serious problems. For example: In Thailand in many areas only about 5 percent of households involved in the inland capture fishery use licensed gears, sampling those households is, therefore, fairly irrelevant to assessing the extent of the fishery; in Indonesia, as likely elsewhere in Southeast Asia, there was a reported increase in involvement in inland capture fisheries of an estimated 40 percent as a result of the economic crisis of 1997, therefore a frame survey undertaken in 1992 is unlikely to be an accurate basis the frame for the Philippines for recent surveys. The frame survey for inland fisheries is apparently being updated.

Surveys are organised by Municipal Officers but based upon hiring labour specifically to undertake surveys. Data collectors are paid per operator interviewed. They are trained and supervised for one week.

Surveys last 15 days and the inland capture survey is supposed to be undertaken every three months, simultaneously with the aquaculture survey. The frame upon which aquaculture statistics are gathered was recently redesigned by BFAR. A farm inventory is planned for next year (designed by BFAR, implemented by BAS).

Two basic approaches are taken to obtaining capture fishery statistics for inland waters:

The Frame Survey of Inland Municipal Fisheries

For the survey of municipal fish landing centres the frame is the List of Inland Municipal Fish Landing Centres (for provinces with LC's). Information collected includes: landing centre category; unloading information; number of boats; daily volume of catch; fishing gears and fishing ground; species. The frequency of data collection is officially a three times a week interview of fishing boat owners or fisherman at sample fish landing centres during peak hours of unloading (for landings centres).

For provinces without Landings Centres, a survey of landings by household is undertaken. For this the frame is the List of Fishing Households (1992). Information obtained includes: unloading information; daily volume of catch; fishing gears and fishing ground; species.

Survey forms for the household survey are based upon questions directed at individuals in the household (presumably the head fisherman); a system which elsewhere has been shown to seriously underestimate household catches because respondents tend to report only their own catch. Questions are asked on fishing ground, fishing gear, species caught, monthly average catch and price information, total number of fishing days, daily average fish catch, average price per kg and remarks. The whole survey is based upon quarterly recall by respondents.

According to the survey manual, inland fishing is defined as "the catching of fish, crustaceans, molluscs and all other aquatic animals and plants in inland water like lakes, rivers, dams, marshes, etc., using simple gears and fishing boats some of which are non-motorised with a capacity of less than three (3) gross MT; or fishing not requiring the use of fishing boats". Inland waters are defined as "a body of water within the shoreline which includes brackishwater and freshwater, such as lakes, rivers, reservoirs/dams, etc." Fishing ground codes in use include "rivers, lakes, swamps/marshes/lagoon, dams/reservoir/irrigation/swim, others (includes creeks, rice-fields, channel, spring, stream, drainage etc.)". The list of freshwater species on forms includes only 20 fishes, 7 crustaceans and 4 molluscs.

Non Probability Surveys

This occurs when scheduled sampling surveys (as above) cannot be undertaken. With non-probability surveys, trends in fish production and price are monitored through interviews with key informants. For inland capture fisheries these include: fishers, fish vendors and boat owners. The system is obviously subjective and also does not capture any information on entry into and exit from the fishery.

BAS has experienced severe budget reductions from 1995 to date. Consequently, due to insufficiency and delay in the release of funds, estimates have recently been generated based on surveys with reduced sample sizes and/or monitoring activities with key informants as respondents. The results of limited probability and non-probability surveys were the basis of generating fishery statistics for the provinces since at least 1995. BAS report that "normally, the information for inland capture fisheries is based upon key informants".

Currently BAS is designing an inland fishery statistical survey for 29 provinces. But this assumes that it will get adequate funding.

Data processing systems appear to be in place and functioning reasonably well. The statistical system is de-centralised to provinces/municipalities. Availability of computer hardware is limited in provinces. The database system was prepared by BAS data programmers etc.

All production from rice-fields is recorded under culture.

The Information Produced

A gradual decrease in production is evident from these reports and this is widely attributed to be due to over-exploitation and habitat/environmental degradation. However, it should be noted that the accuracy of these statistics is unknown. Certainly, from at least 1995 these reports are based mainly upon the perceptions of key informants and not upon statistically valid data.

Inland municipal fish production by fisheries region is shown in Table 2.6. Over the 5 years covered in Table 6, 78 percent of the landings were from one fisheries region (Southern Tagalog).

Table 6 Philippines - inland municipal capture fisheries production by region (MT).

Region	1993	1994	1995	1996	1997
CAR National Capitol	264	247	236	198	254
I Cordillera Administrative	2 190	3 766	1 421	1 274	1 080
II Cagayan Valley	4 226	3 670	4 769	4 829	4 762
III Central Luzon	2 903	3 886	4 377	4 488	3 995
IV Southern Tagalog	161 192	167 357	148 395	139 731	120 085
V Bicol	459	367	243	229	382
VI Western Visayas	3 038	4 144	3 335	2 779	2 288
VII Central Visayas	36	53	32	32	59
VIII Eastern Visayas	-	1	5	4	4
IX Western Mindanao	391	316	615	541	286
X Northern Mindanao	208	116	114	194	131
XI Southern Mindanao	670	560	956	948	987
XII Central Mindanao	8 308	2 969	3 428	3 432	6 713
XIII Caraga	9 382	5 516	6 763	6 555	5 227
ARMM Autonomous Muslim Mindanao	17 508	12 763	11 985	12 706	13 486
Total	**210 775**	**205 731**	**186 674**	**177 940**	**159 739**

Inland municipal capture fisheries production by species category is shown in Table 7. Molluscs, fish and crustaceans account for 66.8 percent, 30.8 percent and 2.4 percent respectively of the reported catches over the five years in question. The high contribution of molluscs to the catches presumably reflects some inclusion of fishing in bays and estuaries although molluscs can also be important in purely freshwater areas. Including molluscs in gross statistics in this fashion can be misleading since a large proportion of the weight is composed of shells. The contribution of molluscs to food supply is therefore seriously overestimated based upon gross weight. But on the contrary, molluscs can have a high commercial value. These data on composition should be investigated in more detail and in particular to separate the molluscs by species (if possible) and in particular to separate brackishwater and freshwater types. However, what is most relevant about these statistics for current purposes, is that such high productions of molluscs from inland fisheries appear to be absent from the production statistics for most other countries. This is likely because production of molluscs is not being properly recorded. There appears no reason to believe that fisheries for molluscs in the Philippines are particularly unique to that area.

Table 7 Philippines - composition of inland capture fisheries production from municipal fisheries (MT).

Category	1993	1994	1995	1996	1997
Fish	70 980	52 321	60 340	49 083	52 929
Crustaceans	4 904	6 223	5 651	6 217	4 969
Molluscs	134 891	147 187	120 683	122 640	101 841
Total	**210 775**	**205 731**	**186 674**	**177 940**	**159 739**

Although there is widespread attention to tilapia farming in the Philippines, it is interesting to note that in 1997, for example, about 35 percent of the total national freshwater production of tilapia arose from capture fisheries; and the latter production is likely underestimated. Similarly, production from capture fisheries for four other cultured groups greatly exceeds that from aquaculture. This capture production would mainly include the exploitation of feral/wild populations but also some fish escaping from aquaculture establishments.

Table 8 Philippines - contributions to reported production of selected species by production system, capture versus culture, for 1997

Species group	Capture fishery production	Aquaculture production
Tilapia	20 935	39 005
Carps (all kinds)	5 717	291
Mudfish	4 547	2 144
Hito (freshwater catfish)	2 396	1 052
Gouramy	2 065	132

Perceptions of Inland Fisheries and Objectives of the Statistics

According to the BAS manual for the inland fisheries survey, "*For the past years, inland fishing has contributed significantly to total fish production. The existing fishery household-based survey has generated statistics monitoring the levels of production. Ultimately, the sub-sector will provide the necessary data input for effective policy formulation particularly regarding food security concerns*".

Unfortunately, the household surveys are unlikely to meet these objectives since they are not being undertaken fully due to funding constraints and data collected on food security aspects is very limited in any case.

The Director of BFAR noted the marked shift from capture to culture that has occurred in inland areas in the Philippines. But in some areas, capture fisheries are still important. BFAR is very supportive of the need to improve data/information. In particular, improved information on vulnerable species, the impacts of introduced species and the importance of inland fisheries for livelihoods and development in rural areas is required. BFAR has strong emphasis on these aspects. Even if undertaken fully, the existing survey methods do not generate adequate information in these respects. There is also a need to delineate areas for fisheries versus culture in order to minimise conflicts between the two sub-sectors. Information is required that is relevant to achieving this aim. This is not currently being generated.

BFAR is currently "not happy" with the quality of inland statistics. BAS agrees, but lays the blame more squarely upon funding problems. BFAR also note that the quality of contracted survey personnel is also a problem. Technical interpretations of the statistics are, therefore, constrained. For example, BFAR staff expect high productions from some regions seasonally but this is not "reflected in reports".

BFAR also regard much of the statistics reported in the field to be based upon projections and not upon reality. They also reported widespread "doctoring" of data to meet production targets. In addition, BFAR suspects wide discrepancies from respondents who do not declare actual harvest for reasons of taxation.

It would appear that the statistics for inland capture fisheries serve no real purpose except to form the basis of national reporting requirements. There appear to be no major national or provincial inland capture fisheries management or development programmes, and certainly none using the statistics as the basis either for policy development or monitoring. Several commentators noted that the inland fishery statistics for the Philippines have little more than "cosmetic" value.

Conclusions and Recommendations

The Philippines inland fishery statistics, in common with all countries, suffer from the attempted application of marine statistical system to inland waters. It provides yet another example of the pitfalls in doing this. Statistical systems based upon landing records, particularly at official landing sites, are especially inappropriate for inland fisheries, largely because, in general, most fish tends not to be landed at official sites (depending upon the area in question). However, the Philippines are to be complimented by adding to their system a survey of household activities for inland fisheries. Unfortunately, this progress is undermined by the doubtful basis of the frame underlying this survey and the practicalities of implementing the surveys, including funding constraints. This also illustrates the dangers of designing statistical systems that rely upon substantial manpower (funding) to undertake them. These systems do not work, and are statistically invalid, under circumstances where designed sample sizes and strategies are not maintained. The result, as has occurred recently in the Philippines, is the continued production of statistics in which there is little confidence.

It is difficult to assess the Philippine statistics based upon the current brief overview. However, even if the statistical surveys were to be implemented according to plan, it is highly likely that the system would still produce gross underreporting from three main sources: (1) inadequacies of the frame underlying the household survey, (2) household surveys focussing on the main fisher as the respondent (a system which tends to exclude informal fishers in the household), and (3) likely deliberate underreporting by respondents. Added to this must be the consideration that in recent times the surveys have been inadequate in terms of coverage and/or based mainly upon the views of trends supplied by key informants. Consequently, it is difficult to assess what the likely figure for inland capture fisheries production for the Philippines actually is. It is also difficult to assess if the recent reported decline in production is realistic.

THAILAND

Thailand is amongst the economically better developed countries in Southeast Asia having undertaken rapid development in the past 30 or so years. However, economic well-being is not evenly distributed. In particular, the northern and north-east regions are economically depressed by comparison with the south and in particular in the vicinity of Bangkok. It is an environmentally diverse country and can be roughly divided into the northern section representing the main land mass and the southern peninsular bordering Myanmar and leading into Malaysia. Most rivers in Thailand have been dammed and consequently the country has a large number of reservoirs ranging from very small to extremely large. There are two significant drainage basins, both with large rivers. That draining N.W. Thailand enters the Chao Phraya system. Its upper catchment is a mountainous area, remote in places, and some sub-catchments are still in reasonable environmental condition. The lower Chao Phraya, however, drains most of the key industrial areas of Thailand including the massive urban area of Bangkok. Consequently it is highly degraded in its lower reaches. The N.E. section ("Isaan") contributes about 184 000 km^2 to the catchment of the Mekong River which forms the international border with Lao PDR for a considerable distance.

This is about 36 percent of the total area of the country. Thailand contributes about 18 percent to the total annual flow of the lower Mekong River. In Isaan, the major sub-catchments are the Mun-Chi basin and the Songkhram River basin. Of all the main tributaries of the Mekong originating in Thailand, the Songkhram is the only one still without a mainstream dam (although it has a considerable number of small dams on tributaries). Despite the extent of damming, recent remote sensing images confirm that N.E. Thailand still has considerable areas of seasonal wetlands (flooded areas). These are obviously located in flat areas and flooded mainly from local rains. Much of this area is already converted to rice agriculture with a substantial degree of irrigation development. Thailand is a major exporter of rice. Most of the lowlands of Thailand are already converted to intensive agricultural uses. Much environmental degradation of rivers has occurred. A reasonable catchment and floodplain system still occurs in the Songkhram and particular the Yom River (a tributary of the Chao Phraya) plus some other localised areas. All of the latter areas still have important and vibrant fisheries. Fisheries in degraded areas, even if a shadow of their former status, are still present. Fishing is a very popular activity in Thailand, having a long tradition. It is considered an integral part of the heritage/culture, particularly in rural areas.

Thailand has a rapidly growing sport/recreational fisheries sector of substantial proportions but it is currently un-quantified. A cursory look in larger supermarkets or department stores will usually reveal angling to be the largest amongst the sporting sections. And most equipment on sale is for use in inland waters. In most rural areas, particularly on holidays, most accessible waters are literally awash with fishers. Often the division between these by motivation (food, income or leisure) is difficult to make. Similarly, the country (in common with most economies in transition) has a very significant ornamental fish industry. The extent to which this relies upon domestic inland capture fisheries is not known, but a proportion of catches from rivers and swamps does certainly enter this industry.

Thailand has a very extensive stocking programme. This has concentrated on reservoirs and rice-fields but also includes rivers and swamps. Largely, stocking is seen as a means of providing benefits to poor communities. There is very limited information on the benefits of stocking in open waters.

Fisheries development has focussed on promoting aquaculture (with some considerable success over the past 15 years) and the management of reservoir fisheries. River and swamp fisheries have largely been ignored, apart from localised research on biology, ecology and limnology. This policy arose partly through insufficient appreciation of both the extent and importance of river fisheries but more so through the perception that little could be done to improve them, particularly in the face of rapid environmental degradation arising from water utilisation and pollution from other sectors. The policy has been very much one of trying to compensate for this trend by undertaking mitigation stocking and developing reservoir fisheries, with aquaculture successfully boosting total production and leading exports from the inland sector. But there is clear evidence of late of changes in attitude. NGO's and local communities are becoming increasingly more influential. Their attentions focus on social justice, livelihoods, biodiversity and the environment. DOF is already aware of and responding to these changes. This is evident, for example, in the growing recognition of the importance of inland capture fisheries (including reservoirs, rivers, swamps, rice fields etc.) to poverty reduction, livelihoods and environmental issues. Co-management is promoted, as is attention to environmental rehabilitation. Thailand represents an interesting case in terms of its inland capture fishery statistics, not dissimilar to Malaysia. Not only does the country have a (relatively) good infrastructure and human and financial resources, it is also at a watershed in terms of re-defining the role of government and fisheries in inland areas.

The Statistical Collection System

Each province has a fisheries office with one "statistician" (often a substitute). Each year this person is in-charge of collecting the statistics.

Actual information is collected by fisheries extension officers, based at district level, in close co-operation with officials at village level. Provinces send the information to the Division of Fishery Economics, Statistics Sub-Division, at DOF (Bangkok). This Division is in-charge of the information system. They forward the reports to FAO and to the national statistics authority (The National Statistics Office, Office of the Prime Minister).

The sampling strategy is based upon water body size (0-5, 5-10, 10-50, 50+ rai[4]). Information is collected by sampling approximately "10 percent" of each category. At each a survey is undertaken by asking a person about production. The person can be anybody considered knowledgeable: professional fisher, local official etc. For each interview, a pre-designed information form is used. This contains sections for gear types used, number of fishers, catches per person per year, total catches (estimated from the former), remarks, and for estimated species composition of total catches (in weight and value). Information requested covers a full year (yearly recall) but is not recorded by month. The total information sample is collected over a period of about 3-4 months during the dry season (February-May).

Water bodies are divided into three categories: (1) reservoirs and irrigation ponds, (2) village ponds (=communal/open access areas, not aquaculture ponds) and (3) "natural" water bodies (including rivers, swamps, streams and canals).

Production statistics are extrapolated largely based upon resource areas. The reservoir survey includes both natural lakes and man-made reservoirs. Seven species and five species groups are distinguished in this survey. Production is calculated on the basis of a nationwide inventory of water bodies, which is updated every five years. Total production for a particular water body is estimated in the above fashion, in close collaboration with local officials. The basis of this appears to be using both or either (i) estimated catches per unit effort related to total effort, and (ii) catches per unit area related to total area. DOF are confident they know the numbers of fishers operating in reservoirs and can calculate yield on this basis. In addition, in the larger reservoirs, landing statistics are gathered from middlemen on a weekly basis. For some of the larger reservoirs, catches are estimated solely through landings records. DOF estimate that based upon previous surveys, about 75 percent of the catch goes through official landing sites. For example, surveys at Ubolratana Reservoir have shown that about 17 percent of the catch goes for family consumption. In reservoirs, "small-scale" production is estimated by subtracting recorded landings from total estimated production. Species composition information is supplemented by observations at landing sites. There is no actual sampling of catches or landings.

In addition, DOF have some estimates of production from dry season "pond-traps" which require a license. (These are large dry season depressions, which trap fish as they retreat from flooded areas. They are fished with a variety of gears). Owners of flooded land will often construct pond traps. Some are natural dry season refuges. Some other types of inland fishing methods/gears require a license (*e.g.* barrage fences) but no catch data are collected. There is widespread non-compliance with licensing requirements in inland waters.

The system for aquaculture is very similar with 10 percent of installations being sampled against inventories held at village/district level. Estimates are based upon yearly reports of production, species, prices and stocking information. Since aquaculture installations are more visible and in fixed locations (compared with fishing operations in open waters), the aquaculture statistics are likely more robust.

Notably, no surveys are conducted for "natural" water bodies (particularly rivers and swamps). In some areas, total production for rivers and canals is estimated by provincial officers based on estimates of standing stock and average yield per unit area (reportedly derived from both previous studies the extent of which is unknown to the mission, and the experience of the officer). The actual methodology involved is unclear. But it is extremely unlikely such an approach gives accurate estimates for rivers, especially floodplain fisheries, particularly as accurate data for riverine fisheries production are rare. It is unclear if floodplain (swamp) fisheries are included under "rivers", but they are quite possibly often not included at all.

The fishery production estimates (capture and culture) are discussed at a meeting at the sub-district level before being submitted to the province; a system which reflects the possibly arbitrary nature of some parts of the estimation process. Provincial officers send the information to DOF (Bangkok) where it is compiled, edited, processed, encoded, and analysed with the aid of a UNIX based system for input and retrieval. DOF have developed their own software for this purpose.

DOF report that estimates vary considerably in quality. Statistics collection personnel have a low status (pay) and continuity of personnel involved is a major problem. Staff at lower levels than the province do not receive special pay for information collection and it is unlikely that this system encourages accuracy of the estimates.

The National Statistical Office is responsible for conducting the marine fishery census every 10 years. There is no comparable census in operation for inland fisheries (particularly for rivers). The Conservation Division of DOF reportedly initiated data collection from some important landing sites in the Mekong since 1995. These estimates are incorporated into the production figures for 1997 onwards.

Production from estuaries and mangrove areas is reported under coastal fisheries production. "Inland" catches are considered to be those exclusively from freshwater. This is not a problem for the north of the country (as there is no coast) but it can be assumed that a significant proportion of the inland catch (*i.e.* that not caught in the sea) from coastal areas in the south is reported under coastal fisheries. This can only contribute to downgrading the perceptions of the importance of the inland sector.

Production from rice-fields is reported exclusively as aquaculture - irrespective of the production system (*e.g.* stocked or natural recruitment). DOF consider that most production now arises through stocking activities anyway although their statistical system is not accurate enough to verify this. Even so, a considerable proportion may still arise through capture fishery related activities. Again, this information policy is to the detriment of capture activities.

There are obviously some serious potential problems with this statistical system. Not least of these is the virtual absence of sampling based information on river/floodplain fisheries. A major potential source of error is also with the inventory of water bodies. Obtaining such information, especially for small water bodies, is quite difficult. Additional constraints include problems with recall and estimations made by respondents. Although some people are good at this, many are not, and almost all under-estimate small-scale production. DOF also admit that their system favours commercial/professional fishers simply because they are more visible and accessible. However, the most serious potential problem is possibly the issue of impartiality of information collection. Provincial fisheries offices (and national DOF) spend a considerable part of their budget on the stocking programme. Often the same personnel involved in stocking are involved in statistics collection. In many countries this leads to mis-reporting through either attempts to disguise discrepancies between reported stocking and actual stocking (it is not known if this occurs in Thailand) or simply through more benign over-optimism on the impacts of their activities. The statistical system in force in Thailand is highly subjective and therefore very vulnerable to this kind of misreporting.

A further problem is that the statistical system is very much production oriented. There appears to be limited information collected on participation in fisheries (including catching, processing and marketing). Again, the best information here is for reservoirs where numbers of commercial/professional fishers are thought to be known reasonably well. There is some information on river fisheries based upon numbers of licensed gears but this is likely meaningless considering the level of non-compliance and the gear categories themselves being unrepresentative of the fishery as a whole.

The Information Produced

Reported catches from inland capture fisheries over the recent 10 year period are shown in Fig. 2-20. As explained, it is believed that these reports reflect mainly production from reservoirs. The overall trend for increasing production (average 136 272MT during 1990-2, to 200 364MT during 1997-9) is explained by DOF as due to stocking. This represents an increase in production of about 47 percent over the ten years in question, which is well within the limits of reason considering the stocking effort. There is, however, no way to check if these reports are accurate (which in any case should be done by DOF not the mission). There is currently no reason to assume that the reports are not representative of the general fisheries situation in reservoirs (within the limits of the constraints to the statistical system as described).

The problem is, of course, how to assess the likely errors due to not properly including reasonable figures for fisheries outside reservoirs. This can only be done, initially, by using cost-effective techniques as outlined in Part I. Some indications of likely errors can be suggested here:

Virapat *et al.* (2000) give an estimated inventory of 28 956 reservoirs in Thailand ranging from 0.01 to more than 1000 ha. They estimate production from these reservoirs, using similar methods to DOF (*i.e.* extrapolations based upon reservoir inventories and yield) to be between 122 314 and 318 909 MT. This in fact confirms that the official statistics (Fig. 2-19) likely refer to reservoirs almost exclusively. The same report also describes reservoir fisheries as being the same as "inland capture fisheries" (production from reservoirs is discussed and reported as total production from inland capture fisheries). This confirms that the perception of inland capture fisheries in Thailand is one of reservoirs. Whilst reservoirs are obviously important, as the aforementioned inventory shows, Thailand in fact does still have considerable river and swamp fisheries, plus some production from rice-fields. In addition, production from inland brackish-water areas is reported as coastal fisheries production.

A recent detailed survey of the Songkhram River Basin in N. E. Thailand (Department of Fisheries, unpublished) has produced much valuable information on fisheries in rivers and floodplains/swamps. The survey was based on reports from villages and random sampling of a statistically valid sample of households. Over 40 percent of village leaders reported that capture fisheries were important in their village for income. Overall, more than 60 percent of households in the Songkhram River basin are involved in capture fisheries. The average catch per fishing household was 224 kg per year. The proportion of the total catch taken from various habitats was as follows: rivers, streams and canals - 34.23 percent; swamps/marsh (floodplain) - 31.32 percent; rice-fields - 22.18 percent; reservoirs - 8.27 percent; lakes - 2.06 percent; aquaculture ponds - 1.97 percent. These figures confirm that capture fisheries in such areas are not only important but cumulatively produce large catches.

Production from capture greatly exceeds that from aquaculture. Although the area is notable for still having reasonable floodplains (although a relatively short flood season) catches from river channels and rice-fields are still significant. Production from rice-fields (which in this area generally are not stocked) averages about 50 kg/household/year (but this includes all households, production for rice-farming households has yet to be estimated). These figures are important when considering the potential extent of inland capture fisheries elsewhere in rural Thailand. Although the Songkhram river has no major dam (reservoir) the extent of fishing in rivers, smaller water bodies and rice-fields is likely not untypical of Thailand.

The potential degree of underreporting in the official statistics is also illustrated by the fact that only 5.5 percent of households listed fishing as the main occupation but 57 percent of households list that part-time fishing is important. But the official fishery statistics are based solely upon households where fishing is the main occupation.

It is widely held that dams have significantly reduced fisheries in major rivers in Thailand. This is probably true and has certainly been used as a major reason to devote most attention to reservoir fisheries and aquaculture. However, the impacts of dams on flooding and river fisheries and upon migratory fish stocks are mainly downstream. Much of the capture fisheries activities in rivers occur in side branches and local swamps and other discrete water bodies where longitudinal migrations (along rivers) are less important. Recent flood cover maps of Thailand show that much of the country is still flooded (including in rivers with major dams). Although the major river floodplains have been severely reduced and degraded, localised rainfall still produces large expanses of freshwater habitat available for fishing. Much of this is rice-fields and canals associated with them. But there are still large cumulative areas of smaller rivers, localised swamps and marshes etc.

What is a reasonable guess as to the possible production for inland capture fisheries in Thailand? This is highly speculative largely because much of the freshwater resources are degraded and the economy is relatively well developed (which tends to down-grade involvement in fishing for income and/or food). But Thailand still has large relatively poor rural populations. For freshwaters alone, a conservative figure of 10 million relatively (*i.e.* within Thailand) poorer rural people catching an average of between 20 and 50 kg per caput per year (outside reservoirs) gives an annual production of 200 000 to 500 000 MT (these indicative catches are not unrealistic; it is 20 kg per caput for river fisheries in the remote mountain areas in Lao PDR, which are not dissimilar to mountainous areas in Thailand, and more than 50 kg per caput for the Songkhram river which is probably typical for rural Thailand). Added to this would be that part of the coastal (brackish-water) fishery caught inland, which would also be significant. These examples do at least show that it would be worthwhile to properly undertake a re-assessment of production estimates for inland capture fisheries in Thailand for areas outside reservoirs. This can be done relatively easily and Thailand has good GIS and remote sensing information and expertise to assist these efforts.

Perceptions of Inland Fisheries and Objectives of the Statistics

In Thailand, inland capture fisheries are regarded as activities undertaken by the poor in rural areas (there are some exceptions but this is mainly correct). They are important for food production and security and have some "economic" importance for household incomes etc. It was clearly stated that inland fisheries in these terms were significantly more important than marine fisheries (which are regarded more as a source of revenue/exports). When asked if this was not an over-simplification, DOF responded that "even a poor marine fisherman is rich compared to a poor rural (inland) fisherman".

There is an admitted over-emphasis on reservoirs at the expense of attention to rivers and other areas. This is partly reinforced by the biases in the statistical system. Recently, more thought has been given to rivers but DOF appear uncertain as to their options for such fisheries. There are no significant management strategies for riverine fisheries other than on-going mitigation stocking. Main problems within the fishery are reported to be non-compliance with regulations and over-fishing. This is particularly so in reservoirs. More recently the government has been seriously promoting co-management approaches to improve governance of fisheries. In rivers, environmental degradation is clearly recognised as the major problem. There is a general feeling that in many areas the river and swamp fisheries are already decimated beyond recognition. This is unfortunately true for those areas. On a more positive note this points to the considerable scope for rehabilitation. But some areas still have important river and floodplain fisheries. Most of these are under immediate threat from further environmental impacts from other sectors (particularly dams). Although aware of the opportunities, DOF has yet to become fully involved and active in river fishery restoration and there is considerable scope for this in Thailand. The recent shift in policies towards being more directly pro-poor and pro-environment should in theory enable DOF to become more involved in this area.

Thailand uses its current inland fishery statistics for: (i) calculating GDP (a requirement from central government), (ii) monitoring the status of inland fisheries (production, production area and stocking activities etc.), and (iii) as a management tool, mainly for large water bodies (reservoirs), to calculate the impacts of stocking etc. The current statistics might meet some of these requirements for reservoirs (although there is obviously scope for improvement) but obviously not so for rivers/swamps. For current purposes, the DOF generally consider that they have the information needed for reservoirs, but that there is scope to improve the accuracy and coverage. However, there was a clear consensus at DOF that different, additional, information is urgently required when trying to develop and implement policies and management aimed at poverty alleviation, improving livelihoods and biodiversity/environment considerations. But there is considerable uncertainty about who is supposed to collect such information and particularly regarding what information to collect and how.

Conclusions and Recommendations

Apart from technical constraints in the reporting system (as outlined above), a major problem with the Thai system is that it seriously biases perceptions of the inland fisheries sector towards reservoirs and aquaculture. It has been an almost deliberate policy to either disregard river/swamp fisheries, or to accept their demise, and compensate for loses through production from other sources. This policy is not unique to Thailand and not entirely without justification; aquaculture and reservoir fisheries have developed well. But in parallel to this, a statistical system has developed that is not only biased towards aquaculture and reservoirs, but towards reporting increases in production in those sectors in response to government management measures. This has likely had a cyclical impact - reinforcing further investments in those sectors, partly at the expense of river fisheries. In hindsight, it would have been nice to have statistics reporting the losses being incurred from river fisheries. But a more interesting question, and not entirely academic, is whether the statistical system itself has contributed to such loss by reinforcing pro-aquaculture/reservoir policies or is simply a result of those policies. We can only conclude that countries should at least be cautious when basing policies on incomplete statistical coverage and be especially vigilant where such statistics reinforce policies.

It is doubtful if the current national system yields information of adequate quality to assess stocking, especially considering its subjective nature. But Thailand can, and often does, obtain better information on stocking through alternative local means. This is usually through a more focussed research process where more specific and detailed information can be gathered. What is certain is that the current information is next to useless in terms of livelihoods, poverty, biodiversity or environment related considerations. Naturally, in relation to its current inland fishery statistics, Thailand has the option of checking the information through verification processes (research) and making subsequent improvements in both accuracy and cover. This should be done where possible. But the current Thai system has certain advantages which should not be discounted. It is (presumably) relatively cost-effective. It is based upon a rather simple technical approach. The information collected is not too technical and can be collected relatively easily. These are valuable attributes for a statistical system. The Thai system should not be discarded as a model for obtaining basic information. Before significant changes, and more importantly new investments, to this system are made, the question of whether the system satisfies modern information requirements should be addressed. According to DOF, apparently it does.

Future directions in information improvement need to consider the changing emphasis in policies. The current statistical system on its own will be a considerable constraint to DOF (and Thailand more generally) becoming more directly involved in poverty reduction, livelihoods, biodiversity/environment and inland fisheries restoration etc. The information generated is simply not particularly relevant to these issues. No matter how much is invested in the current system (within reason), the mission doubts if it will ever produce the necessary information. Thailand has the option to make some cheap and effective improvements to its current system, but to largely leave it alone, and to make new investments in more appropriate approaches for information generation under a wider, modern framework.

Some of the recommendations for cost-effective approaches to obtain better information, specifically an improved "overview", for inland fisheries outside reservoirs are based upon utilising remote sensing GIS approaches (see Part I). It is noted that the Thai Department of Fisheries has a relatively well resourced and competent GIS support unit. There is considerable scope for using this facility to improve information for inland areas and using remote sensing for fisheries environment monitoring purposes. This particularly applies to areas where empirical survey data are weak. Remote sensing is also cost-effective, impartial and accurate for undertaking resource surveys (*e.g.* reservoir inventories and aquaculture installations). One opportunity is to improve co-ordination and utility of resources within DOF by training GIS specialists in inland fisheries applications and inland fisheries specialists in GIS applications so the two can work better together. The technology is particularly useful for natural resources management planning (*e.g.* undertaking impact assessments for major development schemes).

DOF should give some consideration to becoming more involved in the recreational fishery sector (although not at the expense of attention to other more pressing issues of livelihoods and biodiversity etc.). DOF consider that the sub-sector is, and will be, largely serviced by the private sector (but oddly this has not stopped them being involved with aquaculture for which the same can be said). Even so, there is still a need for a government overview. Involvement might be based on co-management approaches and the principle of costs being recouped from the sector (which is more feasible for sport fisheries than other sub-sectors, see Part I and further comments in this part of the report for Malaysia).

In short, Thai inland fisheries are changing rapidly. Therefore, information requirements are also changing rapidly. DOF have already identified most of the opportunities but are unsure how to meet the technical challenges. Hopefully, Part I of this report will assist with this.

COUNTRIES NOT VISITED DURING THE CONSULTANCY

The mission has direct involvement in relevant experiences with inland capture fishery statistics elsewhere in Southeast Asia (Cambodia, Lao PDR, Thailand and VietNam) from two main sources: (i) in 1996 an inland fishery statistics project formulation mission was undertaken by the MRC (Sverdrup-Jensen, Coates and Visser, unpublished), and (ii) since 1993 fisheries research and development work has been undertaken by the MRC, much of which is relevant to the current subject matter including the now comprehensive knowledge of capture fisheries production and statistics in Cambodia and comprehensive and systematic sampling based surveys of river capture fisheries in Lao PDR, Thailand and VietNam.

CAMBODIA

Cambodia has impressive freshwater resources. It lies at the heart of the lower Mekong River floodplains and includes the upper section of the Mekong River delta. As part of this system, the Tonle Sap River joins the Mekong at Phnom Penh, draining vast areas of floodplains to the north-west. Chief amongst these is the area around the Great

Lake, which undergoes extensive seasonal expansion partly through the reversing flow of the Tonle Sap River. The area of this lake alone extends from 2000-3000 km^2 in the dry season to 10 000-12 000 km^2 in the flood season. This floodplain adjoins that of the Mekong mainstream forming a large interconnected expanse of prime fish habitat, much of it tropical floodplain forest. The Great Lake and Tonle Sap floodplains account for some 60 percent of reported fisheries production. There are no large reservoirs but a modest number of smaller water bodies exist. Rice field fisheries are however important.

The fisheries of Cambodia are legendary. However, this is mainly because historical records exist, in particular formal and accessible publications made by the French in the 1930's and 40's. Hopefully, this important archive might encourage others to publish research properly also. Based upon official catch reports over the past 10 years the fishery is less impressive (until reports were revised in 1999); although historically, before the late 1970's reports were much higher. This represents another anomaly of fishery statistics: where published scientific records exist, they are, quite rightly, favoured over official statistics, at least in some circles. The country is often quoted as having the largest inland fishery in Southeast Asia. This is not the case: it is certainly easily surpassed by at least Myanmar and challenged by both Indonesia and VietNam. But these countries have much larger populations. For its size, Cambodia has a very impressive river fishery indeed.

The modes of exploitation are typical for Southeast Asian river fisheries. Where opportunities exist, large commercial/industrial gears are used. Major ones include barrage fences and river bag-nets. These supplement huge cumulative catches taken by a multitude of other gears in what is a very diverse and vibrant fishery. Cambodia also has a well developed and extensive fishing "lot" system whereby most of the productive areas or fishing opportunities are leased out. This is generally achieved through bi-annual auctions. Major lots include bagnets along the Tonle Sap River (which target fish migrating from the Great Lake) and areas of prime floodplain which are fenced-off and usually fished with barrage-fence/traps and other gears within the lot. Some of these fences can be up to 60 km long. The management system closely resembles that for the "Inn" fishery in Myanmar where the system appears to be more intensive, but lease areas in Cambodia may, on average, be larger. The two systems have similar histories (being in place since at least the mid-1850's). The system also occurs in Indonesia, possibly Malaysia and on small local scales in Thailand.

As expected, the fishery is highly seasonal. Scenes at fishing lots during peak periods are still reminiscent of the bye-gone days in many marine fisheries. At these periods, huge quantities of fish are preserved by drying and making fish sauce but especially fish paste. There is considerable participation in fish processing, marketing and transport. Large quantities of fish and fish products are exported to both VietNam and Thailand.

For descriptive, management and legislative purposes the fishery is divided into:

- large-scale stationary gears, where the use of gears or areas is auctioned (the fishing "lots").
- medium-scale mobile gears, where gears are subject to licensing, and
- small-scale or "family" fishing which has open entry but only open access to fishing grounds outside lot areas

The fishing lot system in Cambodia has come under considerable criticism of late. First, the current system is regarded, in places, as being socially unjust because it excludes the rural poor from access to the fishery. In response to this the system is currently under review, apparently with considerable political backing. The objective is not necessarily to demolish a system which, in principle, has much to offer, but to address issues of equity, governance and management. Second, and more relevant to the current report, the fishing rights (auction) system is less than transparent and widely regarded as involving much corruption.

Freshwater aquaculture production is modest at about 13 500 MT in 1999. Freshwater aquaculture is developing, as expected, mainly in areas where there is less competition from capture fisheries.

The country is also interesting for the present purposes because its statistics, and the basis for them, are probably the best researched in Southeast Asia. A Danida funded project, based at the Department of Fisheries in Phnom Penh, has, amongst other things, for the past seven years been researching the actual fisheries production based upon catch-effort sampling and socio-economic surveys. This information, together with the historical records and a number of related recent initiatives, has made Cambodia, in terms of its national inland fisheries, probably the best researched country in Southeast Asia. One odd result of this is that its fisheries are often regarded as "unique", and therefore not relevant elsewhere. But they are only "unique" because we know much more about them, not because they are necessarily different to those in comparable areas. Nevertheless, apart from being one of Southeast Asia's major producers, the country provides very good and credible examples of what is actually happening in the more productive sub-sectors of inland captures fisheries and how this may or may not be reflected in statistics.

The Statistical Collection System

The freshwater capture fisheries data collection system was reviewed by Thor Sensereivorth *et al.* (1999). Recent statistics have been collected from the burden books (lease documents), fishing licenses and interviews with lot owners. The middle-scale fishery is estimated from license information and estimates or reports of catch-effort. These statistics are collected by the provincial fisheries offices before being sent to the Fisheries Department and are based partly upon the annual planned figures. Estimates are made for other sub-sectors.

The large-scale or industrial capture fishery is covered mainly by the means of an activity logbook, which the Lot owner updates with the daily production (catch). The production figures for each month are collected by "data" collectors either based at the provincial fishery unit or at the community level (which might include several villages combined). There are around 5-6 data collectors in every province. Total production is reported monthly, by the provincial fisheries staff, to the Department of Fisheries in Phnom Penh. Traditionally, this occurs after a provincial meeting to discuss and estimate the monthly production figures - a system which illustrates the high degree of estimation in the production figures. All but one province has provincial fisheries staff. Since there is no time to sort fish into species level at the Lot, no data on species are recorded. Instead, fish are graded by value into no more than three categories. The same provincial staff collect information for the total aquaculture production from cages, ponds and pens from households by means of a sampling census. It is, however, assumed that this system is far from ideal and at field level there are doubts as to how extensive the census actually is. Provinces submit a yearly report to summarise the data and make projections for following years. These, unsurprisingly, often form the basis of future actual production reports.

Production from the middle-scale fishery is estimated based upon license records and reported catches. In theory, monthly surveys are supposed to be undertaken. In practice estimates are often made by district fishery officers. It appears that the small-scale fishery has traditionally been assessed, if at all, using a "guesstimate" since, until recently, there was no data on the extent of the fishery.

The National Institute of Statistics (NIS) does not collect data on fisheries or fish consumption and is totally dependant on the DOF to supply relevant data. NIS does produce a Consumer Price Index, which includes a quite comprehensive price listing for fish and fish products at several markets over the country. This is very useful supplementary information. The NIS is officially responsible for the general statistical methodology for all the government departments officially has to approve any methodology applied. However, this is largely ignored by the line departments.

In 1994, the Project for Management of Freshwater Capture Fisheries of Cambodia (Danida/MRC) began a stratified random sampling approach to data collection based upon a frame survey of fishing gears. This recorded all species captured, catch by gear, by month, by season, by sector districts, price and total value landed, initially only for the large and middle scale fisheries. The first comprehensive survey of the small scale fishery was completed in 1995-6 (Ahmed *et al.* 1998). It should be noted, however, that this work continued in parallel to the recurrent statistics collection system, figures for which were not amended in response to this sampling until 1999.

The Information Produced

The figures prior to 1999 are effectively meaningless. In 1999, the official reports were revised, under considerable pressure, partly as a result of catch sampling research that has been undertaken by the Danida/MRC fisheries project. This resulted in roughly an increase by the factor 3.3 on previous reports. But even the recent report (1999) is considered likely an under-estimate.

A partial review of the Cambodia statistics is presented in Thor Sensereivorth *et al.* (1999). A full review of the Cambodia statistics is beyond the scope of this report. This should be done elsewhere and would also be of great benefit to other countries interested in the subject. This review identified the cause of under-reporting was derived from four main sources:

- Under-estimates of the participation in, and cumulative catches from, small-scale family fisheries
- Under-estimates of middle-scale fisheries due to inadequacies in license cover (miscounting gears)
- Deliberate under-reporting by fishers, because licenses and fees are linked with revenue collection and fishers consider landings information as confidential for a number of other reasons
- Under-reporting by local government staff for licensed and lease fisheries, related to revenue collection (the revenue officially collected differs from that actually paid and, therefore, proper catch reports are suppressed accordingly)

Current estimates of the freshwater capture fisheries production in Cambodia are presented in Table 9. Uncertainty continues in a number of areas.

Table 9 Estimates of freshwater capture fisheries production in Cambodia (from Sensereivorth* et al.*, 1999)

Sub-Sector	Annual catch (MT)
Large scale fisheries:	
- Fishing lot	30 000 - 60 000
- Dais (Bagnets)	15 000 - 20 000
Middle scale fisheries	85 000 - 100 000
Family fisheries	115 000 - 140 000
Rice field fisheries	45 000 - 110 000
Total	290 000 - 430 000

First, whilst catches from the bagnets are relatively easy to verify through catch sampling, catches from lease fisheries are difficult to verify because it is often difficult for sampling officials to either gain proper access or, even if they do, to report independently. Even well intentioned officials can be harassed by powerful lot owners. Hence the uncertainty with production from lots. Given the lack of transparency in the lot fisheries, Baran *et al.* (2001), in consultation with most knowledgeable local commentators, applied an arbitrary (but considered conservative) value of three times to the officially reported catches from lots. In addition, most of the current information on catches, and the current official statistics, apply only to the main fishing areas located around the Mekong and Tonle Sap Rivers and floodplains. Areas remote from this will have lower catches per caput but totals would still be significant. This factor contributes to uncertainties with the figures especially for the small-scale family fishery. These fisheries were not included in previous official reports at all.

These figures are between 4 and 6 times the previously reported production in most of the 1990's. Oddly though, they are still higher than the revised figures for 1999. The discrepancy is presumably due to continued reluctance by the people compiling statistics to accept scientifically based sampling over traditional methods, and, despite the inaccuracy of the traditional system which is itself based upon estimates at best, to accept estimates for areas where no data are actually collected.

The Cambodian experiences are highly relevant to the current review in a number of other respects:

- The official statistical system proved reluctant to accept more accurate and representative data, and did not do so until a long time after new figures were available. But this was not entirely because of the aforementioned problems with transparency and governance. A major problem was that the traditional system collected information through a network independent to the research work and with different methods. Despite the availability of better data, it could not be easily incorporated into official statistics. This illustrates the need to either (i) generate improved figures within the existing system, or (ii) if figures need to be changed, change the statistical reporting system first and in particular, modify approaches so they can more readily accept in-direct information. This points to the danger of assuming that improved information based upon rational and credible research will automatically change fishery statistics. Governments should be more flexible in the way they generate statistical information.
- These new figures arose from a significant donor funded investment in research. The information generated is highly valuable and has forced changes in official perceptions of the fishery. But it is interesting to ask if the results only endorsed what people actually already knew about the fishery. For example, Chevey and Poulain (1939) had already estimated production from the Great Lake and Tonle Sap to be 100 000 MT, not that dissimilar to recent estimates, allowing for population growth

(Baran *et al.*, 2001). The overall information generated, of course, has great value well beyond its relevance to fishery statistics, but a very relevant question is should other countries embark on the same kind of programme if revising the statistics is the objective?

- There are doubts about whether the methods used to obtain more accurate recent figures can be sustained (especially so for the small-scale fisheries). They require high levels of training inputs, motivation, supervision and monitoring. Whilst improvements can be made in the traditional system, an option is to use the research information to reassess what the traditional figures mean (which is presumably what happened in 1999).
- Even with the improved information, based upon sampling data, a large error of uncertainty still exists. The estimates in Table 2.9 give range of between 17 and 144 percent for the sub-sectors and 48 percent for total production (based upon the lower estimate of production range in each case). Whilst these levels of accuracy are workable for useful indications of the extent of the fishery, they are all but useless for monitoring overall trends. Why then, continue to collect the data every year?
- In relation to the narrow subject of statistics, the considerable investments in research have shown two important points:
    - o they only confirmed that the recent official reports (to 1999) were essentially bogus (but hopefully more sustained realistic figures will emerge). Even so, current and medium-term figures will likely be based upon re-assessing the figures produced through the traditional means, not necessarily by adopting *prima face* new methods or data.
    - o investing significantly in strengthening the statistical system based upon current methodologies and objectives is not necessarily a good idea, and it may not yield data accurate enough for monitoring and other purposes.

Another problem with the statistics in Cambodia is that they continue to be driven by the quest for gross production data. They are of limited use for management where livelihoods, poverty, food security and environment/biodiversity are becoming more important issues. The mission notes that although some useful information on these latter aspects is now emerging in Cambodia, it arises through research, not through the statistical system. When assessing the recent significant re-estimation of the official Cambodian statistics (for 1999) it is important to keep in mind and separate the contributions of research and recurrent statistics collection systems.

Some other information of considerable relevance to fishery statistics regionally is available for Cambodia (most based upon research, not the statistics collection system). These are included here mainly for the benefit of other countries that might be reviewing their information systems, particularly for rivers.

Such gross variations in catches over the year should be typical for tropical rivers, particularly those with large floodplains. However, catches are also influenced by the extent of flooding in any particular year. This is likely because (i) bigger floods produce more fish, and (ii) the gears are more effective in bigger floods (because stronger currents in river channels are found in big flood years). This phenomenon also likely affects catches for barrage gears.

According to Ahmed *et al.* (1998): fish consumption in floodplain areas is on average of 76 kg/caput/year, compared to only 8 kg/caput/year for other animal products; only 1 percent of fishing households engaged in fishing lots or large-scale fishing, 6 percent engaged in middle-scale (licensed) fishing, whereas almost all households were involved in small-scale fishing; production per household ranged from an average of 647 kg for family fishing households to 3 319 kg for middle-scale fishing households; 78.6 percent of households are actively involved in fishing related activities.

Fisheries yield from Mekong floodplains in Cambodia has been estimated at between 225 and 375 kg/hectare/year (MRC, 2001). Production from un-stocked rice fields is: in the region of 100-125 kg/hectare/year (Gregory *et al.*, 1996, Guttman, 1999), 38 kg/caput/year for rice farmers (APHEDA, 1997), 201 kg/household per year amongst farmers for a 5 month period (Numa Sham and Try Hong, 1998).

Perceptions of inland fisheries and objectives of the statistics

One thing is for certain, Cambodians know fully the importance of their inland fishery. And in that, the country, along with Myanmar, is unusual. But what is revealing, and of immense relevance in this review, is that this appears to have made little difference to their statistics (until recently). There exists this curious separation of perceptions and statistics, illustrated best in Cambodia.

According to Thor Sensereivorth *et al.* (1999):

"The role of statistics is very important and basic for the assessment and solving of problems relevant to the fisheries management. If we can manage fishery statistics properly and correctly, we can make proper plans for fisheries management based on (1) an assessment of the biological and economic effects of a change in fishery regulations or in hydrology, and (2) an early warning of a species in decline and (3) essential baseline data for Environmental Impact Assessments (EIA's)".

It can only be said that this is an extremely optimistic assessment of the role of statistics as the term is currently understood, and that the existing official figures have not assisted these goals in any significant fashion, and recently revised figures are unlikely to help with most. Another problem inherent in such statements and objectives is widespread confusion regarding the nature of "statistics". There is now a lot of information available in Cambodia that will indeed assist with some of these stated objectives, but it was produced by research, not regular (formal) statistics collection. As far as is known, there are no current or planned management initiatives based upon the current statistics (which is perhaps fortunate).

There has been a recent significant shift in emphasis with Cambodian freshwater capture fisheries. Whilst the fisheries retain significant commercial importance, there is increasing emphasis on social justice, poverty reduction, improved governance (co-management approaches) and biodiversity and the environment.

The main problems with the fishery are reported as largely due to over-exploitation and non-compliance with existing regulations (Ahmed *et al.*, 1998). It appears that this is a common gripe amongst fishing communities, as there is little evidence of actual over-exploitation, except perhaps for a number of prominent, but never abundant, species (Coates, 2001). The more usual complaint of habitat loss and environmental degradation in rivers applies less immediately to Cambodia as the resources are still in reasonable shape. But Cambodia's aquatic resources are extremely vulnerable to water management activities and pollution arising mainly, but not exclusively, from upstream. There are signs of growing environmental stress but it is not yet critical. Will the existing statistics enable these influences to be monitored?

It is beyond the scope of this report to advise Cambodia on specific measures it should take to improve its statistics. Better informed advice is available locally, and some local initiatives are already underway. But despite recent improvements in knowledge of the fisheries, Cambodia is yet to offer examples of how actual recurrent statistical systems can be improved and sustained (other than demonstrating the levels of previous under-reporting). The experiences in Cambodia are, of course, highly relevant to statistics, and options for their improvement, in other countries.

To a large extent the statistical system in Cambodia, even if it functioned effectively, suffers from its historical origins whereby a priority has been to track trends in gross production. This it has clearly failed to do. Neither is there evidence that the recent improvement (increase) in the figures will help in this respect. The system also has a bias towards the more prominent gears and this is likely at least in part because of the revenue generating aspects of the sector (which does not mean that that consideration is unimportant).

Inland capture fishery statistics are clearly in a state of transition in Cambodia. In view of recent experiences with the statistics, and the now relatively advanced state of knowledge of the fisheries (in comparison to some countries), the time is certainly ripe for the on-going re-assessment of the whole statistics and information system. Part I of this review recommends that countries should first consider what information they actually need. Only then should they worry about how to get it. Fundamental to this issue in Cambodia, as elsewhere, is for the relevant authorities to recognise that the fishery sector and its objectives are changing, together with its information requirements.

It is peculiar, therefore, that despite the level of knowledge of Cambodian inland capture fisheries, and particularly the recent attention to improving statistics, that this report has to conclude that the country is in the same boat as everybody else in terms of what to do to improve things; although it is better armed than some with information once it has decided.

LAO PDR

Lao PDR is the only landlocked country covered in this report. The country is amongst the poorest in Southeast Asia. It comprises some 202 000 km^2 of the total Mekong catchment which accounts for about 97 percent of the total area of the country. It contributes some 35 percent of the average annual flow of the Mekong. Freshwater resources are dominated by rivers and the country includes some of the most pristine of all the Mekong tributaries. River fisheries dominate the sector. Floodplain/swamp fisheries occur in localised areas and are generally more common in the south of the country than in the north, although nowhere are they extensive. The country has one large reservoir, Nam Ngum, with modest production and a number of smaller reservoirs used for hydropower and mainly irrigation. Rice agriculture is widespread and is being intensified although pesticide use is currently less than elsewhere in Southeast Asia.

Lao PDR still has some impressive fisheries, mainly river-based. Population density is quite low and there is much potential for river capture fisheries to develop further. Aquaculture is poorly developed by Southeast Asian standards. This is likely partly due to the low level of marketing opportunities but also through competition from wild fisheries (including rice field fisheries). Information on trade is inaccurate but Lao PDR is likely a net exporter of fish. Considerable quantities of fish pass informally between Lao PDR and Thailand, especially in the south and along the Mekong River, which forms much of the 1800 km international border between the two countries.

The Statistical Collection System

The Fisheries Division was created only in 1995 as a distinct unit within the Department of Livestock and Fishery of the Ministry of Agriculture and Forestry. No information on national capture fisheries production has ever been collected in a systematic and comprehensive fashion. Some information has been collected for the fishery in the Nam Ngum reservoir, where collection is relatively easy since the local fishers are only allowed to sell their catches to one middleman. Despite this, information on the small-scale fishery in this reservoir, where the catch is consumed directly and not marketed through the middleman, has been lacking.

Although not currently functioning properly for providing fisheries information, a basic structure for data collection seems to be in place and is currently used to collect statistics on livestock, agriculture and forestry. Data collection at village level is performed by means of the village headman, a "model farmer" or the relevant veterinarian worker. Usually at least one, but more often, all three of these are present in each village. Each is responsible for data reporting to the Ministry of Agriculture and Forestry. These people submit completed questionnaires through the district and provincial authorities to the national line departments in Vientiane. However, it is reported that relationships between villagers and government officers are less than ideal and there is widespread under-reporting. The main problem appears to be the usual fear that statistics will be used for taxation purposes. The level of formal training in data collection and statistics, in general, is weak at both provincial and district level.

The National Statistics Centre (NSC) has been developing methodologies and standards leading to a uniform system of data collection. The NSC policy is to work with a decentralised structure where all line Ministries will be responsible for data collection in their own field.

The Information Produced

The official production figures, both for capture and culture fisheries, are based entirely on estimates. In some cases these are more accurately described as guesses. These may or may not include extrapolations using previous documented estimates and, needless to say, may not reflect actual production. Official estimates are derived from yields per unit area for reservoirs and rice/fish culture and a standard figure for river fisheries. The latter figure has not changed much over the years and originates from a study by the University of Michigan in 1973. Singh (1990) re-estimated total production and included more realistic estimates for reservoir fisheries. Again this was based on no sampling data from Lao PDR. This estimate has been used as the basis for recent statistics submitted to FAO.

The recent official figures for total production from inland capture fisheries are shown in Fig. 2-24. The reported increase in production since 1993, and variations between years, are assumed to be explained by re-estimates or perceived increased production from reservoirs. There is no sampling or statistical basis to the information reported in Fig. 2-24.

A household survey was performed by NSC in 1992 comprising 3000 households in 147 villages in 18 provinces. The survey included a limited number of questions relevant to fisheries. The summary information suggests that nationally about 66 percent of the households interviewed own at least 1 fishing net. The NSC has also developed a "Village Book" for the regular reporting of various data.

There have been a number of localised studies of capture fisheries, notably in southern Lao PDR. *e.g.* In the area of Khone Falls, where there is a traditional fishery targeting migratory fishes (Viravong *et al.*, 1994, Singhanouvong *et al.*, 1996a, 1996b, Warren *et al.*, 1998). This work includes some excellent and extremely valuable time-series data for catch-effort for this fishery but is of limited use for estimating production.

Recently, research and survey work has enabled a reasonable re-evaluation of the likely capture fisheries production. Sjørslev (2000) reported results of a sampling survey of fisheries in Luang Prabang province in the northern part of the country. This mountainous province is has high terrain gradients gradient and there are no significant lakes, reservoirs or swamps. There is an extensive network of rivers and streams, which is typical for such areas. A second major aquatic resource is rice-fields. Aquaculture is poorly developed.

The area is regarded as one where capture fisheries production, on average, would be at the lower end of the range for the Mekong Basin. Even so, catches of individual fishers have a mean of 54 kg per year with a variance of 30 to 78 kg. Although not spectacular by capture fisheries standards the significance of the catches is considerable because participation in the fishery is very high (which is normal). In 63 percent of surveyed villages, more than 95 percent of households depend on capture fisheries, with an additional 22 percent of villages having between 75 and 25 percent of household dependents. Fishing was ranked as the third most important household activity after rice-farming and livestock. Only two villages (7 percent) had "professional" fishers, each with about 10 percent of households involved. Overall, 83 percent of households are involved in fishing, and 41 percent of household members, 20 percent of which are children.

The average yearly per caput consumption of fish and other aquatic animals was estimated at 29kg with fresh products accounting for between 16 and 22 kg. Fishery products accounted for about 43 percent of total animal products consumed but about 55-59 percent based upon animal protein equivalent. Margins of error using various methods to estimate total catch (based upon catch-effort data) were high (+ 30 percent). Final estimates were reached with some degree of confidence by combining a number of approaches. The use of fish consumption data injected considerable confidence into the overall estimates both as a way of calculating total production and as a check against catch-effort data.

The survey concluded that total production from capture fisheries was between 10 000 and 15 000 MT per annum (as much as half of which is processed locally after being caught). This wide range (error) in the estimates should be viewed in context. It is the indicative figure, not its absolute accuracy that is important: First, there is much natural variation in such fisheries and therefore trying to be super accurate in any one year is somewhat pointless. Second, and more importantly for the present purposes, official statistics for the province put capture production at a meagre 700 MT per annum (between 4.5 and 7 percent of the likely figure). Apart from the lack of actual data in the official figures, two main factors contribute to the under-reporting: First, it is understood that official reports cover only what is considered to be "proper" ("professional") fishing. Second, they only include finfish landed at regular marketing sites (the survey showed that most fish is not formally marketed and between 20-30 percent of the total catch is not fish but composed of a variety of other taxa - crustaceans, molluscs, insects, amphibians etc. taken especially from rice-fields).

Where imports and exports are known (either nationally or locally) then fish consumption figures can be used to estimate fishery production and are a very credible check for local statistics. As already noted, Lao PDR is unlikely to be a significant net importer of fish, and has no marine fishery. Therefore, most fish consumed will be produced domestically. Lao PDR undertook an Expenditure and Consumption Survey in 1997/8 based upon a nationwide household survey. The inclusion of a limited number of simple questions in this survey, relating to expenditure and consumption of fish, enabled a very accurate indicative figure for fish production for the whole country to be calculated. However, it was important to include in this approach estimates of consumption for fish products (particularly fish sauce, fish paste and dried fish). The resulting estimate of national fish consumption (= production) for Lao PDR is in the region of 200 000 MT (Sjørslev 2000). The largest potential source of error (which could be either positive or negative) in the calculation arises from figures for processed fish (both consumption data and fresh-fish conversion factors). The survey data produced an estimate of consumption (production) of 100 000 MT per annum for fresh finfish alone. The estimate of 200 000 MT per annum is considered reasonable and equates to an average of about 36 kg per caput per annum which is realistic for a country in Southeast Asia with good water resources and a predominantly rural/ agricultural population. The proportion of this arising from the various sub-sectors has yet to be calculated but aquaculture is known to represent only about 14 000 MT nationally in 1998, which was re-estimated at 30 000 MT for 1999 (7 to 15 percent of the total production). Production from rice-fields, however, is significant.

A conservative estimate of capture fishery production of about 150 000 MT per annum is 5 times the officially reported annual figure. Lao authorities are currently discussing how to incorporate more realistic revised estimates of capture fisheries production into their official figures. Why this is problematic is a lesson in reality regarding statistical systems. One difficulty, common to many countries, is that despite the official figures having no sampling or valid statistical basis the system of generating national fishery statistics is incompatible with more accurate data generated through other mechanisms. For example, there is no formal requirement to reconcile estimates in the national fishery statistics and those from the national expenditure and consumption survey. New figures also question the validity of old figures which can, understandably, be taken personally by those involved in their production (also a common problem).

The current official statistics in Lao PDR result in some interesting phenomena. For example, the objective of a recent major aquaculture initiative is to raise per caput fish consumption from 7 to 11 kg per annum (the former figure is based upon official production divided by population number). It is already (or more likely traditionally) likely in the region of 36 kg. That this enables the development target to be exceeded simply by re-estimating consumption is a minor point. What is more significant is that policies are being based upon the official national statistics, despite the general lack of confidence locally in them. But without better figures, what else can be done?

Perceptions of Inland Fisheries and Objectives of the Statistics

Lao PDR clearly recognises the value of its living aquatic resources sector (fisheries). This is exhibited, for example, by the recent establishment of a separate division for fisheries and a significant research institute (LARReC). These developments show that, despite funding and human resource constraints, the country is willing to invest in the sector. This is a welcome and encouraging start. But a significant question is on what basis are sector and sub-sector policies set. This brief review has suggested that whilst Lao PDR appreciates its capture fishery, it seriously under-estimates its true quantitative value and extent. Recent surveys have helped reinforce the recent emphasis but the official figures remain.

It was previously reported (Sverdrup-Jensen, Coates and Visser, unpublished) that the usage of the current data on fishery production is extremely limited in Lao PDR and appears to be divorced from fishery planning exercises, which are, in any case, in their infancy. Whilst there is an element of truth to this, the official figures do still have a major influence on national policies, especially so amongst those less familiar with the sector. In particular, the figures have a major influence on donor perceptions and therefore their investment strategies.

There is a widespread belief, as well as occasional reports, that in Lao PDR that total production from capture fisheries from rivers and swamps is undergoing drastic decline due to over-fishing and environmental degradation. Oddly, there is no substantiated information or data to support this belief. In fact, the official statistics show an increase over the past 10 years. Of course, the latter are relatively meaningless in this context. But the point is that officials, not surprisingly, do not base their opinions on official statistics and this therefore raises the question as to why are they collected in the first place?

These examples also illustrate that official statistics are used or ignored arbitrarily, depending upon whether or not they support a particular policy or perception.

Conclusions and Recommendations

The complete separation of the historical and current fishery statistics from fishery planning should be further encouraged.

Clearly, a major and immediate task for Lao PDR is to re-assess its current official figures for capture fisheries based upon a review of historical and recent information and data for the fishery. Some suggested methods for doing this are included in Part I. Much information is locally available and certainly more than enough to produce very realistic estimates. In this process, information based upon data from credible surveys should take precedent over all other information. Once survey data are accepted (within the normal margin of error) extrapolations based upon resource and population distribution are difficult to challenge.

This must be done by the appropriate Lao authorities, not externally. The current report serves only to illustrate the need to do this. In common with many countries, Lao PDR needs to consolidate a more flexible, interactive and inclusive approach to the generation of national fishery statistics. There are encouraging signs that this is happening. It appears to have already been achieved recently with the figures for aquaculture. Only when this is achieved also for capture fisheries should the information be allowed to influence planning.

What could be done in the future? Lao PDR can perhaps take comfort from the fact that its inland capture fishery statistics are no worse than in many countries, and at least it has not invested significant resources in compiling them. An infrastructure does exist with which to collect data and information. Used wisely this is a significant asset. One danger is that Lao PDR will attempt to use this by duplicating systems in other countries. There is no evidence that this will work, and better information is already on hand and can be used for estimating gross production, more accurately and without significant investment. The more optimistic scenario is that Lao PDR, because it has not already heavily invested in fishery statistics, is ideally placed to consider its options more rationally and impartially than most countries. Fundamental to this process is to clearly establish what information is needed and then to identify the best options for obtaining it.

VIETNAM

VietNam is among the more densely populated countries in Southeast Asia. The highest densities occur in the south especially within the delta of the Mekong River which represents the country's most important agricultural area. Economic development has accelerated in recent years. Almost all freshwater areas are still heavily exploited for fisheries. The major river fisheries are centred on the Red River and its delta in the north, now highly degraded, and more importantly the Mekong delta in the south. Remote sensing flooding imagery shows that up to 40 percent of the area of the delta in VietNam is still flooded seasonally, mainly in the upper section. This is essentially an extension of the highly productive Tonle Sap floodplain system of the lower Mekong in Cambodia. Coastal regions are now largely under flood "protection". A considerable amount of fish migrates into VietNam from Cambodia (and quite possibly the reverse occurs also). The Mekong delta also has a large brackishwater/estuarine fishery in its lower reaches. VietNam also has very extensive rice cultivation and has recently challenged Thailand as the world's top exporter. However, production is intensive with very high pesticide use and rice-fish production has no doubt suffered as a result. Aquaculture is very well developed with 407 000 MT reported national production in 1999.

The Statistical Collection System

Sverdrup-Jensen, Coates and Visser (unpublished report of a trip in 1996) found the fishery statistics collection system in VietNam to be very unclear. It has continued to prove difficult to establish exactly how statistics are collected. One reason for this is that there is a large degree of delegation of the statistical system to provinces and it can be challenging to establish exactly what is happening at that level. In provinces where a Department of Fisheries exists it is responsible for collection and processing of information on fisheries production at the district and village/community levels. This information is heavily biased towards aquaculture statistics. Out of a total of 53 provinces, 23 have a Department of Fisheries including all provinces in the Mekong delta. In general, most provinces now have fisheries extension offices but for inland areas these mainly service aquaculture. In other provinces, staff of the Department of Agriculture and Rural Development will collect the information on fisheries via their staff employed at district level and report directly to the Ministry of Fisheries (MoF), Department of Planning and Investment, in Hanoi. Provinces are requested to report every 3 months and produce a yearly report on the total area and total production. Only a limited number of species are distinguished, in particular, shrimps/prawns, marine crabs, *Gracilaria* spp. and a number of commercial fin-fish (in particular snakeheads and Pangasiid catfishes), which have export potential. All other production (culture or capture) is lumped together and reported simply as "freshwater fish". Since production figures are used as a basis for government revenue and tax it might be expected that this system results in a certain bias in reporting.

The Ministry of Fisheries has no budget to collect their own data and rely entirely on the data supplied by provincial offices. An independent (parallel) system is in place through the General Statistics Office (GSO). This office has, since 1994, mobilised people at community level to ascertain, amongst other things, the total production area and the average production per production method by means of a sample. Again the bias is towards aquaculture. There seems to be some communication at different levels between the two systems, although it is admitted that this co-operation is far from optimal.

There is a licensing system in place for fishing in the larger reservoirs. Licensing systems also occur in open water (river/floodplain) fisheries and these target the larger professional gears. Compliance is not high and relationships between fishers and district officials in general leave room for improvement. The government is promoting improved co-management approaches to try to improve governance and management of the fisheries.

A complicating factor is that four different departments (excluding the Ministry of Fisheries) are responsible for the management of the different inland water bodies. Whilst all might lay claim to revenue from the fishing, few of them systematically collect data on the number of fishers involved or the capture fisheries production on a national basis. The government Ministries or Departments went through a major re-organisation and reform in the mid-1990's and this, together with the still ongoing shift to market oriented economy, does not clarify matters in terms of responsibilities and competence of different offices for collecting data. A detailed investigation of the actual data gathering systems on a provincial, district and village level is necessary to obtain a clear picture of the usefulness and potential of any specific statistics. This can be time consuming and requires significant local knowledge.

A major overhaul of the fishery sector was proposed by the Fisheries Sector Master Plan project (Danida in 1996). The marine fishery remained the main target for changes in the way data are collected. Again the emphasis has been on the export sub-sectors and aquaculture. There is currently an on-going Danida funded project to improve fisheries information systems. This has not fully addressed the needs for inland capture fisheries but is attempting to incorporate some aspects through liaison with the Danida funded MRC Fisheries Programme.

Collecting data on the small scale fishing activities, in general, is not currently considered feasible. Inland capture fisheries are considered only to constitute a minor fraction of the total fishery and aquaculture sector. The government takes the view that the main thrust for growth from inland areas will be from aquaculture. There is a perception, not universally held, that there is probably little point improving the statistics for inland capture fisheries. Needless to say, in the absence of hard data on the inland capture fishery, this attitude is somewhat irrational. In the few areas where improved statistics have been collected it has also been shown to be incorrect (see below). Nevertheless, emphasis by the government on generating export revenue has placed inland capture fishery statistics as a low priority.

Where statistics do exist for inland capture fisheries, based upon information collection, they appear to be founded mainly upon estimates from records of licensed gears. These may or may not include an element of catch reporting by fishers. Some districts may undertake surveys of reports from fishers. Better statistics might be available on a local basis for individual reservoirs, but the mission has been unable to find any that are relevant to obtaining estimates of reservoir fisheries on a national basis.

The Information Produced

Inland capture fisheries production reported to FAO, together with freshwater aquaculture for comparison. Based upon this information, the relative degree of attention to, and investment in, aquaculture would appear justified. It is certainly the case that the aquaculture sector has performed well and the figures suggest it outstrips capture by a significant margin. But the reality regarding inland capture fisheries is quite different. For example, official reports of production from freshwater capture fisheries by a single province in the Mekong Delta (An Giang - see later) have averaged around 65 000 MT per year. It is hard to believe the province accounts for 86 percent of total national capture production from freshwaters; especially considering it is only one of at least 12 other provinces in the delta (subject to definitions on boundaries). An Giang province, being located near Cambodia, still with extensive seasonal flooding, is noted for its inland capture fisheries but a number of other provinces have similar freshwater resources, not least Dong Thap province which is adjacent in the north-east section of the delta (also bordering Cambodia), plus large sections of several others. Even those areas where the annual flooding is now largely eliminated are not expected to have totally insignificant capture fisheries, not least because all still have extensive networks of canals and many still have fisheries on the Mekong distributaries. Also, those closer to the sea begin to have brackishwater/estuarine fisheries (inland).

The first problem in VietNam with the national inland capture fishery statistics (at least as reported to FAO) is that they do not include all available provincial information; or, more likely, the information is not reported to national authorities (unless An Giang is the only province with reports).

Following this information, the apparent 25 percent reported decline in inland capture production over the past ten years would seem to be baseless. Certainly the figures are incorrect in absolute terms but is the trend representative? Has there been a decline in the fishery or decline in reporting? Do the figures represent a degree of subjectivity due to perceptions of what is believed to be happening? Is there actual misreporting (at provincial/district level) to justify management activities in other sub-sectors? For present purposes, these questions are less relevant than the fact the information produced, when viewed in any impartial fashion, does not enable them to be answered. So what then is the purpose of this information?

In addition to these discrepancies in compiling national statistics, at least as forwarded to FAO, recent statistically based sampling surveys of inland capture fisheries have shown that, as usual, the existing reporting/statistical system still grossly under-estimates the fishery. In 1998-9 the MRC commissioned a survey in An Giang province which was undertaken by a local university and provincial and district fisheries officers with technical assistance through the Research Institute for Aquaculture Number 2 (Ho Chi Minh City). A team report was produced (Sjørslev, 2001) and the information produced on freshwater capture fisheries in the area was as follows:

- 66 percent of households rely significantly on capture fisheries either for income or food. This equates to about 1.35 million people who rely to various extents on capture fisheries (out of a total of 2 016 949) in just one province.
- 45 percent of people interviewed reported that they went fishing. This equates to about 900 000 people.
- 9 percent of fishers are children below the age of 15. About 30 percent of fishers are women.
- 5.7 percent of households are involved in either fish processing or trading.
- About one person per 62 households is involved in fish trading (about 60 percent of which are self-employed). This equates to about 32 500 traders in the province.

- By comparison, only 14 percent of households are involved in aquaculture, either solely, or more often in combination with capture fishing.
- Only 25 percent of "professional fishing" households actually operate larger-scale gears such as bag-nets and larger traps/ barrages.
- "Professional fishers" spend about 10 months per year fishing, but "part-time" fishers still spend an average of 7.3 months per year fishing.
- The total catch estimate for "part-time" fishing households was approximately twice that from "professional" fishing households (and the latter also includes some small scale catches from non-licensed gears).
- The fishery cannot be adequately described or monitored by using "professional" (= licensed) fishers as the prominent group.
- 80 percent of the total catch is sold (including from part-time fishing households).
- The mean catch per household was 792 kg/year with a median of 300 kg/year (excluding households using highly productive gears such as bagnets). This estimate includes non-fishing households.
- Consumption of aquatic animals (fish plus other taxa) was 58.4 kg/person/year of which fresh fish (plus other taxa) accounted for 54.3 kg with 4.1 kg/person/year of processed fish. The fresh fish equivalent was 61 kg/person/per year.
- Fish accounts for 75 percent of the total animal food intake.
- 76 species of fish were reported to be caught (and that section of the survey only related to recent catches, the number of species over a full year would be much higher).
- Total production from the capture fishery was estimated at 273 118 MT for 1999. About 28 percent of this is used as fodder/ feed for commercial aquaculture (the region has very significant cage culture particularly for carnivorous snake-heads, *Channa spp.*, and catfish). About 23 percent is likely exported (probably domestically) from the province.

Naturally, when these figures were first produced they were received with some scepticism locally. Fortunately the figures could be verified by making comparisons with other regions. The figures were, for example, remarkably similar to those obtained by a number of independent studies for the same adjoining ecosystem in Cambodia (see Cambodia this document). Catches per household were comparable as were catches per gear, consumption figures and the levels of participation in the fishery. This is not surprising as it is effectively the same fishery. What gives the relatively high production estimate is the relatively high population living in the province (over 2 million people). Estimates of catches per unit area have still to be made (this is complicated because large quantities are caught from rivers and canals where fish may be migrating through the area).

The official provincial report for the capture fisheries in An Giang province for 1999 was 64 000 MT. The estimate from the actual survey was therefore about 4.25 times higher (which is comparable to the error for other similar fishery statistics documented elsewhere in this report). However, the provincial figures are based upon catch reports and estimates for the larger gears (mainly bag-nets, barrages, trawls, big lift nets and stationary gillnets). Interestingly, by applying the same statistical methods as the province, but using the data from the aforementioned actual survey for the same gears and effort, an estimate of 66 679 MT was derived - a difference of only 4 percent. This endorses the survey data. It also shows that the provincial statistics are, in fact, reasonably accurate or at least representative. The problem with the provincial statistics is that they apply only to a small sub-sector of the total fishery.

The aforementioned survey and statistics refer to a single province. The same correction (factor 4.25) cannot be applied to the national figures because we know they do not include all provincial reports. Also, not all provinces may have statistics of the same nature as in An Giang (meaning they most likely under-report even more). What then is a realistic total estimate of freshwater capture fisheries production in VietNam?

A cursory look at the Mekong delta in VietNam suggests, based upon data for An Giang, that the upper half, which includes the major seasonally flooded sections, when allowances are made for resource areas and population numbers, might be producing in the order of 400 000 to 500 000 MT. Based upon production per caput, this is conservative and less than production per caput in Cambodia. Added to this should be a smaller amount for the middle to lower sections of the delta (with limited flooding) but an unknown but likely substantial amount for the inland areas of the estuary/coastal region. A figure of 500 000 to 600 000 MT per annum for the Mekong delta in VietNam is therefore not unreasonable and compares reasonably with the estimates for the Ayeyarwaddy (Irrawaddy) delta in Myanmar, which has some similar characteristics. An average of a conservative production of 35 kg/caput/year (it is nearly twice that in the upper section) gives a figure of 600 000 MT. Whilst such production might be considered high for the Mekong delta, it should be related to resource area and population size.

There are 17 million people living in the VietNamese part of the Mekong delta; this is 1.5 times the total population of Cambodia (including those not living in fishery resource rich areas). Taking a rough figure of 10 percent of the population involved in fishing (very conservative based upon the An Giang data) gives an estimate of around 1.7 million VietNamese fishers in the delta alone (and it is arguably likely twice that). Added to this should be those also involved in fish processing, marketing and transportation. Whilst all of these people may not be involved full-time, they all depend significantly upon capture fisheries. More importantly, so do the other members of their households (multiplying the total dependency by a factor of about 4.0). The entire population also depends upon fish for food security. Added to this estimate for the Mekong total will be production from areas outside the Mekong basin and from reservoirs. This might be speculated to be at least another 100 000 to 200 000 MT per annum.

Calculations in this fashion are unlikely to yield either accurate or accepted estimates. But the analysis shows at least three important things: (i) that the current reported production of 75 000 MT from inland capture fisheries nationally is a gross under-estimate, (ii) any reasonable impartial estimate based upon available data (locally or by comparison with relevant regions elsewhere) would conclude that inland capture fisheries production likely exceeds that from freshwater aquaculture, and (iii) whatever the realistic figure is, it is sufficiently high enough to justify investing some effort into obtaining a more accurate estimate in a more systematic fashion.

Perceptions of Inland Fisheries and Objectives of the Statistics

VietNam is certainly a country which generally seriously under-estimates the importance of its inland capture fishery, particularly so for the Mekong delta. It is hard to say whether this has been due to the fishery statistics or whether the statistics themselves have been influenced by pre-determined policies. In general, there is also the widespread view that the fishery is in decline (primarily through environmental pressures) and that, in any case, there is limited scope to improve it.

The use of the current statistics seems to be limited for reporting purposes to the Ministry level and is purely descriptive. There appear to be no national freshwater capture fishery management actions or plans based on the currently available data (at least for river fisheries). Neither could any be realistically undertaken. It is more likely that the current statistics have encouraged a lack of interest in the sub-sector. There are some local initiatives, with related statistics etc., for reservoirs. These relate mainly to assessing the impacts of stocking programmes.

Conclusions and Recommendations

Obviously, VietNam needs to re-assess its inland capture fishery statistics. A more representative picture of the sub-sector can be obtained with limited cost, using existing information. This might include exploring in more detail the information available at provincial and district levels and especially establishing the basis of that information. Doing this does not necessarily require substantial investments in the statistical system itself.

Regarding improving the current statistical collection system, there are two separate problems: (i) the way in which national figures are compiled (or reported to the national level), and (ii) the relevance of the original statistics. A statistical system including staff is currently in place. There are certainly low cost solutions to improving the current information, where it is already being collected. The example from An Giang suggests that at least for some areas valid corrections can be applied to current statistics, without extra costs. It is not unreasonable to suggest that such changes might indeed result in overall savings. In addition, the replicate collection system by GSO and the MoF could be merged to rationalise the investment of effort (if this has not already been done). There is no technical reason why local authorities, given limited support and advice, could not make many improvements on their own. The problem is very much one of motivation to pay attention to these fisheries. To address that problem, policy changes at national level would help.

This does not mean that VietNam need necessarily invest substantially more in its current inland fishery statistical system. On the contrary, this review concludes that such investments should proceed with caution. A better approach is to first ascertain what kinds of information are required for policy, planning and management purposes. The existing system, provided improvements are made where feasible, even if scaled-down, may provide the current information more effectively and cheaply, and certainly more reliably. It is the additional information that may be required, but is not currently collected, that is important. Investing in the current system may not necessarily provide that. In particular, the current system is unlikely to provide information relevant to monitoring trends in the fishery, livelihoods, poverty and food security aspects or biodiversity and the environment.

It is, of course, for VietNam to set its own policies and priorities. All this review can contribute is to illustrate the dangers of basing policies on poor statistics. The downgrading of inland capture fisheries has been fuelled at least in part by the statistics themselves. This has spiralled into further downgrading of the fisheries. A national policy of promoting commercial aquaculture and export-oriented fisheries is not necessarily inappropriate in itself, and is not being questioned here. Indeed, exports and aquaculture have responded admirably. The danger lies in when the policy results in insufficient attention to an inland capture fishery of the extent and importance of that in VietNam.

The evidence suggests that the inland capture fisheries in VietNam, particularly in the lower Mekong River, are worth sustaining. But VietNam, in common with many countries, is certainly making an error of judgement by assuming that its inland capture fisheries cannot be improved. Evidence from Myanmar in this report, and experiences elsewhere, conclusively show the substantial benefits that can accrue by applying cost-effective enhancement techniques to such fisheries (through better management of the environment and/or stocking). There is much scope for such techniques to be applied to river fisheries in VietNam, particularly since most of the environments are already under substantial management. In common with most countries in the lower Mekong basin, VietNam has yet to adopt closer co-ordination of water and fisheries management activities to optimise resource utilisation for which will require improved statistics and information.

Bibliography

A.D. Dholakia: Fisheries and Aquatic Resources of India, Daya, Delhi, 2004.

Arnold C. Long: Deep Sea Demersal Fish and Fisheries, Cyber Tech Pub, Delhi, 2009.

B.R. Selvamani and R.K. Mahadevan: Marine Capture Fisheries, Campus Books, Delhi, 2008.

C.B.L. Srivastava: A Text Book of Fishery Science and Indian Fisheries, Kitab Mahal, Delhi, 1999.

K.P. Biswas: Economics in Commercial Fisheries, Daya, New Delhi, 2006.

Omprakash Sharma: Handbook of Fisheries and Aquaculture, Agrotech Publishing Academy, New Delhi, 2009.

Rajendra Kumar: Biotechnology and Genetics in Fisheries and Acquaculture, Arise Pub, Delhi, 2010.

Ramakrishnan Korakandy: Fisheries Development in India : The Political Economy of Unsustainable Development, Kalpaz Pub, Delhi, 2008.

S P Malhotra and V R P Sinha: Indian Fisheries and Aquaculture in a Globalizing Economy, Narendra Pub House, Delhi, 2007.

S. Nath and S.C. Dey: The Ecology and Fisheries of Barak River System of India, Narendra Pub, Delhi, 2008.

Tomi Petr: Fisheries in Irrigation Systems of Arid Asia, Daya, New Delhi, 2007.

Umesh C Goswami: Natural and Anthropogenic Hazards on Fish and Fisheries, Narendra Pub House, Delhi, 2007.

V B Sakhare: Reservoir Fisheries and Limnology, Narendra Pub, Delhi, 2007.

V R P Sinha: Fisheries Research Planning and Management in Developing Countries, Narendra, Delhi, 2005.

Index

□□□